Improving Student Information Search

CHANDOS
INFORMATION PROFESSIONAL SERIES

Series Editor: Ruth Rikowski
(email: Rikowskigr@aol.com)

Chandos' new series of books is aimed at the busy information professional. They have been specially commissioned to provide the reader with an authoritative view of current thinking. They are designed to provide easy-to-read and (most importantly) practical coverage of topics that are of interest to librarians and other information professionals. If you would like a full listing of current and forthcoming titles, please visit www.chandospublishing.com.

New authors: we are always pleased to receive ideas for new titles; if you would like to write a book for Chandos, please contact Dr Glyn Jones on g.jones.2@elsevier.com or telephone +44 (0) 1865 843000.

Improving Student Information Search

A metacognitive approach

BARBARA BLUMMER

Center for Computing Sciences

AND

JEFFREY M. KENTON

Towson University, College of Education

ELSEVIER

AMSTERDAM • BOSTON • CAMBRIDGE • HEIDELBERG • LONDON
NEW YORK • OXFORD • PARIS • SAN DIEGO
SAN FRANCISCO • SINGAPORE • SYDNEY • TOKYO
Chandos Publishing is an imprint of Elsevier

CP
CHANDOS
PUBLISHING

882190690

Chandos Publishing
Elsevier Limited
The Boulevard
Langford Lane
Kidlington
Oxford OX5 1GB
UK
store.elsevier.com/Chandos-Publishing-/IMP_207/

Chandos Publishing is an imprint of Elsevier Limited

Tel: +44 (0) 1865 843000
Fax: +44 (0) 1865 843010
store.elsevier.com

First published in 2014

ISBN 978-1-84334-781-1 (print)
ISBN 978-1-78063-462-3 (online)

Library of Congress Control Number: 2014948150

© B. Blummer and J. Kenton, 2014

Typeset by Domex e-Data Pvt. Ltd., India

Transferred to Digital Printing in 2014

Contents

List of figures and tables

Figures

Tables

Acknowledgments

This book evolved from my unpublished doctoral dissertation that was expanded and updated. In that endeavor, I would like to acknowledge again all of the support I received from my dissertation committee including: Dr. Jeffrey Kenton, my dissertation advisor, as well as Dr. Liyan Song, Dr. Sarah Lohnes Watulak, Dr. Olga Kritskaya, and Sara Nixon. In addition, I wish to acknowledge the support provided by Dr. Francis Sullivan, Director of the Center for Computing Sciences. Dr. Kenton and I appreciate the comments by Dr. Anthony Onwuegbuzie on concurrent research design. Lastly I am especially grateful to Dr. Brenda Dervin for clarifying the sensemaking methodology and its impact on information science research.

Barbara Blummer

About the authors

Barbara Blummer is the reference librarian for the Center for Computing Sciences in Bowie, Maryland. She received a MLS from the University of Maryland in 1995, a Master's degree in Communications/Digital Library from Johns Hopkins University in 2005, and an EdD from Towson University in Instructional Technology in 2012. She has published numerous articles in the library literature and presented at many conferences on information literacy. This research represents an expansion and an update of her dissertation study.

Jeffrey M. Kenton is the assistant dean for the College of Education at Towson University. Among his research interests are: instructional technology, technology literacy, problem-solving, assessment, and metacognition. His present work revolves around studying the intersections among classroom technology use, pre-service teacher preparation, content knowledge development, and metacognition.

Summary of the study

To improve education graduate students' information search behavior during problem-solving exercises, this book presents a mixed method study that evaluated the effectiveness of a tutorial designed to enhance participants' metacognitive strategies during information seeking for problem solving. It represents an expanded and updated version of the first author's unpublished dissertation research (Blummer, 2012). The use of the think-aloud protocol facilitated an understanding of individuals' strategies and perceptions as they searched for information to solve a problem. A variety of quantitative data offered evidence of the impact of the tutorial on students' problem-solving abilities. The study focused on individuals' use of specific idea tactics and especially the differences in their problem-solving efforts executed before and after exposure to the tutorial.

The study centers on the first author's unpublished dissertation research that examined the impact of metacognition on education graduate students' information search. Chapters 3–5, 8–10, and 15–17 focus on the metacognitive aspect of information search. Education students' information-seeking skills are highlighted in chapters 6 and 7. Information on the research study is offered in chapters 1 and 10–18.

The book is organized in two parts. The first half of the book discusses the literature on the main themes in the research study, and these encompassed information search, metacognition, problem solving, metacognitive scaffolds, and education graduate students' information-seeking behavior. Chapter 1 provides an introduction to the study. Chapter 2 presents a review of the literature on information research and online search. Chapter 3 defines metacognition and traces its development. Chapter 4 examines the role of metacognition in problem solving. Chapter 5 considers the impact of metacognition on information problem solving. Chapters 6 and 7 explore education graduate students' information seeking and information problem-solving skills respectively.

Chapter 8 focuses on the role of metacognition in online search. Chapter 9 traces the literature on metacognitive scaffolds.

The second half of the book centers on the research study and its findings. Chapter 10 describes the development of the idea tactics tutorial. Chapters 11 and 12 discuss the research methodology, including the problem-solving activity and post-activity interview and the data analysis respectively. Chapter 13 tracks the impact of the Indexes on six participants' problem solving. Chapter 14 provides the findings in relation to the research questions for these six participants. Chapters 15, 16, and 17 discuss the themes that emerged from the study, including: idea generation and mental pattern breaking, participants' adoption of metacognitive strategies and behaviors, as well as the incorporation of metacognitive strategies in information literacy instruction. Chapter 18 offers suggestions on utilizing the tutorial to maximize its effectiveness and modifying it for different user groups. The last chapter, 19, provides the conclusion and recommendations for future research.

Overview of the study

Abstract: Students often experience difficulties locating information despite library training in database search techniques. Research suggests metacognitive strategies including: planning, monitoring, and self-regulating actions could enhance individuals' search in research databases. An idea tactic tutorial that promoted metacognitive strategies was developed to improve education graduate students' searching in research databases for problem-solving activities. Bates identified 17 idea tactics, and nine of these concepts were incorporated in the idea tactics tutorial. We developed three additional tactics based on metacognitive strategies and they are included in the tool. A mixed method study evaluated students' use of the tutorial as well as its impact on their search techniques and outcomes. This work constituted the first author's dissertation study and our book represents an expansion and update of the research.

Key words: library training, education graduate students, metacognition, problem solving, research databases, tutorial.

Introduction

Academic library services provide research training to users. Traditional library training focused on students' information literacy skills and included instruction in utilizing advanced database features and searching relevant materials. However, some students still have difficulty locating resources following library training in database search techniques (Blummer et al., 2012). This likely stems from the multitude of problems users encounter during information search. One novel approach to enhancing students' research techniques highlights individuals' information problem-solving abilities and especially their metacognitive skills. This perspective views information problem solving (IPS) as a form of information literacy that requires students to employ metacognitive skills or the ability to plan, monitor, and evaluate one's own action (Lazonder and Rouet, 2008). IPS researchers equate information problem solving with information seeking in online databases and the web. Moreover, they note the importance of problem solving competencies in fostering students' success in academia and beyond (Walraven et al., 2008, p. 624). To this end, the dissertation study examined the effectiveness of an idea tactic tutorial to enhance participants' information searching in research databases for problem-solving activities. The tool centered on "idea tactics" that expert searchers employ to "help improve the searcher's thinking and creative processes during searching" (Bates, 1979, p. 280). Bates identified 17 tactics, and nine of these concepts are incorporated in the idea tactics tutorial. We developed three additional tactics based on metacognitive strategies and they are included in the tool. This tutorial also contains definitions as well as examples, and it was provided to participants in an online format during a problem-solving exercise.

This chapter discusses the role of metacognition in problem solving during search as well as the lack of research on students' use of metacognition in information seeking. It also highlights the value of metacognitive scaffolds in problem solving and especially the use of online tutorials to deliver skills training.

Background – metacognition in information search

Research on information need, information behavior, and information retrieval highlighted the enormous cognitive demands placed on users during information seeking. Ellis (1989) and Kuhlthau (1991, 2004) suggested that users progress through various stages of information acquisition. Dervin (1983, 1992) maintained that users aim to satisfy an information gap that exists between an individual's experiences and their knowledge. Marchionini (1995) highlighted users' efforts to assess the effectiveness of the information retrieval process especially "how it relates to accepting" the information need and the ability of the retrieved material to support the task (p. 58). Wilson (1999) emphasized the importance of feedback loops in information behavior models due to the "iterative" character of the process that produced "new research questions" (p. 268).

The cognitive demands on users can be particularly excessive in searching research databases. Research by Ahmed et al. (2009) suggested users' search problems stemmed from the failure of database designers to incorporate human computer interface techniques into information retrieval interfaces. The authors developed a prototype interface design that they maintained "improved performance and satisfaction" for novice and experienced users (Ahmed et al., 2006, p. 169).

Some research suggests metacognition could enhance individuals' interactions in research databases. Marchionini (1995) pointed to the importance of metacognition in information seeking. He maintained that metacognition triggered our need for information, enabled "mental models for systems and domains," and monitored "our progress" (p. 14). Likewise, Gorrell et al. (2009) noted the "emergence of interest in metacognition in the context of web search and online inquiry" (p. 447).

Recent studies focus on promoting students IPS skills particularly metacognitive strategies to support online search (Brand-Gruwel et al., 2005; Walraven et al., 2009). Wopereis et al. (2008) illustrated the effectiveness of providing IPS instruction to distance education students in a research methodologies course. This instruction focused on specific sub-skills within five categories, including: define problem, search information, scan information, process information, and organize and present information. Pre-test and post-test results focused on how frequently a skill was performed by the experimental and the control groups. According to the authors, the experimental group performed better following a pre-test and post-test of students IPS skills. Students receiving IPS instruction engaged in text scanning and information evaluation more often than those individuals in the control group. In addition, these students engaged in significantly more metacognitive activities compared to those in the control group.

Research on problem solving also underscored the role of metacognition in promoting favorable outcomes. Salomon and Perkins (1989) referred to general knowledge as how to think well and they believed it supported the development of strategies for "problem solving, inventive thinking, decision making, learning and good mental management" (p. 17). Likewise, Flavell (1978) also linked metacognition to problem solving. According to the author, a "metacognitively sophisticated individual" would approach problem solving by focusing on the "task features" such as the identification of the problem and any sub-problems, as well as tracking "past solution efforts, their outcomes, and the problem-relevant information they yielded" (p. 237).

Other theorists have recognized the significance of metacognition in facilitating individuals' problem-solving skills. Schoenfeld (1982) surmised that cognitive behaviors were affected by task, social environment, and the "problem solver's perception of self and his or her relation to the task and the environment" (p. 1). He highlighted the importance of all three components of cognitive endeavors in problem solving, but noted most students lacked awareness of their potential to "observe, evaluate, and change" their behavior (p. 30).

Sternberg's triarchic theory of intelligence pointed to the role of metacomponents in problem resolution by fostering the recognition and definition of the problem, the gathering of "mental resources" for tackling the problem, the development of steps and strategies for problem solving, and support for monitoring the process and evaluating the solution (Sternberg and Frensch, 1990, p. 89). Frensch and Sternberg (1989) linked problem solving to an individual's flexibility in adapting their thought processes to the current situation. The authors promoted instruction in "learning-to-learn skills" (p. 183).

Need

Despite the importance of metacognitive abilities in influencing information search outcomes, there is minimal research on graduate students' metacognitive activities during information seeking for problem solving. Hess (1999) investigated one graduate student's cognitive processes during a web-based information retrieval session. He pointed to information overload as an obstacle for retrieving material and advocated training users in information skills, defined as the ability to "retrieve, filter, and store relevant information" as well as differentiate it from irrelevant material (p. 7).

While there is some research on individuals' use of metacognitive strategies during information problem solving, these studies are largely directed at younger students. For example, Bowler (2010b) studied the metacognitive strategies of adolescents during information search. Laxman (2010) reported on 25 freshmen students' successful use of an intervention to assist their information seeking in confronting both well- and ill-structured problems. The intervention provided students with search skills as well as worked examples and practice problems to foster the "activation of learners' prior knowledge" (p. 516).

Still, research suggests metacognitive scaffolds offer potential to improve information processing for graduate students as well. Chen and Ge (2006) described the development of a web-based cognitive modeling system to support ill-structured problem solving through question prompts, expert modeling, and peer review. This prototype system was aimed at facilitating scaffolding for instructional technology graduate students in solving instructional design problems. The availability of a case library fostered students' abilities to "perform analysis" and "propose solutions" to instructional design problems (p. 300). The evaluation of the pilot program indicated that the system facilitated students' abilities to utilize "prior knowledge, organise their thoughts, and articulate their reasoning" (p. 301).

Although there are an abundance of studies on the information-seeking behaviors of various professional groups and undergraduate students, librarians have directed little effort to identifying the "research process of graduate students" (George et al., 2006, para. 6). This trend is especially pronounced among studies focused on education graduate students. Still, information-seeking behavioral research supports the development of services and collections to targeted groups. Vezzosi (2009) emphasized the need to explore users' information-seeking patterns to design and plan activities "tailored to users' learning needs" (p. 65).

A pilot study of education's master's students' information-seeking behaviors at a mid-sized public university, based on interviews and a survey, revealed that graduate students had feelings of confusion and uncertainty when researching (Blummer et al., 2012). Several interview participants reported difficulty determining when to stop gathering information as well as in creating the final product. In addition, some survey respondents expressed dissatisfaction with the content of their previous library instruction. The pilot suggested these graduate students were savvy searchers, but required instruction in techniques to enhance their ability to locate and process the volume of information on the web.

Problem solving, literacy in research databases, and tutorial-based library instruction

Librarians differ over the most appropriate focus of information literacy instruction. Johnston and Webber (2003) believed instructional efforts in the United States suffered from a dependency on the Association of College & Research Libraries' definition of the information literate individual. According to the authors, their guidelines reduced "a complex set of skills and knowledge to small, discrete units" (p. 337). Grafstein (2002) observed the information explosion called for an understanding of the "differences between knowledge and information" (p. 200). She pointed to the importance of prior knowledge in individuals' acquisition of new knowledge as well as users' abilities to integrate various ideas. Likewise, Thelwall (2004) predicted that the next generation of scholars would require a new skill set to interact with research from a variety of disciplines. Bowler (2010) suggested librarians instruct students in "how to think about their own thinking" and especially using metacognitive knowledge to enhance problem solving (pp. 38–9).

Research also highlighted the value of tutorials in providing research skills to scholars. Ragains (1997) underscored the role of online and web-based instructional guides and tutorials in his calls for "more aggressive, proactive planning and delivery of instruction" (p. 169). According to the author, librarians required a variety of "ways to reach students" other than one-shot, course-related, faculty-requested training (p. 168). Diekema et al. (2011) reported on the success of an online information literacy tutorial that centered on problem-based learning. The authors noted some students "displayed metacognitive strategies that enabled them to conduct a more extensive research process" (p. 264).

Consequently, idea tactics are utilized as a metacognitive intervention to support education graduate students' information problem solving in research databases. These tactics represent search strategies used by information specialists and compiled by Bates (1979) to "help generate new ideas or solutions to problems in information searching." She described the tactics as part of a "facilitation model" that may help the searcher in an online or print environment (p. 280). In this instance, the tactics are presented in a tutorial and the study measures the impact of the intervention on participants' search strategies and their search outcomes. Table 1.1 lists nine of these tactics and includes three additional strategies designed to promote individuals' metacognitive skills. An initial search served as a pre-test that illustrated participants' problem-solving strategies and database search skills. This information was compared with strategies and search techniques that participants demonstrated following access to the tutorial.

Table 1.1	Idea tactics in the metacognitive tutorial

Tactic	Description
Think	Identify search goals or what you wish to accomplish.
Catch	Recognize an unproductive search and instigate a new approach.
Notice	Consider the appearance of any clues that may affect your interpretation of the question or how to answer it.
Meditate	Analyze the search strategy by incorporating scientific as well as intuitive thought processes for problem solving. This is often described as convergent and divergent thinking. Individuals typically employ one or the other in developing solutions. However, some researchers claim creative problem solving involves both modes of thought.
Change	Instigate a new search behavior, a different keyword, source, or strategy.
Create	Develop a search strategy by identifying relevant keywords, search fields, and databases to access. Research suggests expert searchers adopt a plan rather than follow trial and error techniques.
Wander	Examine the sources for indications of new source opportunities and avenues.
Jolt	Move out of conventional thinking to view the source in an unconventional way.
Identify	Determine personal and system knowledge that may improve search results.
Break	Change standard search habits.
Regulate	Pay attention to your thought processes as well as to how you structure the search process.
Skip	Explore the topic from a different perspective or tackle another component of a multipart query.

Note: Adapted from "Idea Tactics," by M. Bates, 1979, *Journal of the American Society for Information Science*, 30(5), p. 282. Copyright 1979 by John Wiley & Sons. Adapted and printed with permission.

The value of metacognition in promoting favorable outcomes in information search cannot be overstated. Consequently, this research examines the role of metacognition in facilitating information problem solving in research databases.

Research questions

The mixed method study targeted education graduate students, an underserved population in library information-seeking research (Earp, 2008, p. 74). Quantitative measures tracked participants' accesses to the tutorial components, number of revised searches and records examined, as well as the time spent in the tutorial, devising search strategies, and reviewing results. Scores comparing students' initial (pre-tutorial) search with their post-tutorial search were also used. The study's qualitative component centered on a think-aloud protocol that also captured participants' mouse movements during problem solving in Ebsco databases. The study focused on four research questions including the following:

1. *What search techniques did participants demonstrate in their initial search?* This question considers what strategies and skills participants utilized in their pre-tutorial search such as selecting additional databases, employing Boolean operators, truncating terms, accessing the advanced search mode, conducting subject searches, and locating terms from relevant articles.

2. *What general attributes were common among participants in their use of the tutorial?* This question tracks the number of seconds individuals spent in the tutorial and the number of accesses to the various components of the tutorial. It explores how participants used the tutorial. Did participants refer back to the tutorial during their searches or merely utilize it as a one-shot learning tool? How many tactics did participants read and did they access a variety of tactics or stay in one category? Were some tactics used more often than others? How much time did participants spend accessing the various tactics in the tutorial? How frequently did participants access the tutorial?

3. *What search techniques did participants demonstrate in their final searches?* This question compares the search techniques participants demonstrated in their revised searches after exposure to the tutorial. These techniques were not revealed in participants' initial search.

4. *How did the tutorial affect the outcome of the problem-solving activity?* This question compared participants' initial search skills with those demonstrated in subsequent searches. It also compares participants' initial search scores with their final search scores for relevance, ability to answer the question, authoritativeness, and the quality of the response. In addition, it considers the number of revised

searches participants conducted, the number of records they examined, and the time they spent devising search strategies and reviewing results. Were there relationships among the time spent in the tutorial, the number of tutorial accesses, the number of revised searches, and the time spent devising search strategies and reviewing results? In addition, how did the amount of time spent in the tutorial and the number of accesses to the tutorial, and the number of revised searches affect participants' final search scores? The question also examines participants' satisfaction level with the results. Lastly, the question noted any issues that affected participants' problem-solving activities.

Outcomes facilitated the design of a protocol to guide students in applying relevant metacognitive strategies during online search thereby enhancing individuals' information-seeking behaviors. These are discussed in in latter chapters.

Limitations

The small number of students in the sample – eight participants – was a major limitation of the study and prevented the generalization of the findings. The study also attracted participants with more search experience than others. Similarly, some students were more knowledgeable in the task subject area or had enhanced database skills compared to others. Moreover, all of the participants stemmed from one academic institution's College of Education and had similar library training classes.

2

Information research and the search process

Abstract: Information professionals may question the effectiveness of a metacognitive scaffold for enhancing users' search capabilities. Information research is utilized to document the difficulties users encounter during the search process as well as the cognitive and metacognitive aspect of information search. The literature contained references to individuals' use of metacognitive strategies in information search for planning strategies, differentiating among sources, monitoring the process, and evaluating results. Still, studies underscored deficiencies in the user as well as the process that impeded their information-seeking activities. Theorists also described efforts to support users' information search including librarians' awareness of user strategies as well as improvements in search interfaces and database design. Authors failed to consider the role of metacognition in enhancing individuals' information search.

Key words: information models, information search process, information search difficulties, problem solving, users' uncertainties, behavior, retrieval systems.

Introduction

Studies in information behavior and information seeking illustrate the numerous activities associated with information search. Although theorists focused on different perspectives of information use (Ellis, 1989; Dervin, 1983; Kuhlthau, 1993; Taylor, 1962; Wilson, 1999), much of the research acknowledged the complexity of users' information behaviors and especially the social, cognitive, and affective issues that impact it. The literature also contained references to individuals' use of metacognitive strategies in information search for planning strategies, differentiating among sources, monitoring the process, and evaluating results. Still, studies underscored deficiencies in the user as well as the process that impeded their information-seeking activities. Some of these deficiencies included difficulty in translating the problem to librarians and systems, as well as feelings of uncertainty. Consequently, the authors proposed various methods to enhance individuals' information seeking, including identifying users' stage in the information-seeking process and providing relevant support (Kuhlthau, 2004), as well as improving information system design (Dervin, 1992; Ellis, 1989; Taylor, 1962; Kuhlthau, 1999). Unfortunately, none of the authors promoted metacognition strategies to improve individuals' information searching.

This book proposes a metacognitive-based scaffold to help education graduate students overcome the problems they encounter in information search. The scaffold can be adapted for users in other disciplines and academic stages. Although metacognitive scaffolds are popular instructional tools among educational technologists, report of their use for information literacy instruction remains limited. An analysis of the information search process from the perspective of information behavior, information seeking, and information retrieval theorists supports the use of a metacognitive tool for information search instruction.

Early research

Information need

Taylor (1962) was one of the earliest authors to address users' information seeking through his exploration of the problems associated with question formation. He identified four levels of information need, including: actual (visceral), conscious, formalized, and compromised. He defined the fourth level, compromised, as the question that was provided to the information system. Taylor maintained that the question was distorted as it moved through the various levels. He also pointed to three obstacles that affected an individual's interaction with an information system such as the system organization, the type of question and its complexity, and "the state of readiness" (p. 394). The latter, he suggested, referred to the inquirer's state of mind that he described as constantly changing and this influenced their ability to select the appropriate system message. In his summary, Taylor emphasized the need for additional research for "better design" of information systems and especially to consider the "inquirer" as "an integral part" of the process (p. 396).

Information behavior

Wilson (1981) lamented information science's focus on Shannon's (1949) communication model that identified elements such as source, channel, message, coder, decoder, receiver, and noise in users' information-seeking process. Wilson highlighted the complexity of users' information needs and information-seeking behavior that he maintained stemmed from interrelationships among the person's physiological, affective, and cognitive needs, work role, as well as work, social cultural, politico-economic, and physical environments. He argued user studies should consider a "wider, holistic view of the information user" (p. 10), rather than simply how individuals use sources and systems. He hoped the information science field's shift in focus to the user would result in the improvement of library services for supporting users' information needs. In 1999 he proposed a model of information seeking that incorporated Kuhlthau's (1993) notion of uncertainty in users' information behavior with problem solving. He suggested users' resolution of the problem as well as their uncertainty occurred in stages and might include a feedback loop. He believed the use of this model offered potential for including Ellis' (1997) behavioral model that described users' search activities in the problem-solving process.

Dervin's methodology, theory, and framework

Dervin (1983, 1992, 2009, 2010, 2011, 2013) adopted a construction aspect of information search rather than the traditional transmittal perspective of the process. She sought to offer "alternative approaches to the study of human use of information and information systems" with her sense-making concept (1992, p. 61). She compared the information needs concept from the perspective of an observer and a user. She attributed problems with information-seeking research to its positivistic physical science framework that she maintained affected perceptions about information by focusing on "constant, across time-space patterns in human communication behavior" (1983, para. 14). Dervin argued human information processing stemmed from a relativistic tradition and therefore supported an individual's information gathering for sense-making. According to the author, sense-making "searches for patterns in how people construct sense rather than for mechanistic in-put out-put relationships" (para. 16).

In the 1970s and 1980s, the study of information seeking began to include user-orientations (Case, 2002; Dalrymple, 2001; Dervin, 1977; Dervin and Nilan, 1986; Taylor, 1962; Zweizig and Dervin, 1977; Wilson, 1997). Dervin's Sense-Making Methodology (Dervin and Foreman-Wernet, 2003) remains applicable to the study of user orientations in any communicative environment. Library and information science researchers often highlight three aspects of Dervin's model, including: situations defined as the changing time-space contexts in which users construct sense; gaps (internal and external) that users face as they move through changing situational conditions; and the uses to which users put inputs as they make and unmake sense. In library and information science, gaps are most often defined as information needs.

In her 1992 essay, "From the mind's eye of the user: the sense-making qualitative-quantitative methodology," Dervin stated sense-making was a comprehensive approach that contained assumptions, propositions, theory, and methods. She observed sense-making occurred as individuals sought to locate information and resolve the gaps or discontinuities that existed between entities, times, and spaces. She argued how the user conceptualized information was central to the notion of sense-making. In 2003, she pointed out that sense-making, unlike other approaches, focused on the individual as "a theorist involved in developing ideas to guide an understanding of not only her personal world but also collective, historical, and social worlds" (p. 333).

She promoted the application of the sense-making methodology in studying communication such as for interviewing techniques. In 2011 Dervin and Shields stated it had been applied "over a 35 year period to multiple discourse communities" (p. 52). The approach remained especially popular in information science for teaching reference interviewing techniques. She believed the sense-making metaphor supported information seeking, but she pointed out it could illustrate any communication situation (2008). Figure 2.1 outlines the sense-making metaphor that highlights an individual's efforts at "making and unmaking sense as they navigate with their agencies the structural constraints of their situations" (2013, p. 155).

The sense-making approach contains metacognitive implications. For example, Dervin referenced an individual's steps through a situation that she noted "may be a repetition of past behavior" and may also suggest metacognitive experiences (1992, p. 68). Moreover, her explanation of an individual's attempt to define the situation or gap seemingly centers on metacognition knowledge with its emphasis on the users' conceptualization of the "discontinuity as gap" and especially how to

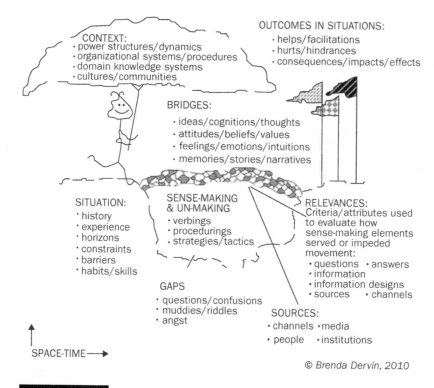

OUTCOMES IN SITUATIONS:
- helps/facilitations
- hurts/hindrances
- consequences/impacts/effects

CONTEXT:
- power structures/dynamics
- organizational systems/procedures
- domain knowledge systems
- cultures/communities

BRIDGES:
- ideas/cognitions/thoughts
- attitudes/beliefs/values
- feelings/emotions/intuitions
- memories/stories/narratives

SITUATION:
- history
- experience
- horizons
- constraints
- barriers
- habits/skills

SENSE-MAKING & UN-MAKING
- verbings
- procedurings
- strategies/tactics

RELEVANCES:
Criteria/attributes used to evaluate how sense-making elements served or impeded movement:
- questions · answers
- information
- information designs
- sources · channels

GAPS
- questions/confusions
- muddies/riddles
- angst

SOURCES:
- channels · media
- people · institutions

SPACE-TIME→

© Brenda Dervin, 2010

Figure 2.1   Dervin's sense-making metaphor

Note: adapted from "Sense-making methodology as an approach to understanding and designing for campaign audiences: a turn to communicating communicatively" by B. Dervin and L. Foreman-Wernet (2013) In: Rice, Ronald E. and Atkin, Charles K. (eds), *Public Communication Campaigns* (4th ed.) (p. 156). Thousand Oaks, CA: Sage Publications. Reprinted with permission

bridge it (1992, p. 69). Metacognitive activities are also described in sense-making interviewing techniques in information studies such as "how the individual saw self as stopped, what questions or confusions he or she defined, what strategies he or she preferred for arriving at answers, what success he or she had in arriving at answers, how he or she was helped by answers" (p. 70). These planning, regulating, monitoring, and evaluating activities imply metacognitive processes.

The inclusion of Dervin's research in this chapter stems from the current authors interpretation of the work as supporting applications in the studies of metacognition in information search. In actuality, Dervin positions her work as explicitly methodological designed to focus on what she calls sense-making and sense-unmaking in any context.

There exist numerous applications of her work in a variety of fields for example in studies of user intersections with media, policy, professional expertise, technology, etc. (Brenda Dervin, personal communication, January 1, 2014).

Information-seeking behavior

Ellis

Ellis (1989) conducted one of the first empirical studies of users' information-seeking behavior and this contributed to the wide acceptance of his findings. His study, which sought to inform information retrieval design, centered on interviews with academic social scientists to ascertain their information-seeking habits. He also aimed to understand their activities and perceptions of the information search process. His analysis revealed a common trend among these academics in their research patterns, although he admitted variations existed among individuals. The author listed six characteristics that reflected the information behavior of social scientists, including: *starting, chaining, browsing, differentiating, monitoring,* and *extracting*. The final three stages, including *differentiating, monitoring,* and *extracting*, appear to resemble metacognitive strategies. He defined *differentiating* as "identifying different sets of sources in terms of the differing probability of their containing useful material" (p. 190). *Monitoring*, he believed, was the researcher's attempts to track new developments in the field through informal and formal sources. He described *extracting* as reviewing a source for relevant materials. In his conclusion, he proposed the design of a flexible information retrieval system that incorporated his findings allowing the user to "follow familiar search patterns" (p. 201).

Four years later, he demonstrated the applicability of his model in illustrating the information-seeking patterns of research physicists and chemists, although he found some differences in search behavior among the researchers. He observed similarity between the information-seeking activities of the chemists and the social scientists with two exceptions. The former researchers verified the accuracy of information and also engaged in ending activities. He identified five information-seeking categories for the physicists: *initial familiarization, chasing, source prioritization, maintaining awareness,* and *locating*. He defined *source prioritization* as "the physicists' views of the importance of the various sources available" and it seemingly reflected metacognitive skills since individuals regulated their cognition by evaluating new knowledge against prior knowledge and made value judgements on the usefulness of the material for their needs. (Ellis et al., 1993, p. 358).

Ellis and Haugan's (1997) interviews with engineers and research scientists revealed similar information-seeking patterns to those researchers in earlier studies. The authors listed eight behavioral categories including: *surveying*, *chaining*, *monitoring*, *browsing*, *distinguishing*, *filtering*, *extracting*, and *ending*. *Filtering* represented a new stage in Ellis' model of search behavior and it resembles a metacognitive strategy. According to the authors, *filtering* encompassed "the use of certain criteria or mechanisms" to "make the information as relevant and precise as possible" (p. 399). In their conclusion the authors noted their study confirmed previous findings that scientists need different information at "different stages of research" (p. 401).

Kuhlthau

The development of Kuhlthau's (1991, 1993) information search process (ISP) model, like Ellis identification of information-seeking patterns among researchers, also stemmed from empirical studies and was widely accepted as well. Her model, the information search process (ISP), evolved from research with high school students and was later verified with a larger diverse sample as well as a longitudinal study with the original participants. The model identified various stages in the search process and it incorporated various constructivists' influences, including Dewey's reflective thinking, Kelly's Personal Construct Theory, and Bruner's belief in the individual as an active agent in the information process. Her research highlighted the importance of users' feelings in the during the search process in designing library services as well as user systems. In addition, Kuhlthau pointed to the importance of studies of users' search strategies as well as information research that focused on users' problems in information seeking such as Taylor (1962) and Dervin (1983).

Kuhlthau (1993) argued an uncertainty principle paralleled the user's migration through the research stages that she identified as *initiation*, *selection*, *exploration*, *formulation*, *collection*, and *presentation*. Some of the stages seemingly contained metacognitive processes. For example, she noted *selection* included "weighing prospective topics against the criteria of personal interest, assignment requirements, information available and time allotted" (p. 343). *Exploration* centered on "becoming oriented and sufficiently informed about the topic to form a focus or a personal point of view" (p. 343).

Her uncertainty principle contained six corollaries and many of these mimicked metacognitive strategies as well. The process corollary centered on the user's construction of understanding and meaning from the information retrieved over time. The formulation corollary was the user's understanding and defining of the topic. The redundancy corollary focused on the user's identification of expected information in the search. The mood corollary included the user's attitude during the search. In the prediction corollary, the user's predictions evolved from constructs "formed through prior experience" and these determined "sources, information and ideas" (p. 351). The interest corollary related to the user's motivation in the search process.

In 1999, Kuhlthau suggested her model be utilized in the construction of information systems especially in accommodating the exploration and formulation stages of the user's search process. She pointed to the impact of the model on librarians' development of services. According to the author, librarians are "attending to the more cognitive and affective attributes of using information for solving problems, for learning and for seeking meaning" (para. 21).

Kuhlthau (2004) identified zones of intervention for librarians to support users' in the process of information seeking. She defined these as an "area in which an information user can do with advice and assistance what he or she cannot do alone or can only do with great difficulty" (p. 129). She recommended matching the level of mediation, such as organizer, locator, identifier, advisor, and counselor, to the particular zone of intervention in the individual's stage in the information search process. She highlighted the role of the counselor in mediating users' information search and listed strategies for intervention, including: collaborating, continuing, choosing, charting, conversing, and composing.

Recently she confirmed the concept's usefulness as a model of information behavior for tasks that require knowledge construction in a study involving 574 students (Kuhlthau, 2008). She maintained the model identified the various feelings students experienced during information seeking. She acknowledged the research showed variations in students' search processes that she related to their "engagement" in the learning process (para. 28). Her findings revealed students that "skimmed through the process and skipped stages ended up frustrated and demonstrated superficial descriptive knowledge" (para. 31). She suggested this study supported the use of the model as a diagnostic tool.

Information retrieval researchers

Marchionini

Information retrieval theorists verified the importance of information-seeking research in informing information retrieval design. Marchionini (1995) observed Dervin (1977) and Kuhlthau's (1988) research highlighted the human-centered aspect of information seeking. He linked Dervin's sense-making approach to "focusing attention on users' needs" and noted its adoption in information science and communication "as a framework for studying the information seeking process" (p. 29). In addition, he maintained "Kuhlthau's model remains robust across different age groups of learners" and it considered "the affective states" of information searchers (p. 29). Foremost, he underscored the importance of information-seeking research in highlighting the problem solving aspect of information seeking that included "communication acts" (p. 29).

Vakkari

Vakkari (2001b) included components of Kuhlthau's (1993) research on the stages of information search process in the development of his task-based theory for information retrieval that emphasized information retrieval and searching activities. His hypothesis stated "stages of task performance are connected to the types of information searched for, to the changes of search tactics and terms and to relevance judgments" (p. 44). The author tested his hypothesis in a study of graduate students' information search over a four-month period. The findings supported the role of Kuhlthau's stages and especially "subjects' mental model" in influencing the type of information sought, the selection of search terms, and the relevance criteria used to evaluate documents (p. 55). In his conclusion, Vakkari pointed to the validity of adopting Wilson's (1999) suggestion of considering information retrieval from the perspective of information seeking.

Summary of information search research

An examination of information studies research highlights the cognitive and metacognitive perspective of information search. The research documented the complexity of the process and the problems users encounter in their information seeking. Taylor (1962) noted users' difficulties in identifying and articulating their information need. Wilson (1999) likened information search to a problem-solving activity. Dervin (1983) emphasized the struggle users encountered in their efforts to make sense of information or experiences. Moreover, Ellis identified multiple stages in researchers information seeking and noted differences among information behavior in various disciplines. Kuhlthau (1993) pointed to individuals' feelings of uncertainty in the information research process.

Yet librarians' and database designers' efforts to address the complexities and difficulties of information search through the development of supportive systems have often failed. A presentation of Kuhlthau's (1993) ISP model to undergraduate students proved effective in reducing students' anxiety during the research process (Kracker, 2002). However, it did not affect students' awareness of affective and cognitive activities during the process, or their satisfaction level with the search. Likewise, Cole's (2001) test of the impact of students' use of information retrieval devices to support their uncertainty during information seeking did not produce higher essay scores for participants in two separate studies. The author surmised the lack of effect highlighted the importance of introducing the device in the appropriate stage of the users' information seeking.

Individuals, and especially students, still demonstrate ineffective search practices, note feelings of anxiety, and also complain of an inability to locate relevant materials while searching library and web resources (Blummer et al., 2012). These included students that received library database training. The failure of information studies to inform the design of relevant support mechanisms stems, in part, from theorists lack of attention to individuals' metacognitive strategies during the search process. In discussing human-computer interactions, Storrs (1994) reminds us "participants must make their interaction intelligible, comprehensive and morphogenic" (p. 184). The latter he defined as "the success or failure of the interaction to achieve the desired state change" (p. 184).

In addition to illustrating the difficulties users confront in information search, and especially the myriad of activities associated with the process, information research literature seemingly illustrated users' employed metacognitive skills in their information gathering. Ellis (1989) pointed to users monitoring, differentiating, distinguishing, filtering, prioritizing, and extracting activities in information seeking. Dervin (1983) noted the role of users' conceptualization of the experience, prior behavior, and preferred strategies in impacting their sense-making. Kuhlthau's (1993) identification of users' selection and exploration activities, and various corollaries associated with the stages in her ISP model also seemed to reflect metacognitive activities.

Lazonder and Rouet (2008) remind us metacognitive skills in online search refer to planning a search strategy, monitoring its progress and evaluating results for "relevance, reliability, and authority" (p. 759). Likewise, Quintana et al. (2005) highlighted the "multifaceted" nature of online searching that encompassed a "range of metacognitive and cognitive activities" (p. 235). They proposed efforts to support students' use of metacognitive skills in online search. The authors differentiated between two types of metacognitive skills. The authors described metacognitive knowledge as referring to knowledge about individual learning capacities, the task, and strategies. On the other hand, they defined metacognitive regulation as "regulating one's own cognition" (p. 236). According to the authors, both kinds of metacognition were required for searching, since they provided "executive control" of the process (p. 236).

Information research identified metacognitive activities as a component of individuals' information-seeking behavior. Consequently, efforts to support students' information-seeking behavior should include instruction in metacognitive techniques as well as database search skills. Teaching students the value of planning strategies, self-regulating, and monitoring the search process enhances users' executive control over the process as well as the outcome. Increased user control over the process should reduce individuals' uncertainty during their information seeking while improving search results.

3

Research on metacognition

Abstract: Throughout the late 1970s and 1980s, research on metacognition focused on understanding the relationship between metacognitive skills and elementary students' classroom performance. Flavell's research on children's memory development in the late 1960s underscored the importance of metacognition in influencing behavior. Markman (1977) linked comprehension to constructive processing, and she believed it was absent in young children. Wagoner (1983) noted a hierarchical relationship among metacognition, cognitive monitoring and comprehension monitoring. Brown and Palincsar (1982) identified two categories of metacognition: knowledge about cognition and regulation of cognition. Metacognition researchers highlighted the importance of supporting students' planning, monitoring and self-regulating strategies through interventions to enhance learning. Within the past 20 years, educators have adopted metacognitive strategies in instructional design for students of all ages.

Key words: memory, metacognition, metacognitive, knowledge, poor learners, metamemory, self-regulating, comprehension monitoring, cognition monitoring, reciprocal teaching, planning, executive processes.

Introduction

This chapter explores the development of research on metacognition. Theorists define metacognition in numerous ways, but generally agree it is knowledge about individual's cognition or "knowledge of self, the task at hand, and strategies to be employed" (Wolf et al., 2003, p. 322). Individuals utilize this knowledge to plan, execute, and regulate the completion of an activity, a task, or a problem. We trace metacognitive studies conducted by prominent authors in the field and especially how their findings led to efforts aimed at improving students' comprehension through interventions. Ultimately, metacognitive research illustrates the role of students' planning, monitoring, and self-regulating their activities in improving individuals' comprehension and learning outcomes.

Early research

Beginnings of a concept

Flavell's research on children's memory development in the late 1960s underscored the importance of metacognition in influencing behavior. He termed memory development "metamemory" and characterized it as the "intelligent structuring and storage of input, of intelligent search and retrieval operations, and of intelligent monitoring and knowledge of these storage a retrieval operations" (1971, p. 277).

In 1977 Flavell emphasized the importance of an individual's metacommunication ability and noted it could be "late-developing" (p. 178). He linked metacommunication to skillful listening and message interpretation. Flavell believed three factors affected children's successful communication: the task demands, its meaningfulness to the child, and the extent to which it required metacommunicative abilities.

The following year, he reviewed studies that supported children's metacognitive development over time or "the acquisition in children of knowledge and cognition about cognitive phenomena" (p. 213). Flavell suggested metacognitive development represented "the ability and disposition to think about 'messages,' in the broad sense, and about the cognitive experiences these messages may engender in people" (p. 233). According to him, young children were unable to think about "the message about the cognitive experiences, or interpretations the message may stimulate, or about possible relationships between messages and interpretations" (p. 233).

Flavell's research with Wellman resulted in further refinement of the metacognition concept including the development of a metamemory taxonomy. This taxonomy recognized the need for "planful memory-related exertions" for some situations (1977, p. 5). In addition, the taxonomy noted individuals' performance in these situations remained dependent on the memory characteristics of the person and the task, as well as the individual's available strategies. The taxonomy also identified sensitivity as well as the interaction of task, person, and strategy variables as two types of memory metacognition. The authors defined sensitivity as a situation that triggered individuals' voluntary intentional remembering.

Metacognitive knowledge and metacognitive experiences

Two years later, Flavell termed these two types of memory metacognition as metacognitive experiences and metacognitive knowledge respectively. He defined a metacognitive experience as a "conscious experience" that concerned "self, task, goals, and strategies" (p. 908). According to the author, metacognitive experiences were "items of metacognitive knowledge that has entered consciousness" (p. 908). He described metacognitive knowledge as "beliefs about what factors or variables act and interact in what way to affect the course and outcome of cognitive enterprises" (p. 907). Moreover, he attributed metacognitive knowledge to prompting individuals to "select, evaluate, revise, and abandon cognitive tasks" (p. 908). Flavell observed metacognitive knowledge and metacognitive experiences were "partially overlapping sets," as he maintained some experiences contained knowledge and some did not (p. 908). The latter, he stated, failed to become a component of our consciousness.

Cognition monitoring

In 1981, Flavell promoted a model of cognitive monitoring that illustrated the interrelationship among metacognitive experiences, metacognitive knowledge, cognitive goals and cognitive actions. The author suggested individuals develop cognitive strategies to foster cognitive goals as well as metacognitive strategies for monitoring cognitive goals. Both, he believed, can produce metacognitive knowledge and experiences. Moreover, he alluded to a developmental aspect of metacognition, suggesting "there might be an increase with age the tendency to notice and attend to metacognitive experiences, and to evaluate their meaning, importance, trustworthiness, and possible implications for cognitive action" (p. 50).

Self-regulation

Throughout the late 1970s and 1980s, research on metacognition focused on understanding the relationship between metacognitive skills and elementary students' classroom performance. Brown and her colleagues (Brown, 1977; Brown and Palincsar, 1982; Reeve and Brown, 1984) explored self-regulation and particularly children's abilities to control and regulate their mental processes. According to Brown and Palincsar (1982), metacognition contained two facets: knowing about cognition and regulating cognition. They likened the latter to executive control processes in information-processing systems that included planning and monitoring activities as well as checking outcomes.

Still, Brown and DeLoache (1977) noted the importance of experience as well as age in confronting tasks. The authors stated "novices often fail to perform efficiently not only because they may lack certain skills but because they are deficient in terms of self-conscious participation and intelligent self-regulation of their actions" (p. 18).

Comprehension monitoring

Markman (1977) linked comprehension to constructive processing and she believed it was absent in young children. In her studies with elementary school children, she demonstrated the inability of younger children to execute instructions mentally or to determine the relationship between instructions and the goal. She emphasized the importance of individuals' awareness of their lack of understanding in order to remedy the situation.

Markman (1981) pointed to inferential processing as a component of comprehension modeling. In this instance, individuals paraphrased information, drew implications, and identified examples to gauge their understanding of the material. In addition, she highlighted the metacognitive knowledge involved in the process, noting that the individuals evaluated "material and task demands" and made "judgments about potential explanations" (p. 75). Ultimately, she maintained that comprehension monitoring remained a conscious process that centered on an individual's recognition of his failure to understand. This remained similar to Brown's (1977) definition of metacomprehension, which Brown described as "ascertaining the state of one's own ignorance or enlightenment" (p. 9).

Wagoner (1983) noted a hierarchical relationship among metacognition, cognitive monitoring, and comprehension monitoring. She linked the latter term to reading comprehension or "comprehension of connected discourse," but suggested metacognition and cognitive monitoring applied to "knowledge about cognition in general" (p. 329). Her review of research on comprehension monitoring led the author to promote "classroom experiments with instruction in monitoring and the incorporation of knowledge about it into pre- and in-service teacher education" (p. 344).

A "fuzzy" concept

Despite the plethora of research on metacognition throughout the 1970s and 1980s, theorists failed to develop a working definition of the concept. Flavell (1981) defined metacognition as knowledge or cognition that "regulates any aspect of any cognitive endeavor" (p. 37). Brown and Palincsar (1982) identified two categories of metacognition: knowledge about cognition and regulation of cognition. They described the latter as executive control processes that centered on planning, monitoring, and checking. Wellman (1983) noted that metamemory was a component of metacognition and he believed it was an "ill-defined concept" with "fuzzy" definitions (p. 33). He identified four common types of metacognition: "factual, long term knowledge about cognitive tasks", "knowledge of one's own current memory states", "regulation of cognitive processes", and "conscious cognitive feelings" regarding the cognitive activity (p. 34).

Four years later, Brown (1987) lamented the lack of consensus on what constituted metacognition. She pointed to the term's "central concerns" that included "conscious control over learning; learning without awareness; transfer of rule learning; relation of age and expertise to various aspects of planning; monitoring and error correcting; general rules for problem solving versus domain specific knowledge; and mechanisms of change" (p. 107). Brown highlighted the importance of the latter in driving metacognitive research and especially studies that employed "interactive processes" (p. 108). According to the author, these experiences are critical for cognitive development and promote internalization of activities such as regulating and self-questioning.

Metacognitive instruction

Impact of memory research on teaching

The link between metacognition and behavior led to efforts that sought to improve students' learning through metacognitive-based instruction. In 1979, Flavell wrote: "increasing the quantity and quality of children's metacognitive knowledge and monitoring through systematic training may be feasible as well as desirable" (p. 910). Two years later, he advocated teaching children oral communication skills through role reversals between speakers and listeners. In this capacity, Flavell believed, children learned "the phenomenological chasm between the mind that already knows and the mind that does not yet know" (1981, p. 57).

Campione and Armbruster (1983) noted the impact of memory research on learning and teaching. The authors observed "from an emphasis on learning and recall of sets of words or sentences, we now see work investigating the comprehension and recall of larger segments of languages up to and including texts" (p. 1). They described their interpretation of training studies as aimed, in part, to understating "the nature of active comprehension and to design instructional programs" to support students (p. 27). Reeve and Brown (1984) maintained the primary goal of intervention research centered on ensuring "that the trained techniques can be used to solve problems different to those on which the skills were taught initially" (p. 5).

"Fix-up" and studying strategies

Armbruster et al. (1983) described two types of metacognitive interventions: those that addressed comprehension failures and others that provided studying strategies to enhance learning. They described the former as offering "fix-up" strategies such as questions to enable students to monitor their learning (p. 14). They listed successful studying strategies identified in the research as outlining, summarizing, self-questioning, and instruction in semantic mapping.

Interactive metacognitive interventions

Reeve and Brown (1984) advocated interactive metacognitive interventions to enhance children's self-regulation abilities. They described successful reciprocal teaching efforts that focused on improving students' metacognitive processes to enhance their text comprehension and reading skills. According to the authors, students assume the role of the teacher "leading a dialogue on a segment of text" (p. 15). The strategies employed in this technique included summarizing, question generating, clarifying, and predicting (Palincsar, 1986). According to Palincsar, work with junior high school students in remedial reading classes using the reciprocal teaching strategies proved successful.

In 1985, Sylwester summarized major findings in research on memory. The author observed these findings had implications for education due to the link between memory and learning. He pointed to a "declarative system that contained who/what/where/when/why" information and a procedural system that "processes automatic motor and problem solving skills" (p. 70). He stated a major implication of research was "to help students develop" connections between concepts as well as strategies to search memory to "draw inferences from limited information within their memory" (p. 73). According to the author, students need to know "how to tie that information to their past experiences, and how to retrieve and use integrated knowledge" (p. 74).

Metacognitive interventions for poor learners

Much of the early research on metacognitive interventions centered on children with learning difficulties. As Campione (1987) pointed out, these learners lack knowledge as well as mechanisms that control their knowledge. The author reviewed studies on metacognitive interventions for slow learners and observed studies that attempted to improve individuals learning through instruction in knowledge about human memory were not successful. However, he pointed to research that taught these children "self-checking routines" as well as "memory strategies" that produced "impressive immediate training efforts" (p. 135). Moreover, Paris and Oka (1986) advocated a "broad cognitive agenda for special education" that centered on instruction that supported self-regulated learning (p. 103).

Palincsar and Brown's (1987) review of the literature identified four categories of interventions aimed at improving special education students' metacognitive skills. These included efforts to enhance students' memory skills, strategies designed to increase individuals' text comprehension, techniques to improve their written work, and instruction to promote their math performance. The authors stated that effective metacognitive instruction contained five characteristics: promotion of task analysis, development of strategies to foster task completion, "explicit instruction of the strategies accompanied by metacognitive information" in their use, feedback on effectiveness of strategy, and instruction on "the generalized use of the strategies" (p. 73). The authors encouraged the use of metacognitive instructions as an "integral part of teaching activity" (p. 73).

Metacognition research for enhancing problem solving

On the other hand, Glaser (1985) analyzed metacognition research for its implications on the nature of expertise and especially problem solving. He observed experts employed self-regulatory or metacognitive abilities that were not apparent in "less mature or experienced learners" (p. 9). He promoted teaching strategies that built on "initial knowledge structures" through "assessing and using relevant prior knowledge," or with scaffolds that offered "organizational schemes" (p. 14).

Recent efforts in instructional design

Within the past 20 years, educators have adopted metacognitive strategies in instructional design for students of all ages. Tessmer et al. (1990) promoted instructional design that highlighted concepts as conceptual tools to foster students' abilities to make "schema-like connections with prior knowledge" (p. 49). To this end, they advocated instructional strategies that incorporated analogies, concept mapping and structuring, as well as transmediation or the "process of translating from one code to another" (p. 50). The authors identified an example of the latter as including students learning about the social hierarchy of whales and illustrating their understanding through sketches. In this instance, learners translated their knowledge from "verbal to visual" (p. 50).

Innovations in learning: New environments for education evolved from a conference hosted by the U.S. Department of Education that sought to locate "examples of instructional programs that aim to enhance student proficiency in understanding, reasoning and problem solving" (p. viii). The book, published in 1996, highlighted the impact of cognitive research on effecting instruction design especially for elementary and middle school classrooms. In the book, Brown and Campione (1996) described their development of the Fostering Communities of Learners program for urban elementary students. According to the authors, the program centered on promoting "the critical thinking and reflection skills underlying multiple forms of higher literacy" (p. 290). The following year, Brown pointed to the program's "metacognitive culture of learning" based on research, sharing information, and performing tasks (p. 403). In this instance, "constructive discussion, questioning, querying, and criticism are the mode" (p. 406).

Educators also embraced metacognition in instructional design at the university level. Case and Gunstone (2002) reported on modifications they incorporated into a science/engineering course in a South African university to promote students' metacognitive development. The article attributed "unlimited test time" and students' maintenance of journals for reflection and other tasks as supporting their conceptual understanding of course content and metacognitive development (p. 468). Doolittle et al. (2006) discussed their use of reading comprehension strategies for undergraduate and graduate students. The authors advocated reciprocal teaching that the authors noted was "based on models and guided practice" (p. 106). They noted it was "well grounded in the literature on social constructivist philosophy and cognitive psychology theory" (p. 108). The authors described their use of reciprocal teaching in five cases and maintained the strategy has "withstood the tests of time, usage, and empirical research" (p. 115).

Summary of research on metacognition

This chapter outlined the impact of research on metacognition in promoting the development of metacognitive-based instruction, such as interventions to enhance comprehension and ultimately learning. Although research suggests metacognition develops with age, theorists also recognized that older children and adults had metacognitive deficiencies and promoted instruction to develop these skills. Armbruster et al. (1983) surmised that "older individuals including high school and even college students often show inadequacies in certain areas of metacognitive knowledge or the use of this knowledge" (pp. 21–2). Consequently, we also explored current efforts to promote metacognition development in students (especially college students). Moreover, Lesley et al. (2007) characterized junior and senior level pre-service teachers as employing a limited number of metacognitive strategies in a literacy class. Research highlights the importance of these strategies in learning, and they remain particularly critical for education majors to enable them to impart these skills to their students. To this end, we present the idea tactics tutorial as a scaffold to promote students' use of metacognitive strategies while information problem solving.

4

Problem solving and metacognition

Abstract: Research on expert and novice problem solvers highlighted differences in their knowledge structures, especially in the organization of information in their long-term memories. Problem-solving research highlighted the importance of memory, a component of metacognition, to support the problem-solving process. These studies also reveal the significance of individuals' creation of mental models and the use of metacognitive skills in promoting optimal results. Metacognitive skills in problem solving include planning, monitoring, regulating and orchestrating the process. Studies of children's problem solving illustrated that individuals with high metacognitive knowledge performed better than those with low metacognitive knowledge. Studies showed a relationship between metacognition and problem solving in older students and adults as well. Enhancing individuals' metacognitive skills improves their problem-solving abilities.

Key words: problem solving, metacognition, metacognitive knowledge, experience, metacomponents, memory, mental models.

Introduction

Information theorists equate information search to problem solving. The Partnership for 21st Century Skills identified problem-solving skills as a competency for the new era since these capabilities support individuals' learning (2003, 2009). They define these as the "ability to frame, analyze and solve problems" (2003, p. 9). Individuals use metacognition while problem solving, and these skills are critical for optimal problem resolution. Educators, especially in the sciences, recognize the importance of individuals' metacognition in problem solving. Ku and Ho (2010) identified metacognitive activities in critical thinking as planning and evaluating activities. Problem-solving theorists described a multi-step process including: identifying the problem, developing a mental representation of the problem, creating a solution plan, noting personal knowledge about the problem, obtaining resources for problem solution, monitoring problem resolution, and evaluation of problem resolution (Bransford and Stein, 1993; Sternberg, 1985). Individuals differ in their capacity for problem solving. Comparisons between expert and novice problem solvers illustrate differences in their storage and retrieval of information from their long-term memory as well as their representations of the problem. Still, as Brown and DeLoache (1977) remind us, "the beginner in any problem-solving situation has not developed the necessary knowledge about how and what to think under the new circumstances" (p. 19). Studies suggest metacognitive training opportunities improve individuals' problem-solving abilities. These types of instruction can also be used to support individuals' problem solving in research databases.

Problem solving and memory

Problem-solving research highlighted the importance of memory, a component of metacognition, to support the problem-solving process. Likewise, Brown and DeLoache (1977) argued the fields of memory development and problem solving were intertwined. Maier (1933) was one of the earliest researchers to identify the role of memory in problem solving. He noted the solution may consist of "parts of past experience which have become integrated" (p. 144). According to the author, if the parts were not previously integrated, the solution evolved from a "spontaneous combination of isolated experiences." However, he pointed out, if the past experiences were previously associated, the problem was solved by "reproductive thinking" (p. 144).

Newell and Simon's (1972) theory of human problem solving emphasized the importance of memory in the problem-solving process too. The authors identified the total knowledge available to the problem solver as a major component of the problem space, or the area where the problem-solving activities occur. This consisted of temporary dynamic information, the knowledge state itself, access information, path information, access information to other knowledge states and reference information (p. 810). According to the authors, the latter two information types were stored in an individual's long-term or in external memory. They differentiated between the knowledge state that the problem solver was working in and the extended knowledge state "for which only access information is available" (p. 811). They emphasized that this "information may be used in decision processes" and "will be forthcoming if it is called for" (p. 811).

Mental models

Resnick and Glaser's (1976) problem-solving model noted the role of memory as well as a mental representation of the task in the process. Their model encompassed three steps including: problem detection, feature scanning, and goal analysis and also centered on an individual's long-term and working memory. In this instance, problem solvers built a representation of the problem in their working memory, searched their long-term memory for past routines, and redefined or revised the problem as needed. The authors also noted the importance of the task environment and suggested individuals referred back and forth from the task environment to the contents of their long-term memory. According to their chapter, redefinition of the problem may be required in the goal analysis phase for the individual to recognize relevant "features or routines" in their long-term memory (p. 214). Pretz et al. (2003) maintained that mental representations were critical to problem solving, and they identified four components of their model: "a description of the initial state of the problem," a description of the resolution or goal, a list of the operators, and an idea of the constraints (p. 6).

Problem-solving research confirms the importance of memory and especially mental models in problem solving. Chase and Simon (1973) attributed master chess players' superior memory recall capabilities for chess positions to their abilities to store information in "larger perceptual chunks" that contained "a familiar subconfiguration of pieces" (p. 80). Chi et al. (1982) compared expert and novice physicists' problem solving, and concluded that differences in their knowledge bases hindered the less experienced individuals' abilities to "generate inferences and relations not explicitly stated in the problem" (p. 68). For example, they noted that novices categorized problems differently and also were less able to gauge their difficulty. According to the authors, intelligent learners formed better representations of problems that contained "inferences and abstractions derived from knowledge structures acquired in past experiences" (p. 71). The authors also suggested expert learners had much "procedural knowledge – how a knowledge structure can be manipulated, the conditions under which it is applicable" (p. 72). On the other hand, they observed that novice learners remained deficient in procedural skills, and this hindered their ability to utilize their factual and declarative knowledge. These findings, the chapter stated, pointed to the importance of improving individuals' procedural skills or problem solving and teaching them to use all "their available knowledge" (p. 72).

Chase and Ericson's (1981) study of an expert's memory use over a two-year period led them to propose their *skilled memory theory*, which highlights the role of memory in problem solving. They defined skilled memory as the "rapid and efficient utilization of memory in some knowledge domain to perform a task at an expert level" (p. 141). The authors identified two characteristics of skilled memory. First, "experts use their knowledge structures in semantic memory to store information during skilled performance of some task" (p. 159). Second, "expert memory involves organized and direct retrieval from long-term memory" (p. 175). The authors concluded that short-term memory lacks the capacity to "handle the large number of intermediate knowledge states" for skilled memory performance (p. 187).

Problem solving and metacognition

Brown (1977) recognized the benefits of metacognitive skills for problem solving. She identified these skills as "predicting, checking, monitoring, reality testing and coordination and control of deliberate attempts to learn or solve problems" (p. 1). Moreover, her work acknowledged the importance of self-awareness in efficient problem solving including: knowing limitations, routines, identification and characterization of the problem, planning and scheduling of problem-solving strategies, monitoring effectiveness of routines, as well as evaluating operations.

Flavell (1976) linked metacognition to facilitating problem solving too. According to the author, problem solving required metacognitive skills that he identified as "monitoring, and consequent regulation, and orchestration of these processes in relation to the cognitive objects or data" to achieve a goal" (p. 232). He believed that children's inabilities to solve problems could stem from metacognitive rather than cognitive deficiencies. Flavell observed that the "child has much to learn about how, where, and when to store information, and how, where, and when to retrieve it" (p. 233).

Studies on children's problem solving demonstrated the role of metacognition in the process. Swanson (1990) studied fourth- and fifth-grade children's use of metacognition in problem solving. He concluded: "high metacognitive individuals outperformed lower metacognitive individuals in problem solving regardless of their overall aptitude level" (p. 312). He suggested high metacognitive skills compensated for ability by providing children "domain-specific problem-solving aptitude" (p. 313). Similarly, Annevirta and Vauras (2006) found that children with high metacognitive knowledge understood the task and evaluated the solution against the instructions more often than their counterparts with low metacognition. Lee et al. (2009) assessed fourth- and fifth-grade children's metacognitive knowledge and problem solving, and concluded that students who selected less optimal responses failed to differentiate between "knowledge of regulation and knowledge of cognition" (p. 98).

Studies showed a relationship between metacognition and problem solving in older students and adults as well. Rozencwajg's (2003) study of the relationship among metacognition, problem solving style, and fluid intelligence among seventh graders revealed a link between students' conceptualization during physics problem solving and higher metacognition. She also found that students who adopted a calculatory style of problem solving scored low on metaknowledge and monitoring, as well as intelligence. She proposed "teaching metacognitive strategies to poor students" to enhance their learning (p. 289). Fukumoto and Kishi (2007) identified metacognitive knowledge as one of the knowledge layers for skilled engineers' problem solving in Japan's boiling water reactor power plants.

Metacognitive experiences and problem solving

Research revealed the two components of metacognition – metacognitive knowledge and metacognitive experiences – impact individuals' problem solving differently. Flavell (1979) described metacognitive experiences as "any conscious cognitive or affective experience that accompany or pertain to any intellectual enterprise" (p. 906). He believed they were more likely to occur during a task due to the importance of individuals' decisions and actions in the endeavor. Efklides (2001) maintained that metacognitive experiences monitored task characteristics and also reflected an individual's goals in task-making. She identified different categories of metacognitive experiences, and some of these included:

feeling of familiarity, feeling of confidence, feeling of difficulty, feeling of satisfaction, estimate of solution correctness, and estimate of effort expenditure. She found individuals' metacognitive experiences were influenced by cognitive ability as well as "personality and other affective factors" (p. 306). Moreover, the author joined Flavell (1979) in linking metacognitive experiences to triggering metacognitive knowledge. Efklides maintained that metacognitive experiences "monitor online cognitive processing" from the individual's perspective, and "online task-specific knowledge" as well as for influencing "control decisions" (p. 315). Her research revealed that metacognitive experiences varied according to the level of "task difficulty" and "phase of cognitive processing (advance, planning, and solution production)" (p. 314).

Akama and Yamauchi's (2004) study underscored the role of metacognitive experiences in problem solving. The authors examined the effect of task performance on individuals' metacognitive experiences. Comparisons of participants' metacognitive experiences questionnaire results before and after the task illustrated differences between those who successfully solved the puzzle and those who did not. The success group "reported significantly higher feeling of satisfaction" confidence, knowledge, and correctness of the solution than the failure group (p. 720). The authors found participants' prior performance affected "Feeling of difficulty, Need to think of the Success group and Feeling of having knowledge after the task for both groups" (p. 720). The study also showed high correlations between individuals' task performance and metacognitive experiences after the task, which the authors attributed to participants' performance. The article maintained that this result supported earlier studies that illustrated "participants can get information from their performance and revise metacognitive experiences after problem-solving" (p. 721).

Metacognitive knowledge and problem solving

Metacognitive knowledge in problem solving focuses on an individual's control of their cognition. Individuals retrieve metacognitive knowledge from memory and it encompasses knowledge about "person, task, and strategy" (Flavell, 1979, p. 907). According to Flavell, metacognitive knowledge typically centered on combinations of two or three of these variables. Foremost, he argued that metacognitive knowledge impacts cognitive events by supporting individuals' efforts to "select, evaluate, revise, [and] abandon cognitive tasks" (p. 908). Likewise, metacognitive knowledge promotes problem solving by fostering the planning, regulating, and monitoring of the process. Sternberg (1985) termed these efforts metacomponents of critical thinking, and he believed they guided problem solving by facilitating the recognition, definition, and resolution of the problem. According to Sternberg, metacomponents enabled problem solvers to develop strategies to solve the problem, orchestrate the resolution, and monitor the event using feedback that evolved during the process.

Planning

Brown and Bransford (1982) distinguished between pre-planning and ongoing planning in problem solving, and they argued that both were important components of the process. They defined preplanning as "formulation of general methods of procedure prior to the actual onset of action" (p. 105). However, they observed that humans and machines plan in action, troubleshoot, monitor, evaluate, and revise during the problem-solving process. According to their report, intelligent systems (man or machine) were dependent on these "executive orchestration" functions, while non-intelligent systems lacked these planning capabilities (p. 105).

A study involving children solving invention problems illustrated the importance of the problem solver's ability to plan ahead and consider alternative goals as components of problem solving (Pellegrino and Schadler, 1972, as cited in Resnick and Glaser, 1976). The research showed that children who were required to verbalize their plans and explain their justification of the strategy were more successful in solving the problem than individuals who did not discuss their plans. Resnick and Glaser (1976) proposed future research consider studying the effect of instruction in verbalization of goals and "probable outcomes" in other tasks (p. 229).

Monitoring and regulating

The problem solver's ability to monitor and regulate the process remains especially important in fostering successful outcomes. Reeve and Brown (1984) argued that children's abilities to gain control of and regulate their metacognitive processes enhanced their problem-solving skills.

Erbas and Okur's (2012) study of high school freshman mathematical problem solving confirmed the need for regulation in the process. The authors identified problem-solving episodes that participants typically engaged in, and these included reading the problem, understanding the problem, planning, exploring, implementing, and verifying. The authors argued that all of the episodes didn't have to occur, or not in the order listed, for individuals to successfully solve the problem. They also emphasized the importance of students' awareness of errors in the problem-solving process. The article stated the "exploration (metacognitive) and implementation (metacognitive) episodes" facilitated students' abilities to "change the inefficient strategy with an appropriate one" (p. 100). The authors noted that "successful students used metacognitive verification" to verify they had answered the problem (p. 101).

Metacognition and problem solving on the web

Although the bulk of recent studies on metacognition in problem solving included research in physics and mathematics, the importance of metacognition in fostering students' problem solving on the web was also demonstrated. She et al. (2012) examined chemistry students' problem solving on the web and observed that the top problem-solving performers utilized more existing knowledge and metacognitive web-searching skills than other students. According to the authors, expert problem solvers viewed the web like a reference "which they can use to verify their existing chemistry knowledge and/or double check the validity of information they obtained" (p. 760). Bowler (2010a) identified students' use of metacognitive knowledge in resolving "the conflict between positive and negative feelings associated with curiosity about the topic" as they searched the web and other information sources (p. 1339). The author surmised that students' metacognition helped them to "find a balance between the desire to explore and discover" or proceed with other aspects of their search (p. 1339).

Similarly, students exercise metacognitive skills in problem solving in research databases too. Students employ metacognitive knowledge in planning search strategies such as deciding what fields to search as well as in the selection of databases and keywords. Students' monitoring activities are equally important, since they track students' understanding of the information retrieved and how it impacts continued search strategies. Likewise, these monitoring activities support students' self-regulation of the task, enabling them to modify search strategies to support new knowledge bases. Lastly, students need to evaluate the search results against the topic as well as the criteria for the assignment. The current revision of the Association of College & Research Libraries' Information Literacy Competency Standards for Higher Education to consider a variety of literacies including students' metacognitive abilities illustrates the Association's recognition of metacognition in supporting students' information search (Bell, 2013).

Metacognitive training and problem solving

Flavell (1976) promoted instructing children as well as adults in problem-solving skills that included examining "task features carefully," searching both internal and external sources for "solution-relevant information and procedures," as well as tracking "past solution efforts, and outcomes" (pp. 233–4). Brown (1977) joined Flavell in supporting metacognitive skill training in "checking, planning, asking questions, self-testing, and monitoring" to enhance children's problem-solving efforts (p. 73). Likewise, Glaser (1976) promoted teaching children self-regulation skills. He theorized that individuals might be taught strategies of feature scanning and analysis to notice "cues that prompt effective actions" while ignoring cues that foster ineffective actions (p. 20). Brown and Reeve (1984) argued that students can be taught self-regulation skills, providing the "instructor takes account of the learner's entering skill level" (p. 17).

Studies suggested that metacognitive training efforts remain successful in improving problem-solving skills for individuals of all ages. Masui and De Corte (1999) aimed to support university students' learning and problem-solving skills by enhancing their orienting and self-judging skills. The authors reported that students who received the metacognitive training were more knowledgeable of these skills than the control group. In addition, the experimental group's knowledge of orienting and self-judging led to improved academic performance.

Furthermore, research confirms the effectiveness of verbalization techniques in supporting individuals' use of metacognition in problem solving. Hacker and Dunlosky (2003) stated that concurrent "verbalization promotes metacognition," and this can foster problem solving, since it forces students to explain, justify, and rationalize their strategies (p. 75). Berardi-Coletta et al. (1995) found verbalization instructions that contained questions that focused the participant on the problem-solving process led to their superior performance, especially for learning and transfer problems. Steif et al. (2010) highlighted the success of a questioning strategy that promoted a "body-centered approach to statics problems" in facilitating students' abilities to apply conceptual knowledge in problem solving (p. 137).

Tajika et al. (2007) verified the importance of self-explanation as a metacognitive strategy in problem solving. The research focused on sixth-grade students who completed mathematical word problems utilizing self-explanation or self-learning techniques, or no techniques (control group). Results of a follow-up ratio word problem test revealed higher test scores for those students in the self-explanation group. Moreover, the authors found differences within the experimental group as well. The authors labeled individuals that generated many self-explanations "higher explainers" and noted these individuals "outperformed low explainers on both the ratio word problem and the transfer tests" (p. 230). The authors believed these differences could stem from high explainers' efforts to monitor their comprehension.

Idea tactics tutorial

The idea tactics tutorial contains metacognitive strategies designed to improve students' problem solving in research databases. These metacognitive strategies encourage students to plan, monitor, and regulate their problem solving. Detailed search examples provide information to foster the development of students' procedural as well as conditional knowledge in database search techniques. For example, expert modeling contains tips on how students can employ metacognitive strategies as well as utilize database features to foster optimal search outcomes. Moreover, search and idea tactic examples include conditional search information that offers rationales for applying tactics and accessing various database features.

Summary of problem solving and metacognition

Problem solving represents a complex cognitive as well as metacognitive endeavor. Comparisons between expert and novice problem solvers highlight differences in their knowledge structures, especially in the organization of information in their long-term memories. These differences allow expert problem solvers to access meaningful information quickly and efficiently, and this impacts the outcome of their problem solving. For example, expert chess players can create representations of problems that are more accurate than those of novice players. Still, Frensch and Sternberg (1989) argued that experts can also experience difficulties in problem solving that the authors attributed to a deficiency in their flexibility and/or their proceduralization, which prevents them from adopting strategies and novel approaches. Studies confirm the role of metacognitive skills in facilitating problem solving in planning, monitoring, regulating, and orchestrating the processes to foster the resolution of the problem. Individuals with high metacognition are better problem solvers, regardless of age or aptitude. Research suggests that individuals' problem solving benefits from instruction in metacognitive techniques. The idea tactics tutorial offers metacognitive strategies for students of all skill levels that enable them to gain control over their cognition while problem solving in research databases.

5

Information problem solving and metacognitive skills

Abstract: Interest in exploring the role of metacognition in IPS stemmed from studies and developments in the field of library science. More important was education researchers' use of the Big Six Skills model to understand how students solve information problems; this focused attention on the role of metacognition in IPS. In the millennium, a group of researchers in the European Union focused on information problem solving and metacognition. Studies revealed that students have difficulties solving information problems in online databases and on the web. The increasing importance of online information led to the development of IPS research that focused on strategies to improve students' problem-solving skills in these domains. The idea tactics tutorial provides metacognitive support for students' IPS in research databases.

Key words: information problem solving, IPS, metacognition, scaffolds, self-regulated learning, evaluation skills, prompts, big six, Big6 model, regulation activities.

Introduction

In the previous chapter, we discussed problem solving and metacognition from the perspective of cognitive psychologists and educational researchers. However, we now consider metacognition's effect on solving information problems. These require individuals' abilities to identify an information need, locate relevant sources, and organize and synthesize the information from various sources. Brand-Gruwel and Wopereis (2006) noted "information problems can be categorized; there are problems that require facts, problems that ask for a description of a construct, and problems that require connecting constructs" (p. 244).

These and other educational researchers joined information science theorists in studying the role of metacognition in facilitating individuals' information problem solving (IPS). The availability of online resources and their use in educational environments increased interest in improving students' IPS skills, especially in online databases and the web. Ultimately, this interest led to research on identifying optimal approaches to enhance students' IPS in online databases and on the web.

Evolution of information problem solving and metacognition research

Interest in exploring the role of metacognition in IPS stemmed from studies and developments in the field of library science. Moore's (1995) work represented one of the earliest studies of users' application of metacognitive strategies while problem solving for information. The author examined sixth-grade students' cognitive and metacognitive strategies as they utilized the school's library materials for an assignment. The author coded data gathered from interviews into three categories: metacognitive knowledge, executive control processes, and cognition associated with information retrieval and use. Her findings suggested students lacked variety in their information-seeking strategies. She also found differences in the quality of students' metacognitive knowledge and their use of executive control processes for planning tactics and monitoring events. She observed "correct interpretation of monitoring outcomes and ability to act upon the interpretation are critical" (p. 27). She emphasized that all students "engaged in higher order activities associated with executive control processes" (p. 27). In the article's conclusion, Moore identified factors affecting students' cognitive and metacognitive abilities, such as their knowledge of the library and its resources, the processes associated with information retrieval, and teacher expectations for the project. The article advocated class assignments that promoted "an understanding of thinking processes" and empirical studies on the information problem-solving process (p. 29).

Big Six Skills

Research on metacognitive strategies in IPS benefited indirectly from the development of Eisenberg and Berkowitz's (1988) Big Six Skills approach to library skills training. The Big Six Skills approach supported the development of students' information literacy through a six-step information problem-solving process including: task definition, information-seeking strategies, location and access, use of information, and synthesis, as well as evaluation. The approach offered an information literacy curriculum geared for K-12 students, but the authors maintained it was applicable for individuals of any age engaged in any situation that required information. The approach was designed "within the context of Bloom's taxonomy of cognitive objectives" and showed similarity to Kuhlthau's model of the library research process (p. 26). According to the authors, the Big Six Skills approach differed from traditional library skills instruction by its emphasis "on developing transferable, higher level thinking skills" that were "linked to the general school curriculum" (p. 28). In addition, numerous revisions to the model to address different learning environments as well as the availability of new technologies fostered its continued relevance and applicability to IPS (Eisenberg and Berkowitz, 1993, 2010).

Initially, the Big Six Skills approach did not directly address the use of metacognition in IPS, but merely referred to "higher levels of thinking" in the process (Eisenberg and Berkowitz, 1988, p. 28). However, in subsequent publications, the authors noted the importance of metacognition in IPS that they described as "evaluating the nature, tendencies, and preferences" of personal information problem-solving processes (1999, p. 114).

The Big Six Skills approach gained wide acceptance in school libraries. Its popularity led to efforts to examine its applicability for skills instruction and services in other library environments. For example, Cottrell and Eisenberg (2001) analyzed academic reference encounters utilizing the Big Six skills model of IPS. The authors concluded that location and access activities were observed extensively, synthesis activities less frequently, and many encounters included only one stage of the model. The authors advised employing the model to determine where the student was in the research process and providing relevant support, including ensuring the individual addressed all the necessary steps. In addition, the article noted that the findings pointed to the need for librarians to support students with the synthesis of information, and the authors recommended that libraries offer synthesis tools such as word processors, spreadsheets, and citation management software. If the latter was not feasible, the authors suggested combining libraries and computing centers, and educating staff in the IPS process.

More important was education researchers' use of the Big Six Skills model to understand how students solve information problems; this focused attention on the role of metacognition in IPS. Wolf et al. (2003) employed the Big Six Skills model as a metacognitive scaffold to enhance eighth-grade students' use of multimedia in solving information problems. A few years later, a group of researchers in the European Union began a series of studies that examined students' IPS based on a revised version of the Big Six Skills approach. Their model, and subsequent research, illustrated the importance of metacognitive skills in the IPS process.

Metacognition in information problem-solving research from the EU

In the millennium, a group of researchers in the European Union focused on information problem solving and metacognition. Brand-Gruwel et al. (2005) utilized a descriptive version of the "Big6" process model to examine IPS on the web by expert and novice students (p. 489). In this capacity, they revised the Big6 model to include general problem-solving skills such as the activation of prior knowledge in the users' definition of the information need. Moreover, the revised model contained five main skills, and each contained sub-skills. In addition, the metacognitive process of regulation, including orientation, monitoring, steering, and testing, was added to the model. The model proposed that regulation activities occurred throughout the problem-solving process and facilitated the "coordination of the process" (p. 491). The study tracked participants' time spent in performing the main skills, frequency in performing the main skills and sub-skills, search strategies in locating information on the web, regulation activities, and the outcome of the final product. The authors noted that experts devoted more time to tasks, especially in "scanning, processing, organizing, and presenting information," as well as more time monitoring and steering their actions (p. 502). The article listed instructional guidelines that emerged from the study and one component addressed enhancing students' regulation of the process (p. 504).

Similarly, Walraven et al. (2009) applied the descriptive IPS model in their study of secondary education students' criteria for evaluating search results, sources, and information available on the Internet. The research question considered how students solved information problems and what criteria they used to evaluate sources. Scores tracked students' time in constituent (main) skills and sub-skills activities, as well as regulation (metacognitive) activities. The results highlighted students' lack of attention to evaluating sources and information that they indicated stemmed from "time pressure, motivation and convenience" (p. 244). The authors surmised that students focused on searching and scanning activities rather than processing the information and organizing the final product. In their conclusion, the authors highlighted the importance of evaluation of sources in instructional opportunities and especially instructing students in IPS to promote its use in "multiple domains, tasks, and situations" (p. 245).

Likewise, Brand-Gruwel et al. (2009) verified the usefulness of their revised model of IPS using Internet (IPS-I model) on students from various age and discipline groups. The IPS-I model was based on the descriptive model for IPS utilized in earlier studies with the addition of three conditional skills including skills for reading and evaluating, as well as utilizing computers. The study demonstrated all students performed the five IPS constituent skills, including: define the information problem, search information, scan information, process information, and organize and present information and participants regulated the process. The authors concluded these were "constituent skills for the main skill called Information Problem Solving" (p. 1215). The research found secondary education students did not engage in monitoring, steering, and orienting during their IPS as often as the other groups. The study also revealed all participants focused on the usability of the source, rather than its reliability and reputation. The authors proposed the findings pointed to instruction in IPS focus on all the skills in the model including regulation. However, they acknowledged some students might have mastered sub-skills identified in the model and not require instruction in these areas.

Improving students' information problem solving

The increasing importance of online information, particularly on the Internet and databases, led to the development of IPS research that focused on strategies to improve students' problem-solving skills in these domains. The majority of these efforts centered on the descriptive model of IPS, but all of the studies included strategies to enhance students' metacognitive skills during the process.

Information problem-solving instruction

Brand-Gruwel and Wopereis (2006) studied the impact of integrated IPS instruction on 15 student teachers' problem solving, utilizing "authentic, comprehensive and whole tasks" (p. 248). Students received cognitive strategies as "Systematic Approaches for Problem Solving" in worksheets as well as mental models about IPS (pp. 249–50). The results showed that students in the instructional group devoted more attention to task requirements and information needs, judged sources more frequently, and spent more time processing information and regulating activities than the control group. In addition, the quality of their final product remained superior to those individuals who did not receive the IPS instruction.

Likewise, Wopereis et al. (2008) evaluated the benefits of IPS instruction to students in a distance education course on research methodologies. This instruction focused on specific sub-skills within the five categories, including: define problem, search information, scan information, process information, and organize and present information. Pre-test and post-test results focused on how frequently a skill was performed by the experimental and control groups. According to the authors, the experimental group performed better following a pre-test and post-test of students' IPS skills. Students receiving IPS instruction engaged in text scanning and information evaluation more often than those individuals in the control group. In addition, these students performed significantly more metacognitive activities compared to those in the control group such as "monitoring and steering the process" (p. 749). The authors credited the instruction with helping students regulate the IPS process, "especially when reflective questions" were included (p. 749).

Argelagos and Pifarre (2012) also utilized the descriptive model of information problem solving in their study of the effect of instruction for developing students' IPS skills over time. The participants were secondary students and the intervention focused on embedding IPS web-based activities in a variety of disciplines over time. The research structured students' problem solving and utilized scaffolds to support students' problem resolution. The post-test results revealed students in the experimental group scored higher for the constituent skill "defining the problem" as well as its sub-skills, "search terms" and "selected results" than the control group. The experimental group had higher scores for task performance than those without treatment as well. The authors observed that the worksheets available to those students in the experimental group helped them analyze the website contents, and the prompts encouraged "them to read and process its information" (p. 524).

Walraven et al. (2010) employed the descriptive model of IPS in their test of the instructional use of two transfer theories to foster secondary students' evaluation skills in IPS. The authors described the high road transfer theory developed by Salomon and Perkins (1989) as representing a "conscious formulation of abstraction stimulating metacognitive skills" (p. 717). On the other hand, they noted that Simons et al.'s (2000) rich representation theory promoted a "good extensive and well organized knowledge base and the domain specific interpretation of the skills" (p. 717). The high road program centered on IPS and the "evaluation of results, sources, and information," and included the use of process worksheets for problem solving (p. 718). The rich representation study highlighted the use of mind map techniques and students engaged in discussions about criteria used to evaluate results as well as completed tasks focusing on "specific criteria" (p. 720). Students in both groups received a "reader on information problem solving" that contained the necessary phases for information problem solving including rationale for the steps and "rules of thumb concerning evaluation criteria" (p. 718). The findings revealed that the differences among the programs in fostering students' knowledge and use of evaluation criteria were minimal. The authors noted that the use of the "rich representation program realized a stronger effect" (p. 725), but it was more difficult to implement. The article stated that evaluation instruction promoted better web searching among students.

In addition to instructing students in IPS, efforts to support students during the process also encompassed the availability of prompts. These prompts ranged in focus and content, but all aimed to promote students' metacognitive skills.

Prompts

Raes et al. (2012) compared different forms of scaffolding to enhance the domain-specific knowledge and the metacognitive awareness among high school students' IPS on the web. The scaffolding included teachers, technology or both. The Web-Based Inquiry Science Environment provided the design to the project that included "a whole-task approach" with embedded instruction that supported IPS constituent skills and sub-skills (p. 85). The authors found that all groups benefited from the scaffolding, especially the teacher-enhanced. Students with low prior knowledge benefited the most from teacher-enhanced scaffolds or a combination of teacher and technology. The type of scaffold used for students with high prior knowledge had no impact on their post-test results. The authors suggested that the technology-based scaffold remained the best for increasing students' metacognitive awareness.

Gagniere et al. (2012) evaluated the use of metacognitive prompts in a collaborative setting, utilizing three steps of the descriptive model of IPS, including: searching, classifying, and presenting the information. The authors maintained that the prompts led to an increased evidence of metacognition in the experimental group during searching. The authors also suggested an indirect effect of the prompts was the activation of the experimental group's use of metanavigation strategies that produced "better monitoring and controlling of processes" (p. 79).

Ifenthaler (2012) compared generic with directed prompts to foster individuals' self-regulation of the problem-solving process. In this study, directed prompts offered information on planning, monitoring and evaluating ongoing problem-solving activities. On the other hand, the generic prompts centered on "general instructions for planning and reflecting on their ongoing problem-solving activities" (p. 42). Data included a pre-test and post-test as well as participants' construction of a concept map. The findings revealed the superiority of generic prompts in improving participants' domain-specific knowledge and their "structural and semantic understanding of the problem scenario" (p. 48).

Stadtler and Broome (2008) tested the availability of *met.a.ware*, a tool that offered metacognitive prompts to participants searching for health-related information on the Internet. The authors described *met.a.ware* as providing indirect support for individuals' use of metacognitive strategies through the availability of ontological categories for note taking. Moreover, *met.a.ware* prompting sought to help individuals monitor their comprehension and evaluate information. The authors reported that participants who utilized the *met.a.ware* tool during their search sessions contained more knowledge about sources than individuals in the control group. The study also demonstrated the superiority of participants' note taking, which the authors attributed to the ontological categories.

De Vries et al. (2008) reported on their efforts to test the usefulness of a portal and a worksheet to support elementary students' reflective web searching in two experiments. The authors defined reflective web searching as promoting ownership over the search questions through interpreting and personalizing web content and adapting web content into meaningful answers. The worksheet asked students to identify the question and what students thought, as well as what they found on the web. The portal contained task categories that offered hyperlinks with meaningful descriptions. The authors concluded that "reflective web searching occurred while searching and through talking" (p. 664). However, they found that students' final answers were "literal adoptions with minor syntactical adjustments" (p. 664). They recommended supporting children "to adapt what they *find and think* into personally meaningful answers" (p. 664).

Idea tactics tutorial

The idea tactics tutorial shares similarity to the scaffolds described above in providing metacognitive support for students' IPS in research databases. However, while the metacognitive skills promoted in the descriptive model of IPS centered on students' regulation processes, the idea tactics tutorial also encourages students' use of planning, monitoring, and evaluation skills. These skills remain especially important in IPS, since individuals need to plan a strategy and evaluate its continued effectiveness throughout the process to achieve successful outcomes. Moreover, in the tutorial, metacognitive tactics are offered as prompts to guide students in selecting new strategies to improve their search outcomes. The tutorial also provides instruction in the use of database search techniques, and some of these strategies parallel steps in the problem-solving process. In addition, the tutorial contains expert modeling of an information search in research databases that illustrates the step-by-step process of IPS utilizing an authentic information need.

Summary of information problem solving and metacognition

The availability of online resources, especially the Internet, and their use in educational environments highlighted the importance of students' IPS skills in the millennium. The majority of IPS research focused on a revised version of the Big Six Skills model of information problem solving. This model described IPS as a five-step process composed of main (constituent) skills and sub-skills, as well as regulation (metacognitive) activities. The research focused on understanding how students solve information problems as well as developing supports for the process. Although the studies identified students' deficiencies in IPS, research on the provision of scaffolds during the process demonstrated their effectiveness in helping students to solve information problems. Foremost, the assessment of these scaffolds illustrates the importance of metacognitive support in fostering successful outcomes for students' IPS in online searching.

6

Education graduate students' information-seeking skills

Abstract: Studies reveal education graduate students lack database search skills, including knowledge of resources and search methodologies. Some studies also point to students' anxiety while performing search activities. Research highlights the importance of library skills instruction in improving these individuals' search strategies, and the literature revealed a wide range of training opportunities developed for this audience. One study indicated students were dissatisfied with their previous library instruction. In addition, very few of instructional efforts identified in the research contained assessment components. However, those efforts that assessed students' learning gains revealed individuals benefited from skills training. The idea tactics tutorial was developed to support the information-seeking behavior and information literacy deficiencies of education graduate students.

Key words: education graduate students, information-seeking behavior, search skills, deficiencies, information literacy, library training, instruction.

Introduction

A literature review of education graduate students' information-seeking behavior from the early 1980s to the present illustrated the difficulties these individuals encountered conducting research in print as well as electronic sources. In 1996, Fabiano observed graduate education students "are neither efficient nor effective library users" (p. 160). Nearly 20 years later, Switzer and Perdue suggested students lacked "a clear understanding of research constraints and fail to compile peer-reviewed scholarship, particularly seminal studies" (p. 4). Recent literature emphasized the importance of the Internet and especially online resources to these students, but authors noted that students lacked search skills and remained confused about selecting sources. Studies also pointed to a variety of library instructional opportunities for these students and the benefits they received from the training. However, the majority of these training efforts lacked formal assessment measures that confirmed their effectiveness in enhancing students' knowledge of library resources. Studies support the value of library instruction in improving students' research skills. O'Hanlon (1988) linked information-seeking skills' instruction to developing teachers' problem-solving abilities, improving their lesson planning, and imparting research skills to their pupils. We believed education graduate students would benefit from a metacognitive approach to library skills instruction. Consequently, we developed the idea tactics tutorial based on education graduate students' information-seeking habits, their information literacy deficiencies, as well as previous library training efforts for these individuals as identified in the literature. This research, outlined in the chapter, highlights the appropriateness of our scaffold in addressing students' difficulties in problem solving in research databases. Ultimately, instructing education graduate students in planning, monitoring, and self-regulating their search strategies offers numerous benefits beyond improving their information retrieval efforts in research databases.

Early research

"Where do I begin?" and other search difficulties

One of the earliest studies of education graduate students library search skills centered on a survey of 100 graduate students enrolled in an educational research course at Memphis State University. The findings revealed students encountered time restraints, difficulty locating materials, and did not consult librarians for assistance (Blummer et al., 2012; Park, 1986). Moreover, Park noted that students described their search outcomes as only "somewhat" successful (p. 14). Most students suffered from an inability to determine where "to begin" (p. 14). Park suggested the results pointed to the need for students to identify their information needs as well as develop skills to interact with information systems (Blummer et al., 2012). Consequently, Park (1986) described the library's development of search worksheet to assist Memphis State University's users with their information search by asking users to identify specific concepts (p. 18) and relevant terms (Blummer et al., 2012).

Evans (1986) referenced Park's findings in his proposal for a research skills course aimed at education graduate students at the institution. "Information Resources for Educational Research" would include a pre-test administered early in the semester "to determine the specific contents of the inclass presentation" (p. 18). The author noted that the presentation would include two parts: a broad general perspective on educational research literature, and instruction in research strategies (Blummer et al., 2012).

A survey of Fordham University's education graduate students' information skills revealed these students would also benefit from library support. Responses to open-ended survey questions and focus group interviews highlighted students' tendencies to avoid special collections and basic reference sources (Libutti, 1991, p. 11). The author noted that students' lack of attention to these resources remained problematic due to the importance of these sources for advanced research.

Hesitancy in utilizing electronic resources

Authors suggested that education graduate students were slow to adopt electronic resources, particularly online journals, in their research efforts. A survey of Rutgers University's education doctoral students' use of library resources revealed many respondents had never used CD-ROMs, online indexes, abstracts, databases, or the online catalog, as well as other libraries' online catalogs (Fabiano, 1996, p. 164). The author concluded that students needed instruction in utilizing these sources and pointed to students' comments on their need for library assistance.

LeBaron et al. (1998) reported similar findings with their examination of education graduate students' use of the Internet at the University of Massachusetts, Lowell. In this instance, students created an e-journal of education-related Internet resources. An analysis of students' contributions to the e-journal revealed that the majority were not retrieved from the search engines recommended by the instructor. Many students utilized sources from the print literature. The authors observed the findings led to more emphasis on "traditional Internet information sources," encouraging students to use "network based research tools," promoting student participation in email listservs, and examination of professional resources (pp. 199–200).

Education graduate students' research skills in the millennium

Lack of information literacy skills

Authors pointed to education graduate students' lack of information literacy skills. Sosin and Deleo (2005) noted that these students lacked technology skills as well as a familiarity with the professional literature. Moreover, the authors maintained that students remained confused about the difference between information literacy and "issues of technology" (p. 212). Four years later, Deleo et al. (2009) queried graduate education students on the meaning of information literacy, and concluded that many individuals remained confused over the definition. The authors stated that all the students in the study described themselves as information literate, but the research found "just over half" of the participants defined information literacy correctly (p. 441). In addition, the study revealed a significant number of participants lacked an understanding of the contents of the library's online catalog as well as the Library of Congress Classification system (p. 441). In their discussion, the authors emphasized the importance of library training for these students and especially brevity in instruction. To that end, they recommended two library skills training sessions for an Educational Leadership and Technology program. The first session would identify students' weaknesses and include the use of clickers and the "turn and talk" methodology, whereby students discussed the question and answer with their closest classmate. A second session would focus on developing specific research skills.

Switzer and Perdue (2011) blamed education graduate students' difficulties in researching and writing their thesis literature reviews to the abundance of information in the education field, coupled with "a dearth of institutional resources for native graduate writers" (p. 4). According to the authors, a librarian and the director of the writing center at the institution, students could locate "piles of information on a given topic in their field," but struggled with performing an exhaustive literature review as well as synthesizing the information (p. 4). The authors maintained that this left many individuals feeling discouraged and overwhelmed.

High use of online journals and the Internet

Earp (2008) surveyed Kent State University's education graduate students' information preferences. The findings underscored the importance of the Internet for research, a preference for online journals, and failure to seek assistance in conducting research (Blummer et al., 2012; Earp, 2008). Earp noted that doctoral students were more apt to seek assistance from faculty, but master's students typically sought help from classmates. She also observed that education graduate students ranked education databases second as sources of important information. In addition, the research revealed barely half of the doctoral students had utilized dissertations for research, and their use was limited to once or twice a semester (Blummer et al., 2012; Earp, 2008).

Dissatisfaction with previous library instruction

Blummer et al. (2012) utilized Earp's survey along with semi-structured interviews with five students to identify the information-seeking habits of individuals enrolled in a mid-Atlantic state's college of education's master's programs. The results supported research that found a high use of the Internet among graduate students in locating information. In addition, the study's illustration of education graduate students' feelings of confusion and uncertainty when researching supported previous findings. For example, two interview participants described problems related to gauging when to stop gathering information for a research paper, as well as in the creation of the paper. Most important, however, was several survey respondents' dissatisfaction with the content of their previous library instruction. The authors surmised that the results pointed to the need for flexibility in library skills instruction and including information on appropriate library database subscriptions, "techniques for gauging completeness, and tips for revising the final product" (Blummer et al., 2012).

Anxiety

Studies highlighted education graduate students' anxiety while performing research-related activities. Green and Bowser (2002) sought to reduce off-campus graduate education students' anxiety through a faculty-librarian partnership in teaching thesis and research courses at the institution's satellite centers. Pre-test and post-tests centered on graduate education students' anxiety levels regarding the thesis process. The authors acknowledged the pilot was small and the results were inconclusive, but they observed a "trend toward reduction of anxiety in the post-collaboration students" for some questions (p. 348).

Katopol's (2012) study of African American students in a graduate education program in a predominately Caucasian institution also confirmed earlier research on students' anxiety when researching and reluctance to seek library help (Earp, 2008; Green and Bowser, 2002). Katopol reported that black students encountered significant information anxiety, and this impeded their information seeking. The qualitative study focused on open-ended interviews that sought to review the information sources the students used and their behavior when performing information behavior tasks. The author stated that participants "felt anxious or lost when engaged in information search," but the research found students typically sought help from their peers rather than librarians (p. 7). Moreover, the study highlighted African American education graduate students' preference for online resources that they typically accessed through the Internet; this finding confirmed earlier research on education graduate students' information-seeking behavior (Earp, 2008; Green and Macauley, 2007). In addition, Katopol (2012) indicated that black students believed "librarians had no knowledge of their racially-related research interests" and would not be able to assist them in their searches (p. 8). The author summarized that these students suffered from information anxiety, which she related to the amount of information they discovered. She also observed that students experienced anxiety when contacting librarians or faculty "who knew little about research on minority populations" (p. 12). The article's conclusion pointed to the need to recognize factors that impeded black graduate education students' information search, such as the inability to find collections that supported their research interests. To this end, the author recommended collaborating with departments to develop collections to support minority interests as well as showing "students the variety of resources" and helping "them become more comfortable with them" (p. 13). Nevertheless, Katopol acknowledged that black education graduate students had similar information needs to other graduate students.

Likewise, a study of education doctoral students identified time and assignments as increasing anxiety among the focus group members. One student suggested that the library, and especially technology-related issues in accessing library information, remained particularly unnerving. She commented that it would have been helpful to have assistance in clearing "those hurdles related to technology on the library" (Miller and Irby, 1999, para. 18).

Importance of instruction to provide "new skills, new knowledge"

Green and Macauley (2007) interviewed doctoral-level education candidates in the United States and Australia, as well as with their university librarians, to identify individuals' information skills. The authors observed that beginning doctoral students utilized familiar sources and Google to find information. The article highlighted the importance of these students' information literacy skills in supporting their research efforts and especially facilitating the completion of their literature review. In addition, the article suggested that students' metacognitive skills supported their research, as the authors acknowledged the value of students' learning schemes. The authors suggested developing instruction based on individual needs (Blummer et al., 2012).

A study at the University of Hong Kong centered on tracking the development of education and engineering graduate students' search skills over time (Chu and Law, 2007). The authors stated that beginning students remained confused over the difference between subject and keyword searches, and that they often obtained insufficient results. Still, the article noted that students gained knowledge with skills instruction over time and improved their search performance (Blummer et al., 2010; Blummer et al., 2012).

Library training for education graduate students

The literature documented the development of a wide variety of library training opportunities to address the deficiencies in education graduate students' research skills. Early efforts were centered in the academic library and included classes in bibliographic training, presentations on the Education Resources Information Center ERIC, the creation of library guides for graduate students, and the development of pathfinders, as well as librarian support for thesis and dissertation research (Blummer, 2009; Clayton and Nordstrom, 1987; Hoover and Clayton, 1989; Pickert and Chwalek, 1984).

Following the millennium, academic librarians often teamed with education faculty to promote education graduate students' information literacy or higher-order thinking skills (Blummer, 2009). For example,

Grant and Berg (2003) facilitated the incorporation of the ACRL's Information Literacy Competency Standards in Higher Education within a doctorate of Educational Technology and Literacy program. In addition, Hooks and Corbett (2005) discussed their efforts to integrate information literacy instruction into a graduate education curriculum through a constructivist approach. Bhavnagri and Bielat (2005) described a project at Wayne State University that included Blackboard as well as librarian-led bibliographic instruction to scaffold education graduate students to develop better search skills and knowledge of research materials.

Most training lacked comprehensive assessment

Unfortunately, the assessment of these training measures was typically anecdotal and provided little indication of their success (Blummer et al., 2010). For example, Pickert and Chwalek (1984) attributed Catholic University's librarians' training program to support the institution's education graduate students, to facilitating their development from "dependent, wary and infrequent users of library information to independent confident and competent producers of scholarly research" (pp. 383–94). Clayton and Nordstrom (1987) stated that their library support for Queens College graduate education students in a required research seminar class received "positive feedback." The authors noted that librarians "deal with more articulate questions from students who are confident about using the library" (p. 53). Likewise, Hooks and Corbett's (2005) integration of information literacy instruction in the curriculum at a college of education lacked an assessment feature as well. However, the authors claimed that students' "academic work" had improved through better writing skills that remained especially evident in their postings on the learning management system (p. 253).

Some instruction contained formal assessment measures

Still, assessment measures were a component of a few of the research training efforts for education graduate students (Blummer, 2009). Franklin and Toifel's (1994) assessment of bibliographic instruction for the University of West Florida's education graduate and undergraduate students centered on comparisons of individuals' pre-test and post-test scores. These tests tracked students' library knowledge and familiarity with the online catalog, as well as knowledge about ERIC and other education databases. The assessment found that all students benefited from the bibliographic instruction, especially undergraduate students. However, the authors noted that this may have stemmed from graduate students' higher pre-test scores than those of undergraduate students.

An assessment of a library training unit for education graduate students in the University of Arkansas' College of Education's Higher Education Leadership program included a quiz on educational resources, a self-assessment of library skills, and an anonymous evaluation of the unit (Blummer, 2009; Murray et al., 1997). The findings supported the success of the training endeavor. Similarly, Bhavnagri and Bielat (2005) reported favorable results for their integration of bibliographic instruction for an education research course at Wayne State University. The authors utilized students' self-assessment and all of the individuals indicated improved library search skills following the instruction.

Beile (2002) conducted a quantitative analysis of graduate education students' pre-test and post-test of library skills and self-efficacy levels to assess library training for the University of Central Florida's education graduate students. In this instance, Beile focused on learning outcomes and self-efficacy levels of students in three instructional environments including: face-to-face instruction, a web-based tutorial available on campus, and an online version for distance education students. The study compared pre-test and post-test results of students' self-efficacy and knowledge of library skills utilizing a Pearson correlation coefficient between the scores. The findings revealed that all students benefited from the instruction and there was no significant difference in students' library skills gains among the three instructional environments. Still, Beile linked prior library instruction to higher scores in both "pretreatment and posttreatment" self-efficacy levels and library skills scores (p. 6).

Idea tactics tutorial

The idea tactics tutorial supports education graduate students' information-seeking behavior and especially their information literacy deficiencies. The tutorial addresses these students' preferences for online resources with its focus on improving their search outcomes in research databases. Moreover, the tutorial's content promotes the use of education-related databases. The scaffold seeks to improve students' search in research databases through a two-pronged approach. First, students are provided with metacognitive strategies to enhance their abilities to plan, monitor, and regulate their search. Second, the availability of database search strategies, which include expert modeling, instructs students in the use of multiple search features. Qualitative and quantitative measures support the assessment of the tutorial's effectiveness in improving students' search outcomes. Quantitative results centered on a comparison of the relevance, the authoritativeness, the ability to answer the problem, and the quality of the students' search outcomes before and after exposure to the tutorial. These results indicated improvements for most students. The qualitative assessment of the tutorial focused on interviews with students, and the majority expressed favorable attitudes toward the scaffold.

Summary of education graduate students' information behavior

Foremost, these studies of education graduate students' information-seeking behavior shares similarities to studies with their counterparts in other disciplines in illustrating the need for library training (George et al., 2006). Students lacked knowledge of education resources as well as database methodologies, despite library training efforts. In addition, many of these individuals experience anxiety while researching. These factors, coupled with the lack of definitive assessments of library training measures for education graduate students, suggest they would benefit from instruction that contained a metacognitive perspective on information search. The idea tactics tutorial offers opportunities to improve students' planning, monitoring, and regulating their search activity. The scaffold also provides database search techniques designed to improve search outcomes. Foremost, improving students' metacognitive skills encourages individuals to take control over all of their cognitive endeavors such as synthesizing their research in the writing papers and especially completing the literature review for their thesis.

7

Education students' information seeking to support problem solving

Abstract: Research on education students' problem solving in open-ended learning environments (OELE) and open environment information systems (OEIS) illustrated that participants lacked metacognitive as well as information-seeking skills. These environments include the World Wide Web, and searching in these ill-structured systems can be challenging to users. Studies illustrated that participants with low metacognition often became disoriented in these environments, and this affected their search outcomes. Research also revealed the importance of metacognitive knowledge and prior subject knowledge on participants' search strategies. Comparisons between expert and novice searchers found that experts demonstrated more metacognitive behaviors than their counterparts during search. Studies suggest that enhancing students' metacognitive skills as well as their database search strategies improves problem-solving outcomes.

Key words: education graduate students, pre-service teachers, problem solving, information-seeking skills, open-ended learning environments (OELE), open environment information systems (OEIS), metacognitive techniques.

Introduction

Studies tracing undergraduate and graduate education students' abilities to locate online information to solve problems reveal numerous deficiencies in participants' abilities, and underscore the need for instructing individuals in metacognitive techniques to enhance their search skills. The location of relevant information remains essential for effective problem solving. Problem solving through open-ended learning environments (OELE) is particularly challenging. Hannafin et al. (1994)

stated that learners' use of metacognitive strategies was critical in OELE for judging relevance and evaluating their "own thinking" (p. 50). In 1999, Hill differentiated between open-ended information systems (OEIS) and traditional electronic information systems. According to Hill, in the latter systems the availability of features such as controlled vocabularies or limiting features shifted the responsibility of the search to the system. However, in OEIS, the user actively navigated and searched the system and assumed "a primary role in processing in information retrieved" (p. 6). To this end, she highlighted the challenges faced by users in these environments, especially naïve users due to their "limited system, subject, and metacognitive knowledge" that affected their "problem solving and understanding" (p. 9). Studies discussed in this chapter center on education students' problem solving in the web as OELE and OEIS. As the research revealed, the ill-structured nature of the web provided participants with diverse opportunities for critical thinking, resource discovery, and scaffolding to support problem solving. Numerous authors view information seeking as a form of problem solving (Brand-Gruwel et al., 2005; Laxman, 2010). As Land and Greene (2000) remind us, information problem solving requires the abilities to identify the information problem and locate relevant materials, as well as synthesize and integrate information from a variety of sources. Ultimately, this research underscores education students' deficiencies in both metacognitive and information-seeking skills. It also suggests that education graduate students would enhance their web and database searching by planning, monitoring, and self-regulating their behaviors.

Education students' metacognition in information problem solving in hypermedia systems

Janette Hill conducted several studies that illustrated the impact of metacognitive knowledge of education students' information search. Her dissertation research in 1995 explored the impact of perceived self-efficacy, as well as system, subject, and metacognitive knowledge on four education students' search for information in a hypermedia system. The research yielded videotaped computer screens of participants' search processes and responses to post-search questionnaires that "focused on participants' reflections of the search" (p. 62). A pre-survey examined participants' metacognitive, system, and subject knowledge. Hill concluded that high levels of metacognitive knowledge "increased the chances for success," which she attributed to students' abilities "to reflect on cognitive processes and to, in turn use this knowledge to inform actions" (p. 101). She also linked metacognitive knowledge to orientation in working in hypermedia systems. The study found that participants with low metacognition were more apt to become disoriented in the system, and their disorientation affected search outcomes. Hill identified metacognitive knowledge as exerting the most influence on the "strategies used while working in Netscape" and she linked participants' level of metacognitive knowledge to success in using the system (p. 125). For example, she attributed Mick's search success to his well-informed actions that were "guided by his high level of metacognitive knowledge" (p. 126).

Importance of metacognitive knowledge

In a similar study, Hill and Hannafin (1997) examined the effect of education students' metacognitive, system, and subject knowledge as well as their perceived orientation and self-efficiency on their World Wide Web search strategies. The findings supported the role of metacognitive knowledge and especially prior subject knowledge on participants' search strategies. The study also linked participants' feelings of disorientation to severe hindering of their search strategies. The article suggested that participants' disorientation interfered with their abilities to "reference" their prior knowledge as well as their metacognitive knowledge (p. 58). The authors observed that "participants with high metacognitive knowledge appeared better able to reflect on their search processes and revise their strategies accordingly" (p. 56). They also noted the importance of individuals assimilating new knowledge into "existing schemata" (p. 61). Their research confirmed the need for instructing users in locating information in open-ended systems.

Metacognitive skills improve search outcomes

Tabatabai and Luconi's (1998) study of education graduate students' information seeking for problem solving also linked metacognitive skills to improved search outcomes. The authors compared the web-based problem-solving strategies of three experts and three novices. The results revealed that experts devoted more time to navigation and metacognitive strategies or planning search strategies, setting goals, and reflecting on the task compared to the novices. The authors observed that the experts began their search with a plan, but "novices did not articulate a plan" and instead utilized trial and error strategies (p. 391). Moreover, the research found experts utilized more search engines and navigational strategies than novices. The study illustrated differences in goal setting among the groups as well. Experts set goals and did not put a "time limit to their task" (p. 391). In addition, the groups displayed different attitudes and feelings during the search. Experts remained "more relaxed, confident, and satisfied" with their search results, but novices "became tired and lost due to information overload" (p. 391). All novices experienced frustration, which the article attributed to a lack of computing skills for utilizing search engines, reducing search results, and evaluating reliability of websites. The authors maintained that the findings pointed to the value of instructing students in developing critical thinking skills, using metaphorical knowledge to map problems, and developing planning and self-regulating strategies to facilitate web searching.

In addition, Land and Greene's (2000) work with pre-service teachers' information seeking on the web highlighted the role of metacognition in problem solving. The authors observed nine pre-service teachers' information-seeking processes to identify strategies used by individuals to judge relevance in resources and their sense-making efforts from "disparate resources to generate a coherent project" (p. 48). Participants worked in groups to locate resources and synthesize the material into a final product. The authors linked differences in outcomes to participants' domain, system, and metacognitive knowledge. The article suggested that all groups illustrated metacognitive knowledge by reflecting and monitoring the search process, but they attributed "effective metacognition" to system and domain knowledge (pp. 57–8). In addition, the findings highlighted the importance of initially establishing goals and subsequently locating resources to develop a "coherent" project (p. 61). To this end, the findings highlighted the importance of goals in problem solving in OELE, especially for ill-defined problems. The article recommended "external support mechanisms that help learners develop strategies for effectively learning with project-based environments" (p. 61) and helping learners to "reflect on and articulate their ongoing understanding in a complex learning environment" (p. 64).

Different metacognitive behaviors among experts and novices

Likewise, Tabatabai and Shore's (2005) research underscored the role of metacognitive skills in enhancing participants' information seeking for problem solving. The authors explored variation among search habits for ten undergraduate pre-service teachers (novices), nine library and information studies graduate students (intermediaries), and ten professional librarians (experts) utilizing a think-aloud protocol. Tabatabai and Shore sought to understand if experts utilized different strategies than intermediaries and novices, as well as the relationship between strategies and the timely success of web search. A pre-survey illustrated participants' information seeking and computer skills, as well as web knowledge. The authors concluded that "experts monitored themselves and the process better" than other participants (p. 232). In addition, experts focused on cognitive strategies such as thinking, reading and planning, while novices "used fewer cognitive strategies than experts" (p. 232). Experts were also better able to rationalize their strategy use.

On the other hand, the authors pointed to novices' tendencies to lose patience and rely on "trial and error" strategies (p. 238). According to the article, "what really differentiated experts and novices was how they dealt with search anxiety" (p. 233). For instance, Tabatabai and Shore noted that experts remained positive, but novices and intermediaries became frustrated. The authors maintained that novices "felt lost, disoriented, and caught in a labyrinth" compared to experts (p. 238).

The study identified evaluation and metacognition as the two most important strategies in facilitating searching success. Moreover, the authors highlighted the role of "meta-affect or awareness of one's feelings" on participants' search experience. The article stated that experts remained "more aware of their feelings" and used them to change their strategies (p. 238); this contributed to their positive attitude toward the search compared to novices, who experienced disorientation. In their conclusion, Tabatabai and Shore highlighted the importance of instruction for student teachers in web searching, such as understanding "criteria for evaluating sites," "thinking and planning" search strategies, reflecting and monitoring the search process, and maintaining a positive attitude during the process (p. 240).

Metacognition in group problem solving

Recent research demonstrated the role of pre-service teachers' metacognition in fostering their resolution of a problem-based learning exercise using multimedia and the Internet in a group setting (Siegel, 2012). The problem-based learning exercise centered on identifying strategies to enhance student learning during a static electricity and atomic structure unit. The group watched video cases of instructors teaching two classes and they also consulted a mentor, the Internet, textbooks, and other materials to gather ideas for improved instructional strategies. Siegel identified three aspects of group metacognition. First, she observed metasocial awareness among the participants, which she defined as identifying group members' experience. Second, she witnessed participants' efforts to monitor understanding for themselves and others as well as reveal the group's knowledge deficiencies. Third, Siegel noted that the group monitored processes publicly and adjusted their goals accordingly. The latter, she maintained, was especially important, as the group shifted the learning issue to instructional questions and that led to their focus on the more "suitable" topic of atomic models and charge separation rather than static electricity. According to the article, the group's final paper provided a professional "instructional rationale for models, misconceptions, and model use" (p. 339).

Education students' lack of computing skills

Low system skills

Research revealed that education students are often handicapped in searching, due to low system skills. Tabatabai and Luconi (1998) attributed novice education graduate students' frustration in web searching to their lack of knowledge of search engines, as well as a lack of methods to reduce search results and evaluate websites. Other researchers point to similar findings. Marks (2009) examined pre-service teachers' understanding and use of technology, and how it impacted their classroom practice. The author found that the students, despite their relatively young age, had "little or no experience with more creative and innovative technologies such as digital cameras, iMovie, blogs, podcasts, personal web pages, and Macintosh computers" (p. 367). In 1999,

Owens suggested that "pre-service teachers may enter upper-level education courses either unfamiliar with or unprepared for using the Internet for teaching related purposes" (p. 134). He surveyed pre-service teachers' Internet use and discovered that nearly three-fourths of respondents had negative experiences. They complained about the time needed to access information and obtain prints, and about difficulty in finding sites to meet assignment requirements. Students also expressed disappointment with the quality of the information found.

Colaric et al.'s (2004) survey of 355 pre-service teachers' knowledge of search engines suggested these individuals required Internet training to improve their web search skills. The authors reported that many participants lacked an understanding of how results were returned, employed simple queries for searches, and remained confused about the operation of Boolean concepts.

Bullock (2013) discussed his experiences as an instructor for *Teaching and Learning with ICT*, a mandatory course for teacher candidates at Simon Fraser University in Canada. The author noted that prerequisites for the course included students' "academic qualifications for two 'teachable' subjects" (p. 111), but he observed that some students still lacked advanced computing skills.

Lack of ICT confidence

Studies reveal pre-service teachers lack confidence in their ICT capabilities as well. Markauskaite (2007) found the University of Sydney's pre-service postgraduate teachers to be only moderately confident in their information and Internet-related capabilities. She stated there were "differences" in the level of their confidence in "advanced technical capabilities" too (p. 566). The research also found that pre-service teachers' confidence in their cognitive ICT capabilities ranged from moderately confident to quite confident, with students "more confident with communication and metacognition than problem solving" (p. 566). The article highlighted the need to enhance students' technical and cognitive ICT capabilities in tandem. Some instructional efforts in this direction included the incorporation of problem-based learning exercises and "problem solving strategies into ICT-related courses" (p. 568).

Institutional obstacles and technology anxiety

Education students' lack of computing expertise stemmed in part from institutional obstacles and technology anxiety. Mukama (2009) utilized interviews and focus group discussions in his study of Rwanda's student teachers' use of information communications technology (ICT) to solve problems. He identified institutional constraints as the small number of computers, the wealth of materials, and difficulty in assessing it. He described individual constraints as "linked to the participant's personal capacity as novice users" (p. 545). He differentiated among three types of ICT users: passive, reluctant, and active. According to Mukama, passive and reluctant ICT users complained of time restraints or technophobia in explaining their avoidance of using computers. On the other hand, the article stated that active ICT users sought to utilize web materials. Mukama proposed that active ICT users be utilized as change agents in fostering technology adoption among their peers. Dutt-Doner et al. (2005) maintained that their collaborative work with teacher candidates revealed that students "had limited training in using technology to transform their practice, limited exposure to information literacy skills" (p. 67). The authors described a case study aimed at infusing technical literacy, web resources, and meaningful teaching experiences into the curriculum of a teacher preparation program.

Metacognition compensates for problem-solving deficiencies

Land and Green's (2000) study of education students' problem solving on the web revealed individuals' use of metacognition can compensate for moderate system and low domain knowledge. The authors described a group learning scenario that centered on the identification of projects for integrating the Internet into the curriculum. The article outlined the stock markets' groups' completion of the assignment that "effectively integrated their project methods, implementation requirements, resources, and rationales in sophisticated ways" (p. 52). The authors noted that the group "demonstrated high metacognitive knowledge, but had only novice-level system knowledge and low domain knowledge" (p. 58). According to the article, the "learners' ongoing discussion of the search process in light of their evolving goal" fostered the effective completion of their project (p. 58). The authors surmised that "discussion occurred because their thinking about where their searching was leading was not synchronized, so their interaction became both a metacognitive and dialectical process around which their project idea evolved and consolidated" (p. 58).

Land and Green contrasted the stock market's group's successful completion of the assignment with another case that had similar system and domain skills, but developed a project that "reflected poor integration of the topic, methods, rationales, and information resources" (p. 53). This case sought to develop various approaches to teaching Shakespeare, but the group's metacognition did not compensate for their low system and domain skills in fostering effective completion of the project. The authors attributed the lack of compensatory metacognition in part to students' failure to admit their low domain and computing knowledge. According to the article, the group "rarely engaged in any metacognitive processing" such as analyzing the difficulties with teaching approaches to Shakespeare and identifying a better approach (p. 64).

Ge and Land (2004) noted the importance of domain specific knowledge in solving ill-structured problems that are often characteristic of those encountered in OELE, such as the web. Still, research demonstrates the power of metacognitive strategies in overcoming individuals' deficiencies in problem solving. Wineberg (1998) contrasted two expert historians' sense-making efforts as they read various primary source documents. The author stated that despite one historian's unfamiliarity with the subject matter, his use of various strategies such as asking questions, "reserving judgments," monitoring responses, and "revisiting earlier assessments" facilitated his sense-making (p. 340). Wineberg concluded that the findings contained implications for learning and especially for teaching students "how to sort through contradictory information and come to reasoned conclusions" (p. 340). Likewise Chi et al.'s (1989) research on students' study habits revealed that metacognitive strategies such as individuals' use of self-explanations helped their understanding and problem solving (p. 177).

Similarly, Doganay and Demir (2011) studied prospective teachers' metacognition based on Namlu's (2004) Metacognitive Strategy Scale, and found higher scores for high-achieving students. The authors maintained that prospective teachers require "metacognitive strategies both for managing their own learning processes better and for teaching those skills to their students" (p. 2037). To that end, Doganay and Demir promoted the teaching of metacognitive strategies to pre-service teachers by "including organizing, self-monitoring, and self-evaluating skills" in instructional designs (p. 2040). Bertland (1986) highlighted the importance of the teacher as a role model for metacognitive behavior in "planning, comprehension monitoring, strategy use and self-evaluation" to impart similar skills to their students (p. 98).

Idea tactics tutorial

The idea tactics tutorial contains metacognitive strategies to support students' problem solving in research databases. These strategies encourage students to plan, monitor, and regulate their search. Use of the strategies can compensate for low system knowledge. Moreover, the tutorial contains information to enhance users' system knowledge as well. For example, information about various database features supports students' problem solving.

Summary of research on education students' information seeking to support problem solving

An examination of the literature on education students' problem-solving abilities, especially from an information seeking perspective, highlights the various deficits that exist in this population. These individuals lack metacognitive skills in planning, monitoring, and self-regulating their information search behavior. Hill and Hannafin's (1997) study illustrated the role of participants' metacognitive knowledge in facilitating users' abilities to refine their search tactics, thereby maximizing the information potential of the web. Likewise, Land and Green's (2000) research revealed that metacognitive knowledge compensated for low subject and domain knowledge, and they believed this was particularly important in information seeking in open-ended environments. This remains particularly relevant, as recent research suggests that education students lack advanced computing skills. As the literature indicated, information seeking to support problem solving represents a complicated process that requires metacognitive abilities, search skills, domain knowledge, and, recently, familiarity with computer systems. Individual deficiencies in these areas foster numerous consequences that affect individuals' problem solving, producing user frustration, ineffective search techniques, lengthy search processes, and unsatisfactory search results. The idea tactics tutorial offers metacognitive as well as system support for students' problem solving in research databases.

Metacognitive skills and online search behavior

Abstract: Information search in online systems, especially bibliographic systems, remains a complicated process that varies among users. Research revealed that students, regardless of their academic discipline, lack search skills and this affects search outcomes. Some of the difficulties that users encounter in online search stem from system errors, their use of incorrect syntax, their failure to identify correct terminology and their lack of mental models. Students are often unaware of their lack of search skills. In addition, they often seek search assistance from friends or faculty rather than librarians. Users' mental models remain especially important in facilitating success with information systems. However, research suggests that students lack mental models for effective web and database searching. Studies in educational technology and information science highlight the importance of users' metacognitive strategies in overcoming these search obstacles to improve outcomes.

Key words: online search, metacognitive strategies, mental models, difficulties, search errors, OEIS, planning, self-regulation, executive control.

Introduction

Tsai (2009) defined online searching and processing in open-ended environments as a "complex cognitive process involving multifaceted cognitive and metacognitive strategies" (p. 473). This is also true for searching in research databases. Chapter 2 outlined the role of cognition and metacognition in information search. Recently Spink (2011) revised her evolutionary information model, developed in 2010 (Spink and Heinnström, 2011), to include metacognition as a component of users' information behavior. References to monitoring and reflecting in the literature's information-seeking models suggested that other theorists recognized the role of users' metacognitive strategies in their information seeking too (Ellis, 1989; Godbold, 2006; Marchionini, 1995). In this chapter, we consider the role of individuals' search skills, as well as their metacognition, in fostering their information seeking. The first half of the chapter discusses the difficulties that users encounter in online search. These difficulties encompassed users' searches in research databases as well as on the web, since studies show that students use a variety of sources to locate information for a topic (Cook-Cottone et al., 2007; Du and Evans, 2011; Lee et al., 2012; Malliari et al., 2011). The literature suggested some of students' difficulties in online searching could stem from their use of Google for information (Du and Evans, 2011; Head and Eisenberg, 2009; Georgas, 2013; Porter, 2011). Tal (2006) observed that "in contrast to the ease of searching in Google, high precision searches in databases require proficiency" (p. 25). Holman (2011) noted that millennials were the Google generation accustomed to locating information on the web and not in library databases. In the second half of this chapter, we analyze how cognitive and metacognitive strategies can improve individuals' searches in online systems. Ultimately, we offer the idea tactics tutorial as a scaffold to support students' online searching. Although we designed the tutorial to improve students' searches in Ebsco databases, the scaffold can be adapted to support information retrieval in other databases as well as the web.

Difficulties with online search

Information search in online systems, especially bibliographic systems, remains a complicated process that varies among users. Porter (2011) reminds us that successful information searching requires the identification of correct terminology and developing an effective search strategy. Du and Evans (2011) described information searching for research tasks as involving "huge mental processing on users' behalf" (p. 305). They noted that users access numerous systems, utilize multiple search strategies, and reform queries, as well as break down, link, and synthesize information. Kim and Allen (2002) stated that information system interaction encompassed multiple cognitive processes, including "information seeking, knowledge acquisition, and problem solving" (p. 109). According to the authors, differences among individuals' cognition affected each cognitive process. Their research highlighted the importance of tasks in affecting search outcomes and activities.

Problems with various types of online databases

Likewise, research illustrated that users encounter difficulties in searching various types of online databases, especially library databases. Borgman (1996) observed that library catalogs contained design problems and thus failed to consider users' search behaviors that included iterative searches over multiple sessions. Mead et al. (2000) argued the newer systems provided enhanced power and speed, but were "only as successful as they are easy to use by all members of the user population" (p. 107). Their research, which studied users' interactions with library databases, revealed that all participants experienced some difficulties with online search regardless of their age and computer skills, especially in utilizing proper syntax. Borgman (2003) concurred, noting: "vocabulary continues to be the most difficult aspect of searching for any type of information" (p. 105).

Avdic and Eklund (2010) surveyed 150 students at Sweden's Orebro University on the difficulties they encountered using library databases. Participants' comments in response to open-ended questions typically centered on their search problems, especially determining appropriate keywords as well as "titles not reflecting the content" (p. 228). An analysis of the survey responses indicated that some participants believed it was difficult to find relevant articles, and they characterized searching as time consuming. The authors linked students' experience in Internet and library database searching to a more positive attitude toward using the library databases.

Inadequate search skills

Similarly, studies found that some of the problems students encountered in information retrieval stemmed from their inadequate search skills. Yang (1997) examined six cases of students' information seeking in a research database and concluded that students' difficulties stemmed from their unfamiliarity "with the conventions of the system, its capacity and limitations, such as the command functions, interfaces, tools, and resources" (p. 87). Research revealed most students, regardless of their academic discipline, lack information search skills. In 1984, Tenopir listed seven common mistakes users made in online searching; many of these are still relevant today. For example, she suggested users had problems constructing Boolean logic, which she maintained was "not intuitive" for many individuals (p. 635). Another common error identified by Tenopir was individuals' use of one search strategy for different databases. She maintained that variations among systems including the availability of an abstract, controlled indexing, as well as differences in subject category codes and terminology, affected the effectiveness of search strategies in databases.

Holman's (2011) study of undergraduate students' information-seeking behavior confirmed these findings. She noted students' inappropriate use of Boolean operators for advanced searches. She also found that students typically employed the same search terms in databases as in search engines.

Simon's (1995) dissertation research, which centered on graduate students' information retrieval practices, revealed that participants used few databases and their use was improper "or in a very narrow manner" (p. 83). She also found that "many students had no idea about search terms or keywords or what it meant to develop a search strategy" (p. 78). Moreover, the author observed that only a few students employed truncation techniques and none accessed the database thesaurus to identify "appropriate search terminology prior to searching" (p. 83). She believed the research contained implications on the importance of collaboration among instructional designers and academic librarians to develop information literacy courses that addressed students' understanding of the following: the availability of resources in their program, constructing a problem statement, utilizing library resources, determining relevance, and integrating information into individuals' research. Similarly, Lee (2008) attributed undergraduate students' problems in information seeking to a lack of knowledge about search skills, the availability of resources, and evaluating material.

Problems searching the web

Studies that compared undergraduate students' information retrieval on the web to searches in library databases found these individuals lacked search skills for both environments and that hindered their information seeking. Porter (2011) tracked 25 millennial undergraduate students' research strategies in the web and library databases as they located information to complete six tasks. The author found that students searched databases and websites they were most familiar with, failed to develop detailed search strategies, searched in natural rather than Boolean language, and typically chose the first result from the hit list. The author highlighted the popularity of search boxes for these students, although she noted they "rarely read instructions related to a search box" (p. 279). In her discussion, Porter suggested millennials' use of natural language strings in the search boxes was problematic, since these queries were interpreted differently in library databases compared to the Internet. She advised librarians to promote the availability of the variety of library resources to students and to enhance their credibility compared to those retrieved from the web.

Georgas (2013) also focused on students' completion of various research tasks in her comparison of students' use of Google with a federated search tool. The author identified the difficulties participants experienced using Google as too many or irrelevant results, abundance of advertisements, insufficient scholarly content, an inability to locate the full citation, and problems finding books. On the other hand, the study revealed that participants encountered challenges utilizing the federated search engine too, including problems locating books, slow speed, and irrelevant material, as well as difficulties with setting limits, navigating, and finding full-text sites.

According to Hill (1999), open-ended information systems (OEIS) such as the web presented additional challenges to users, since these systems lack standardization and structure. She pointed to varying levels of user skills in utilizing OEIS and noted their influence on individuals' interactions in these systems. Oliver and Hannafin (2000) identified navigating and locating information as especially problematic when searching hypermedia systems.

Need for skills instruction

Foremost, these studies pointed to students' lack of search skills, which hindered their information seeking (Holman, 2011). As Taylor (2012) noted, students gave scant attention to the "quality, validity or authority of the documents selected" (para. 33). This remains especially true for education students. Research by Laverty et al. (2008) on teacher candidates' web search skills revealed that students employed "unsophisticated search methods" (para. 10). The authors noted the importance of teaching search skills for professional development and to obtain learning materials for their students. Still, the research revealed that students typically rated themselves as proficient in online searching (Albion, 2007; Avdic and Eklund, 2010). The dichotomy between students' actual skills and perceived skills has focused attention on college students' information search skills. Denison and Montgomery (2012) pointed to concerns for students' capacities to "put forth the effort needed or know how to find scholarly resources that measure up to the academic caliber expected for college level-research assignments" (p. 380).

Failure to seek search assistance

Students' online search skills remain especially important, since studies revealed they typically do not seek research assistance from librarians. A study of undergraduate students' help-seeking while using the web for assignments found that only 21 percent utilized librarians, and the remaining contacted friends (61 percent) or sought assistance from faculty members (36 percent) (OCLC, 2002). Moreover, respondents rated their satisfaction level for help-seeking from librarians lower than that for the help they received from friends. Studies of graduate students' help-seeking also revealed that few contacted librarians for assistance. A survey of Notre Dame University's graduate students' use of the library revealed over half had never consulted a librarian to identify relevant graduate research materials. Kayongo and Helm concluded that these students had very little contact "with librarians or with library outreach services" (2010, pp. 347–8).

In addition to avoiding seeking help from librarians, students do not utilize help features in databases, according to studies. Cool and Xie (2004) queried students on their attitudes and use of the help feature in information retrieval systems. The majority of respondents ranked help features as important, but nearly 70 percent indicated they had never or rarely used them. Consequently, providing students instruction in strategies to improve their online search remains essential for their success in academia.

Importance of mental models in searching information systems

Users' familiarity with information systems remains critical for optimal search outcomes. Westbrook (2006) believed that mental models "drive expectations, preferences, and reasoning in any interaction with the system" (p. 564). Norman (1983) suggested that mental models were conceptualizations that evolved from individuals' interactions "with the environment, with others, and with the artifacts of technology" (p. 7). He noted that mental models are constantly evolving as individuals gain experience with systems, and he believed these representations helped individuals understand their interactions. Foremost, he observed individuals' mental models were likely inaccurate, containing "contradictory, erroneous, and unnecessary concepts" (p. 14). He promoted the need to "develop systems and instructional materials to aid users to develop more coherent, usable mental models" (p. 14).

Users' mental models

Zhang (2008a, 2008b) studied undergraduate students' mental models in using the web for information retrieval systems. The author found that individuals' mental models affected their search outcomes and feelings toward the search. Zhang concluded that individuals' construction of mental models of the web was linked by their experiences and included personal observation, classroom instruction, and communication. Users' mental models' of databases are based on their perceptions of information systems and are modified with continued experience (Zhang, 2013). Zhang's (2013) study of users interaction with Medline Plus suggested that individuals' development of a mental model of one system evolved from their experiences with another system. According to the author, this centered on "assimilating new elements into the mental models and modifying the existing elements" (p. 168). Yang's (1997) examination of six students' information seeking in a database over time revealed a progression of mental models that "appeared to move from chaos to order, and fuzzy to clear, and they were clearly open to change" (p. 86).

Foremost, research highlights the importance of users' mental models of information systems in influencing their search behaviors. As Connell (1995) reminds us, "the more one knows about a system the more effective he or she will be in using the systems" (p. 507). She underscored the importance of users' mental models in identifying appropriate library databases as well as library records. She pointed to "specific entry" concept in cataloging that assigned record descriptors based on narrow subject headings (p. 506).

College students' lack of mental models in searching databases and the web was noted by Holman (2011). She observed students searching the web and databases, and concluded that most individuals lacked a robust mental model, and this affected their search precision. She found students understood search engines' efforts to match keywords to indexes, but she argued that participants failed to apply the knowledge to searches and did not "troubleshoot particular problems" (p. 25). In addition, Slone (2002) observed that users' understanding of systems stemmed from "mental models, expectations and experience" (p. 1153). Still, she noted the use of mental models can be problematic if users develop similar mental models for dissimilar systems such as online-catalogs and the web. Zhang (2008a, 2008b) seemingly concurred in her prediction that students' mental models of the web as an information retrieval system would affect their behaviors with other databases.

Metacognitive techniques in online search

In addition to users' creation of mental models, information studies and educational technology theorists highlighted the role of other cognitive as well as metacognitive processes in online search. Yang (1997) studied five novice students' information seeking in a database, and concluded it was an "integrative processes" dependent upon cognitive and metacognitive processes that encompassed "goal-driven planning, strategic deliberation, and physical action" (p. 79). She described the executive control process as setting goals, "defining the task, reviewing and planning," reflecting, and "cross-referencing the resources," as well as "reasoning, and affective responses" (p. 79). The article suggested that executive control processes encompassed individuals' development of plans to achieve goals and their scheduling of activities to support their tasks. Yang highlighted individuals' reflection activities in information seeking that including monitoring the process and "providing feedback on the effectiveness of the strategies used for accomplishing their goals" (p. 80). According to the author, the process was not "sequential or logical" but "nonlinear, evolving, iterative and opportunistic" (p. 81).

Studies of individuals' search behaviors suggest they utilize metacognition in information search, and this can improve outcomes. In addition, educators promote metacognition as a mechanism to improve users' retrieval of relevant information. These theorists maintain that information seeking can yield "a loosely–connected cluster of articles of varying relevance and contrasting opinions" (Brem and Boyes, 2000, p. 2). According to the article, searchers may "overlook inconsistencies or conflicts" when searching, because they "think they know what the article is about" (p. 2). The authors promote metacognition in online searching to "monitor what we know and how we know it" (p. 2).

Likewise, research reveals differences among students' metacognition. Hill (1999) stated that users of information systems such as OEIS had "multiple levels of knowledge domains, including metacognitive, system, and subject" that affected their experiences (p. 9). According to Hill, "the limited metacognitive abilities of naïve users" hindered their use of the system (p. 10). She characterized the search process as dependent on the users' search terms, the analysis of the results and their subsequent strategies to improve the search. The article alluded to the importance of monitoring and self-regulation in information search in OEIS, emphasizing the need for users' attention to the task and especially to "be self-directed, and adapt to their interactions with the system" (p. 21).

Role of metacognition

Research confirms the link between online search and users' metacognition. Tsai and Tsai (2003) developed a framework outlining individuals' information search strategies on the Internet from their research with college students. The framework included three domains: behavioral, procedural, and metacognitive. The latter domain included "purposeful thinking," "selecting the main idea," and "evaluating information" (p. 48). Six years later, Tsai and Tsai's framework was validated with the Online Information Searching Strategy Inventory (OISSI). This research, conducted by Meng-Jung Tsai, utilized the OSSI to evaluate high school students' search strategies. The study also examined the impact of gender and students' web search experiences on information search strategies. Tsai found no differences for gender or web experience in students' use of metacognitive strategies. In her conclusion, she linked metacognitive strategies to fostering the integration of prior content knowledge with new information as well as the "self-awareness, self-monitoring and self-regulation of the searching process" (p. 482). She pointed to earlier research that suggested metacognition was the "most critical variable" in successful outcomes. Consequently, she advised that future studies should center on assessing and improving students' metacognitive strategies in online search.

Epistemic metacognition

Mason et al. (2010) studied the influence of college students' epistemic metacognition on their learning while searching the web for information on a learning task. They defined epistemic metacognition as thinking about "the simple/complex and certain/uncertain nature of knowledge" as well as about the "reliability of information sources and evidence in support of knowledge claims as justification for knowing on the web" (p. 612). The study sought to examine four dimensions of epistemic metacognition: simplicity, certainty, source, and justification of knowledge. The authors found that most students' epistemic metacognition focused on evaluating the credibility of sources (93 percent) and/or knowledge justification to "access the veracity" of the information (46 percent) (p. 620). They noted that students who reflected on both levels "outperformed" students that "evaluated only the source accessed" (p. 627). The article concluded: "epistemic metacognition plays a role in transforming the information accessed into knowledge" (p. 627).

Metacognitive knowledge

Bowler (2010b) found evidence of 13 categories of metacognitive knowledge during teenagers' information search. She described these in a taxonomy that included "balancing, building a base, changing course, communicating, connecting, knowing that you don't know, knowing your strengths and weakness, parallel thinking, pulling back and reflecting, scaffolding, understanding curiosity, understanding memory, understanding time and effort" (p. 28). She suggested that metacognitive knowledge comprised a fourth dimension in Kuhlthau's (2004) information search model that included behavioral, cognitive, and affective processes. Moreover, Bowler concluded that librarians should "teach students how to think about their own thinking" (pp. 38–9).

Executive control

Lazonder and Rouet (2008) equated metacognitive skills in online search to planning the search, monitoring its progress, and evaluating results for "relevance, reliability, and authority" (p. 759). Quintana et al. (2005) highlighted the "multifaceted" nature of online searching, which required users' metacognition skills (p. 235). They described metacognitive knowledge as knowledge about individual learning capacities, the task at hand, and strategies. On the other hand, they defined metacognitive regulation as "regulating one's own cognition" (p. 236). According to Quintana et al., both kinds of metacognition were required for searching, since they provided "executive control" of the process (p. 236).

Guthrie et al. (1991) promoted a cognitive model of document search that involved goal formation, category selection, extraction of information, integration, and recycling. The authors studied students' cognitive processes as they searched online to locate information in three formats that contained marked categories including a table, a directory, and prose. Their findings indicated that students "engage in selective inspection as they search documents to locate information" (p. 313). The research noted that students who used efficient strategies had fewer errors and performed the task in less time. The authors suggested that students' inefficient searching was related to the "lack of a metacognitive system" to direct the process (p. 313). The article described this system as an executive process that directed the cognitive components to support the document search. Guthrie et al. noted an executive system that was "explicit, deliberate and conscious may be more effective than one that is not" (p. 313). They maintained that awareness of cognitive processes in the model of document search was more important than overall strategy. Moreover, they believed interventions that enhanced students' awareness of "their own cognitive operations," as well as their performance in the search process, would improve their outcomes (p. 322).

Planning

Likewise, Navarro-Prieto et al.'s (1999) study of web searchers revealed more experienced searchers developed a plan for finding the information and also remained flexible in their use of strategies. Their research also revealed that novice searchers began with very broad questions and narrowed their search terms with "words suggested by the search engines" (para. 23). According to the authors, the study's results fostered the expansion of their model of web searching behavior from the user, the task, and external representations to include individuals' cognitive strategies. Navarro-Prieto et al. suggested that these strategies evolved from users' past search experiences as well as the structure of the information presented.

Bannert (2006) cited research that noted students got "lost in hyperspace" and experienced feelings of disorientation in these environments (p. 360). She attributed these experiences, in part, to students' failure to perform metacognitive activities to promote web-based learning. She noted the need for learners to "analyze the situation," orient themselves to the task, identify learning goals, plan procedures, instigate searches, judge relevance, and evaluate learning (p. 360).

Self-regulation

She et al. (2012) designed three web-based problem solving tasks for undergraduate chemistry students. In this research, the scaffold included instructors' division of each task into four steps to foster students' problem solving. The authors examined the total web pages students viewed, their keyword searches, their use of task-relevant keywords, and individuals' information filtration, modification, and reconfirmation strategies. They described the last two strategies as metacognitive activities, since these required students to "evaluate and judge the accuracy between what they already know and what they get from the web" (p. 752). The findings revealed that "the more metacognitive web-searching strategies" students performed, "the better task performance" was (p. 758).

Narciss et al. (2007) maintained that individuals' self-regulation remained especially important for learning in hypermedia environments due to the large volume of information available, "non-linear structure," and "technological inconsistencies and limitations" (p. 1128). Research suggests that many users would benefit from strategies or tools to support their interaction in hypertext systems including promoting self-regulation skills (Azevedo, 2002).

Wolf (2007) recognized the complimentary nature of self-regulation and information search. She promoted the convergence of information literacy and self-regulation as fields of study due to the interrelationship among the disciplines. According to the author, both disciplines shared attention to the need in information search to review results and adjust strategies accordingly. To this end, she maintained that instructional efforts for information literacy and self-regulation should be integrated.

Idea tactics tutorial

The tutorial contains a variety of information to support students' online searching activities. First, it offers metacognitive strategies to help students plan, monitor, and self-regulate their information searching. Research supports the use of executive control processes in promoting search success. Second, it provides database search tips designed to enhance information seeking in Ebsco databases. These search techniques also expand users' knowledge about the Ebsco databases, and this can foster their development of an accurate mental model of the system. For example, the tutorial offers explanations of subject searches, Boolean searching, truncation, selecting relevant keywords, and applying limits. Screenshots of the database interface as well as results pages also fosters users' system knowledge. The tutorial also offers information on other database features such as limiting by search methodology as well as utilizing cited references and locating additional database records that cite an article. Enhancing students' abilities to create accurate mental models of databases and systems improves their search outcomes. Moreover, research suggests that monitoring behaviors enhances users' development of mental models (Greene and Azevedo, 2009). Consequently, the idea tactics tutorial facilitates users' creation of mental models by providing detailed information on Ebsco databases as well as encouraging users' monitoring behaviors.

Summary of research on metacognitive skills in online search behavior

Users encounter a myriad of problems interacting with online systems to locate information. Some of these difficulties include inexperience with technologies, failure to select appropriate keywords, evaluate results, and revise strategies, as well as a lack of mental models. Search difficulties are also linked to task complexity. Traditional information literacy instruction has often failed to address all of the issues of information search. As Diekema et al. (2011) noted, Lupton and Bruce (2010) termed this instruction as generic that provides tips on how to search databases, but not how to "process, analyze, and apply" the information (p. 262). Individuals still demonstrate ineffective search practices, note feelings of anxiety, and also complain of an inability to locate relevant materials while searching research databases (Ahmed et al., 2009; Blummer et al., 2012; Markey, 2007).

Users lack control over the system design and often have limited influence over their information retrieval task. However, providing individuals with interventions that contain database search techniques as well as metacognitive strategies can enhance their online searching. Denison and Montgomery (2012) identified three types of student groups in information seeking: experienced critiquers, technology admirers, and extrinsic motivators. The authors believed the design of "brief online tutorials or handouts that offered step-by-step suggestions for retrieving information" (p. 388) would suit all groups. Moreover, they maintained that technology advisors and extrinsic motivators would especially appreciate the self-paced learning offered from these modes of instruction. The authors also supported "offering students suggestions on how to find alternative search term" to reduce their frustration with information seeking (p. 388). The idea tactics tutorial addresses the recommendations of the authors and also contains metacognitive support for students' problem solving in online databases. It offers numerous strategies to foster success in students' information seeking.

9

Promoting metacognition

Abstract: This chapter discusses the role of metacognitive interventions in improving students' learning, and particularly problem solving in hypermedia systems. Research supports the use of scaffolds to guide learners in identifying learning needs, evaluating findings and revising search strategies when necessary. Our review of metacognitive scaffolds focuses on print- and computer-based interventions designed to encourage students' use of planning, monitoring and self-regulating their learning in open-ended learning environments and online databases. We highlight the importance of prompts in scaffolds for facilitating metacognitive behaviors and offer examples of their use in supporting students during online search. Studies point to the importance of considering the individuals' mental capacities in designing these interventions. Research notes the effectiveness of question prompts in fostering metacognitive activities during ill-structured problem solving.

Key words: metacognitive scaffolds, interventions, self-regulating, monitoring, reflecting, expert modeling, adaptive scaffolding, pedagogical agents, college students, metacognition, problem solving.

Introduction

Hill and Hannafin (1997) remind us that weak metacognitive knowledge and skill affected the abilities of web searchers to define learning needs, evaluate resources, and revise learning strategies. Hannafin et al. (1999) linked scaffolding to facilitating students' learning in open learning environments. They argued that metacognitive scaffolds are especially important in guiding learners in "how to think during learning," reminding learners to reflect on the goals, and in considering the relationship between the resource and the information need (p. 131).

Lin (2001) identified one technique for promoting metacognition as strategy training, which she believed included modeling effective learning strategies and online procedural prompts. Research supports the effectiveness of metacognitive strategy training from human- or computer-based scaffolds. Metacognition training, by focusing on strategies to enhance an individual's mental processing (such as in planning, monitoring and self-regulation their behaviors), supports their problem solving in online systems. Consequently this chapter examines the effectiveness of metacognitive scaffolds on students' learning and problem solving in hypermedia systems.

Metacognition instruction

While the foundation of metacognition studies centered on improving children's academic success, researchers also noted the potential for instructing adults in techniques to improve their metacognition. Brown and Palincsar (1982) linked intelligence to planning and executive control functions, and noted the tendency for humans as well as computer programs to remain deficient in these areas. Flavell (1979) maintained there was "too little" cognitive monitoring for adults as well as children. He also suggested a role for cognitive monitoring in teaching children and adults how to "make wise and thoughtful life decisions" as well as "comprehend and learn better in formal education" (1979, p. 910).

Osman and Hannafin (1992) discussed incorporating metacognitive strategies into instructional design. They identified four design types based on the training approach and the strategies' relationship to the lesson content. They noted embedded strategies incorporated instructional strategies "directly within a lesson" (p. 91). On the other hand, they described detached strategies as "taught independently from the criterion lesson" (p. 91). Osman and Hannafin further divided embedded and detached strategies into content-dependent and content-independent. The former focused on specific content, while the latter could "be applied across lessons, tasks, and skills" (p. 91). The authors warned against developing strategies that "compete for task-essential cognitive resources" (p. 94). In addition, they promoted the utilization of higher-order strategies for adults and individuals with substantial subject knowledge for instructional design.

Metacognitive scaffolds

Wood et al. (1976) described scaffolds as a tutor that enabled "a child or novice to solve a problem, carry out a task or achieve a goal which would be beyond his unassisted effort." The authors viewed "scaffolding" as a process whereby the tutor manipulated elements to facilitate the learners' abilities to focus on components "within his range of competence" (p. 90). Lin and Lehman (1999) likened scaffolds to devices that "support learning in situations where students cannot proceed alone" (p. 840). Research suggests that scaffolds can encompass "tools, strategies, and guides" that may be human or non-human devices (Azevedo et al., 2004, pp. 345–6). Ultimately, as Wolf et al. (2003) maintained, teachers and designers can assist learners in building strong metacognitive skills through the use of interventions. Studies evaluating metacognitive interventions suggest that these tools improve students' online inquiry and especially problem solving. Bannert (2006) described interventions as metacognitive support devices designed to "increase students' learning competence" through "systematic instruction" (p. 361). A comparison of college students' learning following exposure to a metacognitive support device revealed "higher amount of metacognitive activities" such as "better transfer performance" than the control group (Bannert et al., 2009, pp. 832–3).

Teachers have traditionally sought to encourage students' use of effective learning strategies, and many of these centered on improving individual's metacognition. Recent research illustrates the role of instructors as metacognitive scaffolds in their efforts to promote students' planning, monitoring, and self-regulating behaviors.

Instructor-led scaffolds

Wopereis et al. (2008) embedded information problem solving instruction in a distance education course to increase students' abilities to solve web-based information problems utilizing websites and news groups. The online training emphasized the use of metacognitive activities, including monitoring, steering, and testing during students' problem solving. The authors concluded that students in the experimental group who received the instruction "regulated" the information problem-solving process more often than those in the control group, and the researchers suggested this promoted "effectiveness and efficiency" in problem solving (p. 749).

Hadwin et al. (2005) examined how teachers scaffold students' self-regulated learning (SRL). The authors paralleled the evolution of graduate students' self-regulated learning with the compilation of their research portfolios. The data centered on an analysis of student–teacher dialogue over time for instances of teacher-directed, co-regulation, and student-directed SRL in task definition, goal setting/planning, and enacting. The research revealed a statistical decrease in teacher-direct regulation and a statistical increase in student-direct regulation over time. Hadwin et al. maintained the findings confirmed their hypotheses that "metacognition facets would become more prevalent as students developed experience and proficiency with the task" (p. 432). To this end, the authors highlighted the importance of designing computer-supported tools for learning to "target specific phases and facets of SRL" (p. 438). They also noted the need to "compare the effectiveness of static versus dynamic computer supported tools" for promoting SRL "at different phases and across different facets" (p. 438).

Adaptive scaffolding and pedagogical agents

The use of adaptive scaffolding and pedagogical agents represent cutting-edge metacognitive interventions in open learning environments. Azevedo et al. (2004) demonstrated the effectiveness of adaptive scaffolding in monitoring college students' understanding in hypermedia and providing subsequent support. Similarly Miao et al. (2012) discussed their development of a process-oriented scaffolding agent (POSA) to support individuals' learning in inquiry-based learning environments. However, Azevedo et al. (2010) pointed to challenges in detecting, modeling, and tracing learners' self-regulated learning processes with pedagogical agents. In addition, Hadwin et al. (2005) remind us that "some static tools will be adequate" depending on the phase and facet of self-regulated learning (p. 438).

Consequently, our review of metacognitive scaffolds focuses on print- and computer-based interventions designed to encourage students' use of planning, monitoring, and self-regulating their learning in open-ended learning environments and online databases. As the research reveals, these interventions, by promoting students' use of metacognitive strategies, fostered problem solving in online systems.

Metacognitive scaffolds to support information problem solving

Studies describing the use of metacognitive scaffolds in information problem solving on the web illustrates their role in promoting students' use of metacognition. Zhang and Quintana (2012) examined the effectiveness of a scaffold designed to support middle school students' web searching for inquiry planning, information search, analysis, and synthesis. In this research, students worked in pairs to solve an information problem utilizing the Digital IdeaKeeper scaffold. The control group merely accessed Google for their information problem solving. The findings revealed that students who utilized the scaffold accessed fewer sites and spent more time reviewing their sites than the control group. The experimental group also took less time to complete the search. In addition, these students monitored and planned their strategies more than the control group. Zhang and Quintana highlighted the importance of structure for online inquiry to promote integration, efficiency, continuity, metacognition, and task.

Raes et al. (2012) studied the effect of teacher- and technology-assisted scaffolding for high school students' information problem solving on the web. The research sought to improve students' domain knowledge as well as their metacognitive awareness. The experimental groups included teacher-enhanced, technology-enhanced, and both forms of scaffolding. The findings highlighted the importance of prior knowledge for effective technology-assisted scaffolding. Students with low prior knowledge made significant gains in teacher-enhanced or combination scaffolds. Students with high prior knowledge performed well regardless of type of scaffold. Raes et al. recommended a variety of scaffolding methods to "support a diversity of students" (p. 91).

Wolf et al. (2003) embedded metacognitive scaffolds into a database to illustrate the effects of providing support to students' information problem solving. These metacognitive scaffolds centered on the use of prompts in Eisenberg and Berkowitz's Information Problem Solving (EBIPS) model. The prompts "directed students in the ways to think" (p. 326). In this study, 17 eighth-grade students utilized the scaffolds to complete an assignment, while an equal number of participants conducted research without extensive EBIPS support. The findings supported the role of metacognitive scaffolds in enhancing students' research skills. According to Wolf et al., the products created by students with access to the EBIPS model were more accurate, contained a greater variety of resources, and reflected an increased attention to detail than those assignments completed by participants in the control group.

Prompts

The incorporation of prompts in scaffolds has proven especially effective in encouraging students' use of metacognitive strategies in online environments. Instructional prompting constitutes mechanisms aimed at fostering a range of cognitive and metacognitive activities during a learning task (Bannert and Reimann, 2012). These prompts can include "questions, incomplete sentences, explicit execution instructions or pictures" (Ifenthaler, 2012, p. 2). According to Bannert and Reimann (2012), prompts facilitated students' recall of information, and fostered task execution, as well as their use of cognitive and metacognitive strategies. The literature highlights the use of prompts to activate a wide variety of students' metacognitive behaviors in online learning environments.

Gagniere et al. (2012) demonstrated the effectiveness of metacognitive prompts in supporting collaborative information search among college students. Participants worked in pairs to locate information to "define, explain, and review what is online press" (p. 76). In the experimental group, students received prompts to support cognitive strategies for information search and classification as well as presentation. The study revealed more evidence of metacognitive behaviors in the experimental group especially during information search and a higher incidence of collaboration among these individuals. Gagniere et al. also reported an increased evidence of metanavigation strategies in groups benefiting from the prompts.

Self-regulating

The provision of prompts to enhance students' self-regulation for problem solving remained especially popular in the literature. Azevedo (2005) defined self-regulation as individuals' efforts at planning, monitoring, regulating, and controlling their "cognition, motivation, behavior, and context" (p. 201). Chen and Ge (2006) suggested that prompts encouraged individuals to engage in self-questioning, monitoring, and reflecting activities. They also maintained that system-generated questions facilitated problem solving by guiding students in representing and solving problems.

Lin and Lehman (1999) demonstrated the significance of prompts in assisting undergraduate education students to self-regulate their learning for problem solving during computer-simulated laboratory experiments. The study's participants received various types of prompts, including: reason justification (students provided the reasons for their actions), rule based (students explained the rules and conditions), and emotion focused (students described their feelings). There was also a control group that did not receive prompts. The results revealed that students who received the reason justification prompt performed better than the other groups in the post-test for solving far transfer problems. Lin and Lehman described these as problems that were "contextually dissimilar" and "more complex" (p. 847). Bannert's (2006) findings also linked prompts to "better transfer performance" (p. 370). In this instance, 24 undergraduate psychology and education majors utilized reflection prompts to navigate a hypermedia system. Those individuals receiving the intervention illustrated better far transfer performance than the control group. Bannert highlighted the importance of utilizing far transfer tasks in evaluating the effectiveness of metacognitive interventions.

Kramarski and Michalsky (2010) studied the effectiveness of the IMPROVE metacognitive method on expanding pre-service teachers' technological pedagogical content knowledge (TPCK) in hypermedia systems. The IMPROVE method centers on the introduction of new ideas, metacognitive questions, review, and "obtaining mastery, verification, enrichment and remediation" through self-regulated learning (p. 436). The authors described the instructional approach as providing comprehension, connection, strategic, and reflection questions as prompts to enhance participants' self-regulated learning through their planning, monitoring and evaluating efforts. The findings revealed that students in the IMPROVE group had higher development of TPCK for comprehension and design skills, and they exhibited more self-reflections on the comprehension task than the control group. Kramarski and Michalsky concluded that the "provision of metacognitive support is necessary to understand the rationale and effective procedures of self-regulation" (p. 445).

Reflecting

Huttenlock (2008) reported on the use of an advance organizer as a prompt to enhance college students' metacognitive strategies and search results during an ill-structured problem-solving activity. The print-based advance organizer contained reflective questions designed to facilitate users' abilities to explain and think about their actions. In this study, three participants searched databases utilizing the organizer and three completed the exercise without benefit of the tool. The findings noted that participants who utilized the advance organizer employed "deliberate and focused" metacognitive questioning in their interactions with the instructional tool (p. 109), and also incorporated the questions into their individual search behaviors. In addition, they reflected more on their search outcomes and strategies compared to those participants who did not use the advance organizer. Huttenlock found that the advance organizer was used instead as a worksheet because it was not used consistently among the participants. She maintained that the "key to its effectiveness" was its ability to foster questions and reflections during searching (p. 132).

On the other hand, Kauffman et al. (2008) investigated the availability of automated instructional prompts in fostering individuals' problem solving in a web environment. Half of the study's participants – 54 undergraduate pre-service teachers – received self-reflection and problem-solving prompts to enhance their abilities to scaffold the process. The reflection prompts were designed to encourage students to consider "how well they solved the problem and to evaluate and revise solutions" (p. 119). The authors concluded that students who received the prompts, especially those focused on problem solving, remained more skilled at representing the problem, developing solutions, and constructing the argument than those that lacked the intervention. Kauffman et al. (2008) concluded that both types of prompts remained important, since the reflection prompts promoted self-monitoring.

Likewise, Saito and Miwa (2007) evaluated a feedback system that encouraged users to reflect on their problem-solving process while seeking information on the web. The authors defined reflection as a "cognitive activity for monitoring, evaluating and modifying one's thinking and process" (p. 215). In this study, 19 university freshmen conducted web searches to solve information tasks utilizing the feedback system that offered "visual support for their search processes," as well as question prompts to encourage students to reflect on their search activities (p. 217). An equal number of students performed similar web searches without the benefit of the intervention. Pre-test and post-test comparisons revealed participants in the experimental group improved their search performance "more effectively than in the control group," which Saito and Miwa attributed to their use of reflective activities (p. 226).

Evaluating

Stadler and Bromme (2007) also explored the role of metacognitive prompts in fostering web-based inquiry. They sought to illustrate web searchers' abilities to form representations of document contents and web sources utilizing metacognitive knowledge. To this end, the study centered on providing participants with evaluative prompts, monitoring prompts, both prompt types and no prompts during a web search session. According to the results, individuals receiving evaluating prompts appeared more knowledgeable about the sources and demonstrated more abilities to justify the credibility of a source than their counterparts in the study. In addition, participants who received the monitoring prompts had more knowledge about the facts. Stadler and Bromme concluded that the study supported the role of metacognition in forming document models for managing multiple documents on the web.

Expert modeling

Many of the metacognitive scaffolds described in the literature included expert modeling. Chen and Ge (2006) evaluated a cognitive modeling system aimed at helping students solve ill-structured problems. The system aimed to support students' higher-order thinking using question prompting, expert modeling, and peer reviews. Participants consisted of graduate instructional psychology and technology students who worked on cases guided with procedural and reflective questions, and the solutions. In the last component of the intervention, which centered on peer review, students provided feedback to peers (p. 301). According to the authors, the tool "helped the students to activate their prior knowledge, organize their thoughts and articulate their reasoning" (p. 301).

Osman (2010) investigated embedded online prompts for improving physics students' metacognitive awareness and problem-solving skills. The scaffold provided students with expert modeling, as well as procedural and self-assessment prompts during individuals' physics problem solving. Miholic's (1994) metacognitive awareness inventory served as the pre-test and post-test. The results illustrated that students' problem-solving skills and metacognitive awareness increased over time. Students also reported increased attention to thinking processes, increased recognition of the importance of planning, and increased checking for accuracy in the problem-solving process. The author surmised that "perhaps it is the metacognition about the strategies, rather than the problem solving strategies" that develops students' problem-solving expertise (p. 10).

Importance of matching prompt type to individuals' learning needs

Research demonstrates the effectiveness of prompts in promoting students' metacognitive behaviors. However, studies note the importance of considering the individual's mental capacities in designing these interventions. Ge et al. (2005) looked at different types of questions such as elaboration, question guidance, or no question prompts to determine the role of prompts on graduate students' cognitive and metacognitive strategies in the problem-solving practices on the web. Their findings supported the role of question prompts in fostering cognitive and metacognitive activities to support ill-structured problem solving. They linked the effectiveness of prompt type to the user and suggested that "question prompts required relevant prior knowledge and sufficient schema in order to be effective" (p. 234). Ge et al. concluded that question prompts worked best "when students had sufficient schemata" about a domain, "when they were free of pre-assumptions" with poor problem solvers, and to "facilitate cognition and metacognition" (p. 235).

Generic and direct prompts

Likewise, Davis (2003) focused on the differences between generic and direct prompts in promoting reflection among middle school students working with the Knowledge Integration Environment software and curricula. She described generic prompts as open ended and aimed at encouraging students to think aloud. On the other hand, she defined directed prompts as offering "hints about what to think about," and geared for fostering planning and monitoring (p. 102). In this research, middle school students worked in pairs to locate science information from the web, and their completed projects constituted the primary source of the data for the study. Students' beliefs were measured among three dimensions, including autonomy that viewed science learning from the perspective of internal or external responsibility. Davis concluded that the generic prompts promoted "productive reflection," which fostered students' abilities to "expand their repertoires of ideas and identify weaknesses in their knowledge" that facilitated "knowledge integration" (p. 116). She argued that these prompts remained especially suited for middle autonomy students in helping them to "perform at higher levels of coherence than directed prompts" (p. 126).

Ifenthaler (2012) reported similar results in his study that compared the effectiveness of generic and direct prompts in promoting self-regulated learning among 98 college students. In this instance, students were assigned to one of three groups: generic, directed, or no prompts. Students read an article about the impact of virus inflections on the immune system and answered questions about influenza and HIV infection. Students also created a concept map to illustrate their understanding of the process. According to the results, participants in the generic group gained more domain-specific knowledge as well as structural and "semantic understanding of the problem scenario" (p. 48). Ifenthaler concluded that generic prompts provided more autonomy for learners in self-regulating their problem solving. Still, the author pointed out that directed prompts may be more effective for students who lack a set of problem-solving skills.

Similarly, Ge and Land (2003) studied the effect of question prompts in collaborative group problem solving; they suggested they were effective in helping students focus on the questions, but of limited value in fostering individuals' question generation, elaboration, or clarification of their own or their peers' understanding. Likewise, Davis (2000) compared middle school science students' use of activity and self-monitoring prompts, and concluded that students used the prompts in different ways. Davis argued that "prompts can play a variety of roles in learning environments" if designers "craft the form and frequency of the prompt experience" (p. 834).

Idea tactics tutorial

Consequently, we designed the idea tactics tutorial to encourage students' use of metacognitive strategies especially in generating questions about their search strategies, elaborating on keywords, and evaluating and clarifying results. We offered the tutorial before and during the learning activity, to maximize students' use of the information presented in the intervention. Our scaffold incorporated prompts that included questions, incomplete sentences, and explicit execution instructions as well as pictures. The interface contained questions that guided users to directed prompts that offered specific instructions to users on how to improve their search strategy. We utilized these strategies since we believed our participants were novice searchers who lacked prior knowledge on selecting the appropriate problem-solving strategies to satisfy their information need (Blummer et al., 2012; Ge et al., 2005). Moreover, the tutorial also borrowed from Chen and Ge's (2006) and Osman's (2010) metacognitive interventions in its efforts to offer expert modeling. The tutorial describes sample searches and also contains detailed explanations of search strategies to enhance students' Ebsco database search skills. The combination of directed prompts as well as expert modeling provides metacognitive as well as database search support for students' problem solving in online databases.

Summary of research on promoting metacognition

The research on metacognitive instruction, and particularly computer-based interventions, illustrates the importance of efforts to support individuals' metacognitive skills in facilitating searching and learning in hypermedia environments. Studies link scaffolds to promoting individuals' metacognitive skills, especially self-regulating, monitoring, and reflecting activities. These skills increase individuals' abilities to process information in hypermedia environments and they remain particularly critical in supporting problem solving. Still, as the literature demonstrates, a large number of studies of metacognitive strategies focused on middle school students and undergraduate students' use of a metacognitive scaffold in open-ended learning environments such as the web. However, our research examined graduate students' use of a metacognitive scaffold to support their problem solving in research databases.

10

The metacognitive scaffold: the idea tactics tutorial

Abstract: We sought to develop a scaffold to support education graduate students' problem solving in research databases. A phenomenographic study on education graduate students' information-seeking behavior informed the creation of the scaffold. In 1979, Bates described various information search tactics or idea tactics utilized by information specialists performing complex searching. Consequently Bates' idea tactics (1979) served as the focus of the tutorial, since they resembled metacognitive strategies and they were aimed at facilitating information search. Ebsco database search techniques were included in the tutorial to enhance students' information search skills. Dreamweaver software supported the development of the web-based tutorial. A pilot study revealed problems with the tutorial's interface that we addressed with the assistance of a web design expert.

Key words: tutorial, Bates' idea tactics, scaffold, metacognitive strategies, pilot, database search techniques.

Introduction

The components of a scaffold as well as its design remain critical in fostering its use as well as the effectiveness of the tool. The idea tactics tutorial evolved from research that explored the information-seeking habits of education graduate students. These studies identified students' weaknesses in utilizing online databases, their failure to consult various resources and librarians, and their anxiety in information searching, as well as their preferences for training opportunities. Consequently we developed the tutorial to address these issues. Moreover, the literature review of education graduate students' information problem solving suggested students would benefit from metacognitive support while problem solving in online databases. To that end, the tutorial provides idea tactics that are delivered as sentence prompts that encourage users to execute metacognitive strategies to promote their planning, monitoring, and self-regulating behaviors during the search. These idea tactics stem from strategies utilized by information specialists during information search when they experience difficulties in locating appropriate materials. As Davis (2000) argued, prompts "can enable sophisticated knowledge integration when they encourage students to monitor their progress and identify new connections among ideas" (p. 834).

Research that informed the scaffold's creation

The idea tactics tutorial is aimed at scaffolding students while problem solving in a research database. Azevedo and Hadwin (2005) stated that "scaffolding involves calibrated support for diagnosed learning targets" (p. 370). They highlighted the importance of diagnosis in creating scaffolds that they believed determined how to individually design support for the learner, task, or content (p. 375). A literature review of education graduate students' information-seeking behavior identified the numerous problems students experience while information seeking (Blummer, 2009; Catalano, 2010; Chu and Law, 2007; Evans, 1986; Green and Macauley, 2007; Park, 1986; Pickert and Chwalek, 1984; Switzer and Perdue, 2011).

Phenomenographic study on education graduate students' information-seeking behavior

The bulk of the tutorial's content evolved from the findings of Blummer et al.'s (2012) phenomenographic study on education graduate students' information-seeking behavior. Foremost, this research illustrated the need to include support beyond database search skills to improve students' information problem solving in research databases. The survey, based on Earp's (2008) survey of Kent State University's education graduate students' source preferences, highlighted students' propensity for online resources. The data also revealed that many students suffered from anxiety and uncertainty when searching. Some respondents stated they had difficulty selecting appropriate databases for course-related research. Moreover, a few survey respondents' comments to another open-ended survey question indicated that they did not view their previous library training initiatives as beneficial. While the interview participants, who were self-selected, appeared more confident in their search abilities, they appeared unaware of the diversity of databases that would support education research. Both groups of study participants noted a preference for online materials that stemmed, in part, from their time restraints when searching.

Blummer et al. suggested that the study revealed several library training opportunities for education graduate students. Students' preferences for electronic resources and their time limitations while researching supported the use of an online library training tutorial. The article recommended the tutorial contain content aimed at enhancing students' information online search capabilities as well as provide information on education-related databases. In addition, the authors suggested a flexible tool that would be relevant for users with different levels of database search skills. Moreover, the article highlighted the importance of a variety of learning environments for education graduate students and especially instruction aimed at relieving the anxiety students' experienced while searching.

We designed our idea tactics tutorial to improve education graduate students' research skills as well as reduce their uncertainty while searching. To enhance students' database search skills, we included tips on searching Ebsco databases as well as information on education-related resources. We sought to address students' dissatisfaction with their previous library training by adopting a metacognitive perspective on information search instruction. Research on education students' use of metacognitive strategies while problem solving in hypermedia highlighted the role of planning, monitoring, and self-regulating their behaviors in promoting successful search results. To that end, we embedded tips on searching Ebsco databases within metacognitive strategies to provide extensive scaffolding for individuals' information problem solving.

Bates' idea tactics

In 1979, Bates described various information search tactics utilized by information specialists performing complex searching. She identified 17 idea tactics designed to foster the development of new ideas during search. Bates observed that "new ideas are often blocked or limited by one's current thinking" during problem solving (p. 281). She also highlighted research by George Miller, who underscored the role of location in human information processing. According to Bates, the location concept remains central in some of the idea tactics. The idea tactics resemble metacognitive strategies and Bates noted that these were aimed at helping "improve the searcher's thinking and creative processes in searching" (p. 280). According to Bates, these tactics could be employed in "bibliographic and reference searches" as well as "manual and on-line systems" (p. 280). The author described the tactics as helping searchers overcome obstacles in locating information. She categorized the tactics as a component of a "facilitation model of searching" that enabled individuals to search "more efficiently or effectively" (p. 280). She also suggested the tactics could be useful in teaching search techniques.

Idea generation and mental pattern-breaking tactics

Bates divided the idea tactics by type including idea generation and mental pattern breaking, but she admitted there was some overlap between them. She defined idea generation tactics as assisting individuals in developing new strategies and concepts to foster improved search techniques. Mental pattern-breaking tactics, she argued, supported pattern breaking by consciously or unconsciously encouraging individuals to adopt a new "mental structure or pattern" in viewing the problem (p. 281). According to the author, half of the mental pattern-breaking tactics comprised the "introspective sort" while the others were "more the arbitrary sort" (p. 281). The former approach, she maintained, was deliberate, as searchers gained awareness of their mental structures and changed them. However, she believed individuals could arbitrarily change "a part of [their] thinking or behavior," providing a new perspective on the search (p. 281).

The tutorial's tactics

The tutorial contained 12 metacognitive strategies, and nine of these represented Bates' ideas tactics. Three idea generation tactics were incorporated: Wander, Think, and Meditate. On the other hand, six of

Bates' mental pattern-breaking tactics were incorporated in the tutorial: Jolt, Catch, Notice, Break, Skip, and Change. We created three other tactics – Identify, Regulate, and Create – to represent additional metacognitive-based strategies. We hoped that Create and Identify would underscore students' planning of search strategies, and we utilized Regulate to encourage individuals to revise their strategies when necessary. All of the tactics were designed to promote students' use of planning, monitoring, and self-regulating their behaviors while problem solving in Ebsco databases.

These tactics were presented as prompts in complete or incomplete sentences, and they were aimed at facilitating the user's execution of the strategy. For example, the Change tactic advised users to instigate a new search behavior, a different keyword, source or strategy. A graphic that illustrated an individual at a crossroads underscored the change concept of the tactic.

Database search techniques

Initially, we sought to focus the scaffold on metacognitive strategies promoted in Bates' idea tactics. However, since the aim of the research was to improve education graduate students' information problem solving in research databases, we modified the scaffold to include database search techniques. We hoped the inclusion of Ebsco database search techniques would underscore the application of Bates' idea tactics during problem solving in research databases. A senior reference and instructional academic librarian served as a consultant in the incorporation of relevant database search techniques for this audience.

Search examples were embedded in the tactics. Each tactic contained an information problem-solving scenario that outlined the user's strategies in solving their information need. These examples offered students information on Boolean operators, selecting databases, limiting results, choosing keywords, using subject terms, truncating words, evaluating results, and considering synonyms. Some additional material was provided on specifying methodologies, as well as utilizing Ebsco's "times cited in this database" and "related records" features.

Creating the tutorial

We opted to utilize software tools that were available in-house, to reduce costs. The web-based tutorial was created in Dreamweaver version 8 due to its availability and familiarity to one of the authors. Despite the age of the product, it offered capabilities that remained suitable for the novice as well as more experienced web designers. Microsoft Office 2007 provided additional tools that were utilized in the creation of the tutorial. Microsoft Paint supported the editing of the screenshots for the database search examples. Microsoft Word clip art was used to locate images to enhance the appearance of the indexes. These appeared adjacent to the metacognitive tactics, to reinforce the tactic's concept. We incorporated hover text that described the image for interpretation in a text reader. In addition, hover text was used for describing the learning outcomes to maximize the screen's white space and promote readability. Microsoft Publisher supported the creation of the number bullets that appeared in the search examples. These examples offered a step-by-step guide on the search strategy and results. Coutinho et al. (2005) remind us that "when people are trying to learn, feedback that includes explanations of problem solutions (and not just the solutions themselves) improves task performance" (p. 321). They pointed to research that suggested explanations facilitate individuals' abilities to monitor, implement, and assess strategies promoting metacognition.

Pilot studies

First pilot identified tutorial's weaknesses

We employed pilot studies to test the tutorial's usability. Two graduate students participated in the first pilot of the tutorial. In this instance, the students searched various Ebsco databases for information on their research question. Camtasia provided a screen capture and audio recording of their problem solving. Following a review of their results, each student read the tutorial and initiated new searches on their topics. Follow-up interviews with the pilot study participants, coupled with a review of the Camtasia files, identified areas for improving the learning tool.

Pilot participants experienced difficulty navigating the main index page, which they attributed to the lack of outcome headings such as relevance, evaluation, numbers, and strategy. One of the participants commented that she wanted to "quickly review the index and determine where to go next." In addition, on the strategy, number, relevance, and evaluation index pages, the participant suggested matching the text color of the tactic headings to the definitions, to promote readability.

This pilot study also revealed the need for the inclusion of learning objectives on all of the search example pages. Both of the study participants commented on their inabilities to determine the key concepts of the page. Both participants suggested this information appear at the top of the page where they could "immediately know what I'm supposed to get from the example."

A review of the Camtasia files supported improving the navigation and design of the tutorial. The files also illustrated the need to emphasize the importance of subject terms in enhancing the relevancy of the results, since participants appeared reluctant to utilize this search strategy. While reading a search example page, one of the participants remarked: "So this says to use subject terms but I'm not exactly sure what the difference is." The other participant referred back to the tutorial several times during her search in an effort to improve her results. In the follow-up interview, she suggested the tutorial highlight the definitions for subject terms and truncation.

Modification of tutorial's interface

Consequently, the researcher, working with a web design expert, modified the tutorial's interface to enhance its readability. These enhancements focused on reducing image sizes and dense text on all of the index pages. For example, the lengthy description of the lesson outcomes on the index page was replaced with mouse-over text. To improve navigation from the main index, four headings were created to guide readers to the appropriate page. These headings were situated along the left side of the page, since web usability studies support reading from left to right. Likewise, a title was added to each search example page that listed the tactic and its focus, to facilitate navigation and comprehension of this component of the tutorial. Lastly, the content on these pages were revised to include explanations of subject terms and truncation for each instance of its utilization in a search.

Second pilot

The second pilot, in late August 2011, provided a final opportunity to test the tutorial. One education graduate student volunteered for the test. In this instance, the participant was provided with the laptop that contained the tutorial, Camtasia, and access to the Ebsco databases. The student conducted her initial search, skimmed the tutorial's Index pages, and focused on the Change tactic example, since she hoped to reduce the number of her hits. She subsequently revised her search, adopting the tactic example's suggestion to include more keywords to narrow the focus of her search. Her results decreased from 244 to 14 hits. Although she examined the Evaluation and Strategy Indexes pages for additional ideas, she opted not to search again, noting all of the articles found were relevant to her topic and would support her teaching.

The tutorial

We designed the tutorial to serve as a scaffold for supporting education graduate students' problem solving in research databases. It can be used as a self-paced learning tool or in conjunction with a class. The Main Index (Figure 10.1) lists the objective of the tutorial and describes the origin of the idea tactics. In addition, it notes their similarity to metacognitive strategies and their role in improving individuals' search outcomes by promoting their planning, monitoring, and self-regulating behaviors.

The tutorial centers on the Main Index that contains links to four indexes: relevance, number, evaluation, and strategy. These index topics represent common obstacles users encounter during information search, including: irrelevant hits, too few or too many results, and the need to evaluate records and results, as well as revise search strategies. The indexes are designed to direct users to the appropriate information to improve their search outcome. Users are encouraged to "select tactics based on your search needs." Each of these four indexes describes three idea tactics to support efforts directed at addressing the search difficulty. For example, the number index shown in Figure 10.2 offers tactics aimed at broadening or narrowing the search.

Each of the four Index pages provides access to database search examples that highlight idea tactic strategies. These examples are aimed at providing users with an overview of various database features available in Ebsco as well as strategies to enhance search results. All example search pages contain titles as well as learning objectives and database screenshots. Figure 10.3 displays the Meditate tactic example.

Metacognitive idea tactics tutorial

Learning
outcomes

The objective of this tutorial is to enhance individuals' search strategies and to increase their satisfaction level with the results. In the earlier questions, you began to identify areas where your search could be improved. This tutorial offers idea tactics (Bates, 1979) used by professional searchers to improve outcomes. These tactics also resemble metacognitive strategies designed to promote individuals' knowledge of their cognition. All of the tactics offer the potential to improve your searches. They highlight efforts aimed at planning, monitoring and self-regulating search activities.

Select tactics based on your search needs.

RELEVANCE - Require assistance in selecting search terms?

> These tactics help users select relevant search terms.

NUMBER - Dissatisfied with the number of your hits?

> Click here for strategies that focus on broadening or narrowing searches.

EVALUATION - Reviewing your results?

> Click here to learn tactics that center on evaluating search results to improve subsequent search outcomes.

STRATEGY - Do you need to devote more attention to devising a search strategy?

> Access these tactics.

Bates, M. J. (1979). Idea tactics. *Journal of the American Society for Information Science, 30*(5), 280-289. |

Figure 10.1   Main Index of the idea tactics tutorial

Metacognitive idea tactics tutorial

Tactics to Broaden or Narrow the Search

MEDITATE - Analyze the search strategy by incorporating scientific as well as intuitive thought processes for problem solving. This is often described as convergent and divergent thinking. Individuals typically employ one or the other in developing solutions. However, some researchers claim creative problem solving combines both modes of thought.

- Example: I am interested in graduate students use of self-regulating learning strategies. Click here to see my search strategy and how I can broaden or narrow the search results.

CHANGE - Instigate a new search behavior, a different keyword or source, or strategy.

- Example: I am going to focus on graduate students use of monitoring as metacognitive strategy. Click here to see my strategy and the results.

CREATE - Develop a search strategy by identifying relevant keywords, search fields, and databases to access. Research suggests expert searchers adopt a plan rather than follow trial and error techniques.

- Example: I need to highlight the use of self-monitoring or regulating in problem solving among graduate students. I am want to access a large number of hits, around 100. Click here to see the search strategy and results.

Bates, M. J. (1979). Idea tactics. *Journal of the American Society for Information Science, 30*(5), 280-289.

Figure 10.2   Number Index of the idea tactics tutorial

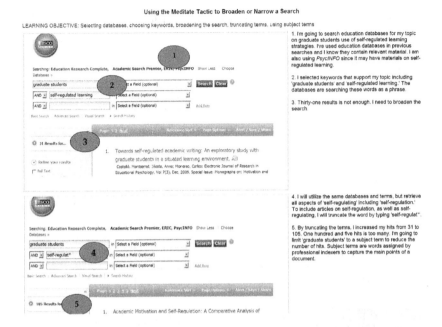

Figure 10.3 Meditate idea tactic search example that illustrates Ebsco search screen. Reprinted with permission.

Content focuses on educational perspective

We focused the tutorial's content on research databases that would remain relevant to our users: education graduate students. We believed an education perspective would help sustain their interest and confidence in the tutorial as a learning tool. In addition, we created examples to underscore the importance of metacognition in problem solving. These examples highlight self-regulating learning strategies, monitoring, problem solving, and graduate students' study habits, as well as the use of database search features in supporting information search. Likewise, we promoted the use of education databases (ERIC, Education Research Complete, Academic Search Premier, and PsychInfo) in our examples, to encourage education graduate students' use of these resources.

Task support

According to Azevedo and Hadwin (2005), scaffolds provided support for "the learner, the task, or the context" (p. 375). The idea tactics tutorial was aimed at supporting education graduate students in the task of information problem solving. Azevedo and Hadwin (2005) also pointed to scaffolding different types of learning such as domain, system, and metacognitive. The idea tactics tutorial offered scaffolding on all three components of students' learning. Students received information designed to enhance their use of metacognition as well as Ebsco database system knowledge and search (domain) knowledge. The tutorial's search examples contain additional information on metacognition and how it facilitates students learning. Moreover, database search information is included in the examples as well.

The tutorial was available to students prior to their problem-solving activity. It was provided in online and print formats. In addition, students were offered the opportunity to consult the scaffold during their problem-solving activity.

Resembles an instructional agent

In its final version, the tutorial contained support features characteristic of an instructional agent. Clarebout et al. (2002) identified four modalities of support provided by instructional agents in open learning environments: executing, showing, explaining, and questioning. Three of these modalities were present in the idea tactics tutorial's examples. For example, expert modeling *showed* students how to formulate search strategies to locate relevant information. An analysis of search strategies adopted offered *explanations* for the rationale behind the approach. Finally, one example contained a *question* to help guide the student in thinking about the search to select appropriate keywords and databases.

Ercegovac (1989) recognized the potential of Bates' idea tactics in improving individuals' online searching. She proposed the tactics' use in context particularly to provide support when necessary. According to Ercegovac, the "system could be programmed to 'understand' users' intentions, plans, and goals" and provide relevant assistance (p. 30). She envisioned a system with the capability to understand when the user was "stumped" by knowledge of the individuals' search goals (p. 30). In this instance, the system response would constitute a display of similar searching problems and their resolutions. Ercegovac termed this "Cognitive System Engineering" and noted that it contained implications for user assistance in online systems (p. 31).

The idea tactics tutorial lacks the capability to diagnose users' search problems and offer relevant assistance. However, the scaffold allows the user to decide what assistance is needed based on their initial search results and to act accordingly by accessing the most relevant index and implementing appropriate strategies. The user maintains control over their search and its subsequent outcome, and gains experience and knowledge in the information problem-solving process.

Summary of the idea tactics tutorial

The idea tactics tutorial was designed to support education graduate students' problem solving in research databases. It was modeled after Bates' idea tactics, which resembles metacognitive strategies. These idea tactics encourage students to think metcognitively in planning, monitoring, and self-regulating their search strategies. The scaffold also contains database search techniques. Example search questions provide expert modeling that guides the user in considering appropriate keywords and syntax as well as relevant databases. Detailed explanations offer the reader the rationales behind the use of search strategies. This two-pronged instructional perspective to scaffolding education graduate students' information problem solving from a metacognitive as well as database training approach fosters individuals' search outcomes.

11

Methodology: the think-aloud problem-solving activity and post-activity interview

Abstract: Our mixed methods study aimed to evaluate the impact of a metacognitive scaffold for supporting students' information problem solving. It represents the first author's unpublished doctoral dissertation. We detail our research methodology, which included the use of the think-aloud protocol as students performed search tasks in a research database. Students consulted the metacognitive scaffold for ideas to improve their search. Screen capture software illustrated participants' thoughts and movements during the activity and represented the research instrument. Information processing theory informed the theoretical framework for the study. The participants consisted of eight students, enrolled in graduate programs, who located materials using the Ebsco databases on the library's web page. A follow-up interview allowed individuals to verbalize any comments about the activity and the scaffold.

Key words: problem-solving activity, post-activity interview, data analysis, coding research methodology, usability study, mixed methods, think-aloud protocol, Camtasia.

Introduction

Research by Blummer et al. (2012) illustrated education graduate students' need for a variety of library training opportunities. Our mixed methods study aimed to evaluate the impact of a metacognitive scaffold for supporting students' information problem solving. It represents the first author's unpublished doctoral dissertation. The idea tactics tutorial offers metacognitive strategies as well as expert modeling of information problem solving in a research database. Mayer (1998) recognized the importance of metacognition in problem solving too. He argued that problem solvers required domain specific skills as well as metaskills, which he defined as metacognitive knowledge such as "knowledge of when to use, how to coordinate and how to monitor various skills in problem solving" (p. 53). Moreover, he advocated modeling the effective use of strategies in academic tasks. In this chapter, we detail our research methodology that included the use of the think-aloud protocol as students performed search tasks in a research database. Screen capture software illustrated participants' thoughts and movements during the activity. A follow-up interview allowed individuals to verbalize any comments about the activity and the scaffold.

Mixed methods research

Our mixed methods study employed both qualitative and quantitative approaches. Hoepfl (1997) described the goal of quantitative studies as seeking "causal determination, prediction, and generalization of findings." On the other hand, she argued that qualitative studies focused on "illumination, understanding, and extrapolation to similar situations" (1997, para. 5). Onwuegbuzie and Teddlie (2003) maintained each approach contained strengthens and weakness. They suggested that "quantitative researchers tend to be more preoccupied with results than with their interpretations" (p. 361). However, they observed that qualitative research often lacks attention to "the analytic technique used and the major features of the analysis" (p. 362). To this end, Onwuegbuzie and Teddlie viewed mixed methods research as a middle ground that offered the strengths of both approaches.

Campbell and Fiske (1959) first proposed the mixed methods concept in research design to enhance validity. The authors promoted a "matrix of intercorrelations among tests representing at least two traits, each measured by at least two methods" (p. 104). In 1998, Tashakkori and Teddlie observed that there was a "rapidly growing area of interest" in mixed method approach (ix). Johnson and Onwuegbuzie (2004) defined mixed methods research as "the class of research where the researcher mixes or combines quantitative and qualitative research techniques, methods, approaches, concepts or language into a single study" (p. 17). They noted that mixed method research existed in the middle of a continuum with quantitative and qualitative measures at either end.

Johnson et al. (2007) pointed to its importance for identifying research questions as well as providing answers. As Bazeley (2006) observed, "there is no single approach to undertaking a mixed method study" (p. 64).

Although mixed methods research offers the benefits of both methodologies, proponents noted it requires more time commitments and cost for the researcher due to the need for the analysis of both types of data (Creswell, 2003; Johnson and Onwuegbuzie, 2004). Mixed methods studies also demand researchers' familiarity with both paradigms. Moreover, Leech and Onwuegbuzie (2009) observed that the concept of mixed methods was "still in its adolescence" and therefore could be confusing to researchers (p. 266). To this end, we consulted quantitative and qualitative experts as well as individuals familiar with mixed methods research in developing our study, which centered on a triangulation design strategy.

Guiding theory

Information processing theory informed the theoretical framework for the study of education graduate students' metacognitive abilities and information-seeking behavior. Information processing theory is based on Miller's (1956, 1960) concepts of chunk and Test-Operate-Test-Exit (TOTE). According to Miller, individuals' abilities to chunk information, or recode it into units, allowed them to increase the amount of material they could successfully remember. His research on recoding coupled with Newell, Shaw, and Simon's work in 1957 and 1958 on complex information processing systems altered Miller's beliefs about what "guides behavior" (1960, p. 2). In his publication *Plans and the Structure of Behavior*, he likened man to a computer that contained plans, strategies, executions, and images. Miller described plans as hierarchies of instructions that identified the order of operations. On the other hand, he defined images as "organized knowledge the organism has about itself and its world" and he believed that included "values" as well as facts (p. 17). According to Miller, the feedback loop or TOTE represented the basic unit of analysis for behavior. He suggested that individuals' actions resulted from a system of TOTE hierarchical units that were controlled by plans or processes. Although he acknowledged plans were inherited, he suggested that variations in their source, span, detail, flexibility, speed, coordination, retrieval, and openness as well as stop-orders fostered different behaviors among individuals.

According to Miller, individuals' problem solving was a cyclical process that centered on information collection and included revision in images, predictions, and testing. He argued that individuals solve problems by utilizing images rather than systematic plans because these were inefficient. Miller suggested that as individuals compared "what is" to "what ought to be" (1960, p. 174), they created images that served as potential solutions to problems. He believed individuals' images were based on values and facts. Moreover, Miller attributed obstacles in the problem-solving process to the inability of the image to represent the "problem situation" (1960, p. 174). On the other hand, he maintained that the formation of heuristic plans fostered the development of solutions to well-defined problems.

Human processing theory points to a general plan for human behavior, and acknowledges similarities among individuals' information-processing skills. Foremost, the theory illustrates that the iterative nature of problem solving is reflected in the process of information collection, revision, and testing of the alternative images. This vision of problem solving suggests it is controlled by cognitive as well as metacognitive strategies, as individuals continually regulate the process to develop new solutions. The theory also recognizes differences among individuals' metacognitive skills. Lastly, the theory highlights the role of the problem or information need in controlling the process. In this instance, a well-defined problem can be solved by a different approach compared to its ill-structured counterpart. According to Miller, well-defined problems enable the searcher to "recognize the solution" while more complex problems do not have an easily identifiable way of revealing "what he is looking for" (p. 170).

In our study, participants verbalized their plans and strategies while problem solving in a research database. The use of the think-aloud approach facilitated the identification of cognitive as well as metacognitive behaviors, and illustrated the tutorial's impact on participants' search strategies.

Think-aloud protocol

Research on the think-aloud protocol highlights its effectiveness in capturing users' cognitive processes during information problem solving. The technique's use in psychology dates to the late eighteenth century and numerous psychologists noted the credibility of the approach for predicting behavior (Miller, 1960). Ericsson and Simon (1984) said the protocol supported an interpretation of human cognition from an information processing perspective that stipulates "recently acquired" information is stored in the short-term memory (p. 11). They described the method as a "powerful means for gaining information" about cognitive processes that control behavior (p. 30). Still, they emphasized the importance of providing proper instructional procedures for participants to enhance the validity of the responses.

Helps students identify strategies to improve understanding

Thinking aloud helps students identify strategies to improve their understanding of text. Instructing teachers to use think-aloud in the classroom improved the reading comprehension of their students (Fisher et al., 2011). Ortlieb and Norris (2012) employed think-aloud to enhance kindergarteners' understanding of science texts. Baumann et al. (1993) reported on the impact of using think-aloud to assist students in "monitor their reading comprehension and employ fix-up strategies" when needed (p. 192). Coiro (2011) promoted the use of think-aloud as a strategy instruction to foster students' online reading comprehension. Israel and Massey (2005) discussed the use of the think-aloud protocol to promote reading comprehension among middle school students. They maintained that the think-aloud approach enabled students to monitor their comprehension. Their research suggested thinking aloud helped students identify strategies to improve their understanding by activating prior knowledge, relating text to prior knowledge, inferring, and reflecting.

Illustrates users' strategies in navigation

The think-aloud protocol remains especially effective in illustrating users' search strategies while navigating databases and the web (Huttenlock, 2008; Van Waes, 1998). The think-aloud method has been used in studies tracking individuals' metacognition while information searching. Huttenlock's (2008) dissertation research employed the think-aloud protocol in her study of education students' use of an advance organizer while searching a research database. In addition, Gazda (2005) utilized the think-aloud protocol to track metacognitive search behaviors of 14 nursing students as they navigated through a hypermedia system. He categorized their metacognition as organizing, monitoring, and modifying their navigation. Gazda observed that the most efficient searchers had the least instances of disorientation, while the least efficient searchers experienced the highest number of these feelings. In his summary, he noted the interrelationship among individuals' hypermedia search strategies, navigational efficiency, and metacognitive behavior in instructional hypermedia environments.

The think-aloud methodology remains popular for evaluating websites and databases, but it should be used with other data collection methods. Hoppmann (2009) employed the think-aloud protocol to examine users' "point of frustration" when searching the official website of the European Union. She listed several advantages to the think-aloud approach. First, it can be employed in studies with a limited number of participants. Second, the strategy involves minimal cognitive processes because the protocol stems from the individual's working memory. Third, the technique remains appropriate for quantitative and qualitative studies. However, Hoppmann noted that as the demand on the users' cognitive process increases, thinking aloud may prove difficult for the participant. To that end, she advocated incorporating the strategy in combination with other data collection methods. Her website usability study included data from questionnaires, think-aloud protocols, and in-depth interviews.

Task-based usability study

Our problem-solving activity resembled a usability study since it tracked participants' interactions with the tutorial and its impact on their search in a research database. Database usability studies highlight their effectiveness in revealing participants' thoughts and feelings as they utilize the software. Tenopir et al.'s (2008) usability study of the University of Tennessee's staff and students' interaction with the ScienceDirect database employed the think-aloud protocol to illustrate participants' feelings and thoughts during search. An analysis of the transcripts revealed positive, negative, and neutral responses associated with participants' feelings. The authors linked individuals' cognitive activities to four categories: software system, search results, search strategy, and task. The outcomes revealed that users experienced more positive than negative feelings and all thoughts typically occurred during users' views of the search strategies and results. Moreover, participants were more likely to have negative feelings with thoughts concerning the system, search strategy, and task.

Employing the think-aloud method with task-based usability studies are effective strategies for evaluating individuals' use of a product. Likewise, George's (2008) usability study of software that allowed individuals to search multiple databases simultaneously included the think-aloud protocol. Participants were asked to complete six tasks that resembled "real-world" (p. 18) searches. Following the task activity, participants answered a questionnaire that rated their experiences based on a five-point Likert scale. The study's findings fostered a list of recommendations aimed at improving the usability of the software.

Evaluation of a library website using the think-aloud protocol enabled an understanding of how easily students could locate information on the site. Stephan et al.'s (2007) usability survey of the University of Mississippi's Libraries' home page highlights the relevancy of these studies in supporting information-seeking research. Participants tackled eight tasks involving simple and complex searches that required students to access the library home page and the catalog as well as commercial databases. Quantitative data collected included the number of clicks to reach a source, the time required to complete the task, if the task was completed, and participants' satisfaction level in completing the task. Observers also gathered participants' comments or any additional qualitative information that reflected users' feelings of indecision or frustration. Although the study did not meet the established benchmark of 75 percent completion rate on all tasks, the survey did foster the redesign of the website and led to the promotion of instructional techniques for interacting with the library's databases.

Research instrument

The research employed one instrument including the screen capture software Camtasia. The data collected by this tool and the timeline for its collection appear in Table 11.1. Camtasia served as a screen capture tool for tracking the audio and video recordings of participants' activities and hence illustrating the impact of the tutorial on individuals' search behaviors. An initial database search served as a pre-test of participants' use of database search techniques.

Table 11.1	Data collection procedures and the timeline for their collection	

Instrument	Data type	Timeline for collection
Camtasia	Qualitative audio file and screen capture	During problem activities for initial and revised searches
Camtasia	Qualitative audio file	Post-activity interview

Camtasia

Camtasia supports the think-aloud protocol by creating a video that captures individuals' mouse clicks and menu navigation, as well as comments to foster an in-depth analysis of the activity. The literature on screen capture software supports its use with the think-aloud protocol. Goodwin (2005) employed Camtasia as a tool to capture participants' screen movements and voice during a Texas A&M University's Libraries' website's usability study. She noted that the software reduced errors associated with having a human recorder and also decreased the labor intensity of the project. According to Goodwin, the software's capability to save the data into a file allowed for its subsequent review and manipulation. She described the software's learning curve as "flat" and the recording mechanism as "easy" (p. 620). Goodwin linked the software to facilitating the library's effort to gather administrative support for a website redesign project. Corbus et al. (2005) also utilized Camtasia in their evaluation of Hunter College's Library's website. An analysis of the recordings from screen captures of participants' movements allowed the librarians to identify and correct problems with the site.

The participants

A convenience sample was used in the study. Enrollment in a graduate education program was the only requirement for the study. Volunteers were solicited from classes in a College of Education's graduate programs in a four-year public institution located in a metropolitan area in the mid-Atlantic region of the United States during the fall 2011 semester. The participants consisted of eight students, including two males and six females of various ages, enrolled in graduate programs. Individuals contacted the researcher to schedule a problem-solving activity.

Participants were provided with access to the idea tactics tutorial following an initial search activity.

Students were encouraged to participate in the problem-solving activity as well as the subsequent interview and signed the consent forms required by the university's institutional review board. Participants were compensated for their time with a $25 gift certificate from a vendor of their choice. This reward may have affected students' motivation for joining the study, but it remained a necessary component of the research to ensure optimal participation.

Participant-generated problems

The task-based activity focused on participant-generated information problems to increase the incentives for volunteering and also to maintain individuals' interest throughout the activity. Participant tasks centered on gathering information for a class assignment. Mayer (1998) observed that problem-solving skills should be learned within "realistic problem-solving situations" (p. 53). He promoted a metaskills perspective that centered on modeling the effective use of strategies in academic tasks. Mayer also noted the importance of motivation in problem solving. Our study borrowed from Mayer's approach in its focus on students' search of a research database using an authentic information need. In addition, Mayer pointed to interest theory, stating: "students think harder and process the material more deeply when they are interested rather than uninterested" (p. 57).

The activity

A College of Education conference room at the university served as the location for the think-aloud problem-solving activities and the post-activity interviews. Students were provided with a laptop that contained Camtasia as well as the tutorial. This enabled participants to access all of the study's components, including the library's subscription databases, from one device. A mouse was available for use with the laptop if desired by the participants. At the start of the activity, individuals produced their information problem. On the problem-solving activity day, the researcher began the process by describing the study, supplying: an explanation of purpose of research, information concerning the video and audio recordings, and an assurance that the results would be confidential.

Participants signed a consent form that also promised the anonymity of their participation. In addition, individuals were given an opportunity to ask for clarification of any of the components of the study.

Students were instructed to locate materials for their problem using the Ebsco databases on the library's web page. They verbalized all of their movements through a think-aloud protocol as they gathered information for their topic. Following one or two initial searches that served as the study's pre-test, each participant responded to evaluative prompts that tracked their satisfaction level with the various aspects of the search such as the number of results and the relevancy of the material. These prompts aimed to guide participants in adopting appropriate revision strategies for subsequent searches. At this point the idea tactic tutorial was introduced for participants to review. The participant instituted additional searches on their topic following exposure to the tutorial. After conducting the search, the participant again responded to the evaluative prompts and conducted revised searches until they appeared satisfied with the results or opted to stop searching. Participants were encouraged to think aloud and consult the tutorial if they were not satisfied with their search results. Participants' revised search time did not exceed 30 minutes.

The screen capture software created a video of participants' voices throughout the task and their cursor movements. This allowed for an examination of the search terms, menu selections, databases chosen, search strategies, and result sets, as well as their comments during the task. The files were saved in Camtasia's default file format, camrec.

Follow-up interviews

Northcutt and McCoy (2004) described interviews as a "critical component" of qualitative studies (p. 197). Johnson et al. (2007) listed interviews as a form of data collection in mixed methods research. We conducted semi-structured interviews following the task completion portion of the activity using an interview guide. This guide ensured all participants received the same questions, and these were designed to gather participants' comments about the activity and especially to reveal any difficulties they experienced in the study. Creswell (2009) argued that qualitative research interviews centered on few open-ended questions that "are intended to elicit views and opinions from the participants" (p. 181). Moreover, he reminds us that "a good interviewer is a good listener" (2007, p. 134). These interviews enhanced the interpretation of the think-aloud protocols by allowing participants to provide an explanation of their research strategies during the session, including any obstacles they encountered as well as their satisfaction level with the search results. All interviews were audio-taped and transcribed verbatim by the researcher.

Summary of the problem-solving activity and interview

The mixed methods study focused on education graduate students' information problem solving in a research database. A follow-up interview tracked participants' comments about the activity. Camtasia screen capture software and participants' use of the think-aloud protocol tracked students' thoughts and movements during their information search, and this constituted the research data. Foremost, we focused on concurrent and sequential data collection and integration of the results. Ultimately, we hoped our mixed methods perspective would combine the advantages of qualitative and quantitative forms of inquiry in evaluating the effectiveness of the metacognitive tool on students' information problem solving.

12

Methodology: the data analysis

Abstract: In this chapter, we outline our methodology for the analysis of the results. We employed descriptive data to reveal individuals' use of the tutorial as well as their feelings about the scaffold and their searches. On the other hand, we utilized statistics to provide an objective view of the intervention's impact on participants' problem solving. NVivo assisted with the creation of codes in the analysis of the descriptive data. SPSS facilitated the analysis of the frequency counts that tracked participants search behaviors' during their problem-solving activity. Our mixed methods study centered on a concurrent triangulation design that sought to confirm, cross-validate or correlate the findings. To promote triangulation, we utilized numerous data sources and methods of analysis, as well as two researchers and a co-evaluator.

Key words: quantitative, qualitative, mixed methods, codes, legitimization, concurrent triangulation, Camtasia, NVivo, construct validity.

Introduction

The use of a variety of tools and procedures in the analysis of the results highlighted the mixed methods design of our study. Onwuegbuzie and Teddlie (2003) described seven stages of mixed methodological data analysis process: data reduction, data display, data transformation, data correlation, data consolidation, data comparison, and data integration. We utilized these strategies in our efforts to construct meaning from participants' problem solving and post-activity interview. We hoped an integration of the findings, and especially correlating the quantitative results with the qualitative data, would illustrate the tutorial's impact on students' information problem solving. We employed descriptive data to reveal individuals' use of the tutorial as well as their feelings about the scaffold and their searches. On the other hand, we utilized statistics to provide an objective view of the intervention's impact on participants' problem solving. Our mixed methods design included the "combination of quantitative and qualitative approaches" in data collection and analysis (Creswell, 2009, p. 203). We present this information through the use of six pseudonyms that describe participants' problem solving.

Concurrent triangulation design

Creswell et al. (2003) noted the variety of mixed methods designs as well as the lack of consensus on the types that existed, their names, and their visual representations. The authors delineated six major design types utilizing four criteria: implementation, priority, integration, and theoretical perspective. Still, they acknowledged variations within these design types "to fit a particular research situation" (p. 223).

Our mixed methods study centered on a concurrent triangulation design. Creswell (2009) described this approach as a popular mixed method strategy that was aimed at confirming, cross-validating, or correlating findings within a study. In this strategy, data integration occurred in the interpretation phase and also addressed the degree of convergence of the findings. The use of qualitative and quantitative approaches strengthens the validity of the findings by offsetting "the weakness inherent within one method with the strengths of the other method" (p. 213). Onwuegbuzie and Johnson (2006) offered additional features of data analysis in a concurrent mixed design. First, they argued that researchers do not build one approach on the other. Second, in this design the results are consolidated after the analysis and interpretation of each data type. Third, this design included the creation of a meta-inference from the integration of qualitative and quantitative inferences.

Utilization of quantitative and qualitative analytical techniques

The analysis of our data followed the fundamental principle of mixed methods data analysis in our utilization of "quantitative and qualitative analytical techniques either concurrently or sequentially, at some stage beginning with the data collection process" for interpretations (Onwuegbuzie and Teddlie, 2003, p. 353). During the data analysis, we examined each data source in its entirety prior to integrating all of the results for the final interpretation. In the analysis of our qualitative data, we focused on what Creswell (2009) termed as "making sense out of text and image data" and this constituted an "ongoing process" that included organizing materials, reading, coding, and identifying themes and interrelations among themes (pp. 183–5).

"Quantizing" our qualitative data

The analysis of our qualitative results also yielded some of our quantitative data. The screen captures of individuals' problem solving supported the creation of frequency counts that tracked individuals' searches as well as their access to the tutorial. The use of a stopwatch enabled data on participants' time spent in the tutorial and devising search strategies and reviewing results. Tashakkori and Teddlie (1998) refer to this technique as "quantizing" and they note its popularity in mixed methods research (p. 126). Creswell et al. (2003) described data transformation as a variation of the concurrent triangulation design that they noted occurred during the data analysis phase. Still, they warned that "there is still limited guidance for how to conduct and analyze such transformation in practice" (p. 229). To that end, we adopted Miles and Huberman's (1994) suggestions in developing "clear decision rules" for quantizing the data (p. 214). They remind us that "this is not an operation to be taken lightly" (p. 214).

Legitimization and validity

Onwuegbuzie and Teddlie (2003) highlighted the importance of legitimizing inferences derived from mixed methods research. Onwuegbuzie and Johnson (2006) defined the problem of legitimization as "difficulty in obtaining findings and/or making inferences that are credible, trustworthy, dependable, transferable and/or confirmable" (p. 52). The Qualitative Legitimation Model, developed by Onwuegbuzie (2000), offered strategies for integrating various types of validity and assessing the "truth value of qualitative research interpretations" (Onwuegbuzie and Leech, 2007, p. 239). We adopted various techniques to address the threats to external and internal credibility illustrated in the model. These techniques promoted legitimation of our analysis including:

- triangulation of the data sources;
- the use of an audit trail;
- member checking;
- weighing the evidence;
- checking for researcher bias;
- making contrasts;
- reviewing outliers; and
- incorporating rich descriptions.

For example, to promote triangulation, we utilized numerous data sources and methods of analysis, as well as two researchers and a co-evaluator. We maintained an audit trail of all of the materials that evolved from the study. We employed member checking by requesting clarification from participants' comments and search behaviors during the post-activity interview. In one instance we contacted a participant for additional information on their comments during the activity. We weighted the evidence in considering the data gleaned from the screen captures as more reliable than participants' comments during the activity, since the video recorded actual search behaviors. We sought to eliminate researcher bias by including another investigator, an academic reference librarian, in assisting in the assignment of codes and the ratings of search results. We contrasted participants' problem solving in their initial search to their efforts following exposure to the tutorial. We sought to understand outliers in search results by recreating searches. Lastly, we offered a rich description of individuals' problem solving by detailing their use of syntax, fields, databases, limits on searches, and search results.

These legitimization techniques resemble procedures for ensuring validity in qualitative research. Creswell and Miller (2000) define validity procedures as "strategies used by the researcher to establish the credibility of their study" (p. 125). The authors argued that validity procedures utilized by researchers were linked to their paradigm assumptions as well as their lens (or the perspective of the researcher, the study participants, and individuals outside of the study) as well as. Guba and Lincoln (1994) defined a paradigm as "a set of basic beliefs" or "worldview," and identified four, including: positivism, post-positivist, constructivist, and critical theory (p. 107).

In our study we focused on the participant lens in seeking to understand how individuals utilized the tutorial and how the scaffold affected their problem solving. Still, we recognized the role of the researcher and their perspective in shaping the study. Moreover, we adopted a post-positive or systematic researcher paradigm in highlighting the importance of validity and seeking the "quantitative equivalence of it" and employing methods to establish credibility (Creswell and Miller, 2000, p. 125). Foremost, we sought to incorporate as many validity procedures as possible to strengthen the credibility of our findings.

Construct validity

Researchers point to different types of validity and procedures designed for their measurement (Tashakkori and Teddlie, 1998). Our study considered construct validity. This refers to how well an experiment supported its objective. Shadish et al. (2002) suggested that construct validity was promoted by "clear explication of the person, setting, treatment, and outcome constructs of interest," "carefully selecting instances that match those constructs," assessment of the match "between instances and constructs" and "revising constructs descriptions" if necessary (p. 66). In addition to these considerations, construct validity in this research was facilitated by the triangulation of the data and especially in comparisons made among the various data types. Shadish et al. (2002) also promoted triangulation that they described as "the need to use multiple operations to index each construct when possible (e.g. multiple measures, manipulations, settings, and units)" (p. 81). Likewise, they encourage insurance that the multiple operations "reflects multiple methods so that single-method confounds (e.g. self-reports) can be better assessed" (p. 82). In the current study, the diverse data sources included quantitative and qualitative results from the think-aloud protocol, screen captures, the post-search interviews, and the scoring of the first searches and last search.

Internal validity

Hoepfl (1997) defined internal validity as "the extent to which the findings accurately describe the reality" (para. 56). Internal validity of our findings from the quantitative data were strengthened by the triangulation of the data, which included the number of revised searches conducted, the time spent devising search strategies and reviewing results, the number of records opened, the number of results, the number of accesses to various components of the tutorial, and scores on participants' search results. The triangulation of the qualitative component included information from the think-aloud and the screen captures as well as the post-search interview.

Internal validity for the qualitative component of the study focused on the Camtasia files that recorded each participant's problem-solving activities. Transcripts from the think-aloud protocol activity supported the validity of the qualitative data by revealing participants' thoughts and motivations in utilizing search strategies and the tutorial during their problem-solving activities. In addition, the post-search interviews provided a validity component through their focus on identifying participants' motives in their search strategies, their satisfaction level with the results, as well as any obstacles they encountered during the problem-solving process.

The initial search served as a control measure for illustrating the impact of the tutorial on individuals' problem-solving behaviors. The triangulation of the material that included both qualitative and quantitative measures strengthened the findings. Internal validity was also strengthened by comparisons among the various data types. For example, participants' search behaviors in the initial search including search techniques utilized, databases accessed, and scores for relevancy, quality, appropriateness, and authoritativeness of the results were compared with their strategies utilized in subsequent revised searches after exposure to the tutorial.

Lastly, intercoder agreement supported the internal validity of the transcripts in the code assignment process and the search score ratings. The researcher and a co-evaluator, both librarians, mutually agreed on the creation of the codes. The use of the NVivo software, and especially the code descriptions that allowed the researcher to describe the definition of each code, strengthened the validity of the process. Intercoder reliability was also used for the rating assignment of all the search results. In this instance, each search outcome was assigned a rating for the results' relevance, its authoritativeness, the quality of the response, and its ability to answer the problem.

External validity

Researchers equate external validity to the "ability to generalize findings across different settings" (Hopef, 1997, p. 59). Cronbach (1975) suggested that social science researchers adopt hypotheses rather than generalizations in describing their research. He maintained that this allowed the researcher to consider controlled and uncontrolled conditions. According to Cronbach, "when we give proper weight to local conditions any generalization is a working hypothesis, not a conclusion" (p. 125). Merriam (1998) offered strategies for the promotion of external validity. These strategies included offering detailed description of the study, providing information on the commonality of the research, and incorporating multisite designs. Creswell (2009) observed mixed methods research required attention to validity issues in qualitative and quantitative research. He described validity in qualitative research as "determining whether the findings are accurate from the standpoint of the researcher, the participant or the readers of an account" (p. 191). Foremost, he identified external validity in quantitative research as generalizing "beyond the groups in the experiment" or "to past or future situations" (p. 162). Although we offer strategies for modifying the idea tactics tutorial for other user groups, these are presented according to what Cronbach (1975) described as a working hypothesis, rather than a generalization.

Reliability

Reliability includes the degree to which a study can be replicated (Merriam, 1998; LeCompte and Goetz, 1982). Lincoln and Guba (1985) pointed out that reliability was threatened by "any careless act in the measurement or assessment process, by instrumental decay, by assessments that are insufficiently long (or intense), by ambiguities of various sorts" (p. 292). Merriam (1998) offered techniques to highlighting dependability and consistency in the data collected; these included providing details about the researchers' "assumptions and theory" about the study, promoting the triangulation in the research, and maintaining an audit trail (p. 206). Creswell (2009) defines qualitative reliability as ensuring that the "researcher's approach is consistent across different researchers and different projects" (p. 190). Gibbs (2007) listed measures to improve reliability in qualitative studies, such as reviewing transcripts for errors, ensuring consistent coding, and utilizing a team approach to the data analysis. Consequently, in our study we focused on the accurate transcription of the audio files as well as on their coding through intercoder reliability. Moreover, we offered evidence of our assumptions and theories regarding the research, utilized triangulation techniques, and maintained an audit trail of the data collected.

Transcripts of problem-solving activity using prefigured codes

We followed the ethnographic approach outlined by Pink (2007) in the analysis of the transcripts from the problem-solving activity and post-activity interview. Pink described ethnography as a "process of creating and representing knowledge (about society, culture, and individuals)" that remains as accurate as possible to the context "through which the knowledge was produced" (p. 22). She noted that the outcome was affected by the attitudes and views of the researcher and the subject as well as their relationship to each other. Consequently she advocated a reflective approach in video analysis that highlighted the contexts of the video's production and especially the "subjectivities and intentions" of the participants (p. 123).

Prefigured codes based on Bates' (1979) idea tactics

To that end, the interpretation of the think-aloud protocol Camtasia files in camrec format were transcribed and coded. The problem-solving transcripts were coded using prefigured codes based on Bates' (1979) idea tactics that were listed in the tutorial including all of the Indexes as well as the tactic examples to track participants' use of the tactics. For example, participants' views of a specific index page, such as the Evaluation Index, and subsequent efforts to evaluate results to improve outcomes in their revised search, led to the coding of the transcript as "application of Evaluation Index." Likewise, participants' views of the Change tactic example as well as comments about the tactic were coded as "comments about the Change example and participants time spent on the page." Frequency counts recorded participants' number of accesses to the various components of the tutorial as well as the length of time they spent in each section. The number of seconds that participants devoted to devising strategy and reviewing results was also recorded, using a stopwatch.

Transcripts of problem-solving activity and post-search interviews using open coding schemes

Constant comparative method

The researcher also coded the transcripts from the problem-solving activity and post-search interviews utilizing an open coding scheme to capture the issues that emerged during participants' problem-solving activities (Creswell, 2007). We adopted the constant comparative method outlined by Glaser and Strauss (1967). This method focuses on numerous comparisons among transcripts to ensure accuracy in the identification of codes. Coding remains an iterative process that includes creating and merging as well as the elimination of codes. Glaser and Strauss identified four stages in the method: comparing comments or actions in categories, integrating categories, developing theory, and "writing the theory" (p. 105). Theory development in this instance required the researcher to consider an abstract perspective in analyzing the qualitative material. In the current study, codes were developed considering themes characteristic of information search. The researcher identified commonalities among the transcripts and developed codes accordingly. This information highlighted the search activity, problems that participants encountered in the process, participants' views on the search tactics the utilized, techniques they employed in their problem solving, their satisfaction with the search results, and any additional information they chose to offer.

Inter-coder reliability

Coding occurred in several phases by two individuals, one of the authors and a co-evaluator, both reference librarians, to support inter-coder reliability. The author reviewed each line of every transcript to identify various idea tactics and dominant themes that emerged during the activity and post-search interview. Transcripts were compared and reviewed numerous times to ensure the accuracy of the content as well as the context in developing the codes. This facilitated the creation of the code tree that illustrated relationships among codes. For example, the themes that emerged for the initial search among all the participants included: choose databases, results review, and initial strategy. On the other hand, in reviewing the results of their revised search participants focused on interest, subject terms, keywords, page length, refinement of concept terms, filtering, full text availability, and the number of results.

Following the identification of the codes, all of the transcripts as well as the codes were provided to the co-evaluator for his comment and suggestions. The co-evaluator, one of the university's senior reference librarians with experience in NVivo coding, noted some inconsistencies and provided suggestions for the renaming of some codes and the creation of additional codes for several categories. For example, he recommended placing "errors" under "Search Obstacles" and dividing errors into "initial," "continuous," and "Ebsco." This suggestion was adopted with one modification. The "obstacles" node was changed to "Participants Perspectives-Search Obstacles" and the "Errors" node was placed under "Search" following discussion between the researcher and co-evaluator. In addition, the "Instruction" node was deleted, since it was represented in "librarian" under "Reflections-General."

QSR NVivo

NVivo version 9 qualitative analysis software facilitated the coding process. Creswell (2007) noted the advantages of using software in qualitative research for data storage and access. He also suggested computer programs fostered data analysis and the product's mapping capability could support visualization for relationships among codes and themes. However, Onwuegbuzie and Teddlie (2003) warned against using the computer program as a "substitute for a through reading of the text" (p. 372). NVivo version 9 contained the ability to facilitate code assignment by importing transcripts and searching text for keywords or phrases. Another feature of this product allowed users to track their coding processes through the creation of code definitions. We focused on creating the index or tree system to illustrate relationships between codes. This software was purchased and loaded on a laptop and provided to the co-evaluator.

Participant searches

Transcription of the Camtasia files allowed for a recreation of participants searches. In this instance, each search participants performed was recorded including the syntax, keywords, and databases utilized as well as the number of results received. The inclusion of [YOUR] after the search string indicated the query did not yield any hits and Ebsco reverted to Smart text searching to return results based on keywords.

Final product

The co-evaluator also assisted with the rating of the search results from the problem-solving activity. This represented the outcomes for all of participants' search results from their Ebsco database searches, including those performed before and after exposure to the tutorial. One of the authors and the co-evaluator rated each search using a five point Likert scale based on the results' relevance, its authoritativeness, the quality of the response, and its ability to answer the problem. A five represented the highest rating. Evaluators gauged the relevance of the search results by how closely the articles matched the topic. The authoritativeness of search results was determined by the scholarliness of the articles, but since participants were searching an academic database, all search results, except zero, received a baseline rating of three. Individuals who checked scholarly or peer-reviewed materials received higher scores.

Quality of the response was judged according to a variety of factors, including improvement occurred over a previous search (if available), as well as the number and cohesiveness of the topic in the results. Lastly, evaluators considered the results' ability to answer the problem. Rating of the search results occurred in two phases. In the first phase, the researcher viewed the search results from the Camtasia files. In the second phase, the researcher recreated the search utilizing the same keywords, search techniques, and databases employed in the participants' initial search. Searches were rated based on these results as well as the results the participant received during the activity. The information was provided to the co-evaluator for his review and comment. Comparisons between the first search and the last search determined the degree of improvement following access to the tutorial. If participants conducted numerous searches prior to accessing the tutorial, the average ratings of these events were utilized for the first search scores.

The ratings for all of the participants' first and final searches were transcribed, and appear in Appendix A. Academic Search Premier was the default database. Any additional databases participants accessed, as well as their search syntax, keywords, and the number of results they received, are also displayed.

IBM Statistical Package for Social Sciences (SPSS)

Bar charts and scatter dot plots were created using SPSS software version 20 (Appendix B). Prvan et al. (2002) described SPSS as a "widely used professional statistical package" (p. 70). The product was developed in 1968 (Hilbe, 2003) and has attained recognition as a "premiere statistical software package" (Hilbe, 2004, p. 168). According to the *IBM SPSS Statistics 20 Brief Guide*, the software has the capability "to take data from almost any type of file and use them to generate tabulated reports, charts, and plots of distributions and trends, descriptive statistics, and complex statistical analyses" (*IBM*, 2011, iii).

We utilized SPSS to illustrate the impact of the tutorial on participants' problem solving from a quantitative perspective. The following data was utilized to create the diagrams: total number of accesses to the tutorial, total time in tutorial, the total time devising search strategy, total time reviewing results, number of revised searches, number of records opened, and search scores for relevancy, authoritativeness, the ability of the responses to answer the question, and the quality of the response for the initial and final searches. Diagrams relevant to the findings are included in Appendix B.

Summary of the data analysis

Onwuegbuzie and Teddlie (2003) viewed data analysis as a cyclical process that included data collection, data analysis, data interpretation, and legitimization. Likewise, our data analysis, which followed the concurrent triangulation strategy, focused on the cyclical process outlined by Onwuegbuzie and Teddlie. The qualitative data stemmed from participants' comments during the problem-solving activity and post-activity interview. The quantitative data was derived in part from the screen capture software and included frequency counts of participants accesses to the tutorial, as well as their time spent in the scaffold and in devising search strategies. Participants' search results ratings also remained a component of the quantitative data. Both data sources were analyzed separately prior to their integration for a general interpretation of the results. Various tools such as NVivo and SPSS supported the analysis of the data. We also identified threats to internal and external credibility as outlined in Onwuegbuzie's (2000) Qualitative Legitimation Model to enhance the validity of our findings. Ultimately, our research results led to suggestions for refinement of the tutorial to enhance its effectiveness in developing users' metacognitive strategies during their information-seeking activities in research databases.

13

The indexes

Abstract: Gorrell et al. (2009) noted the importance of providing metacognitive support in web searching, especially for assisting users in planning, monitoring and evaluating their search. The idea tactics are arranged in four indexes that represent common difficulties users experience during information search. The chapter outlines the development of the Relevance, Number, Evaluation, and Strategy Indexes to improve individuals' search results. The chapter also presents research on the roles of relevance and strategy as well as broadening and narrowing and evaluation techniques on dissertation study participants' search outcome. All of the names utilized in the case descriptions are pseudonyms, to protect the identities of the participants. Four out of six participants improved their search outcomes following exposure to the tutorial.

Key words: relevance, number of results, evaluation, strategy, experts novices searching, broadening, narrowing, Bates' idea tactics, problem solving, participants.

Introduction

Our study explored the role of the idea tactics tutorial in effecting participants' problem solving. The tutorial centers on Bates' (1979) idea tactics, which resemble metacognitive strategies to enhance search results. The tactics are arranged in four indexes that represent common difficulties users experience during information search, including devising a strategy to locate an optimal number of relevant materials and evaluating results. This chapter describes the impact of the Relevance, Number, Evaluation, and Strategy Indexes on six of the eight participants' search behaviors. All of the names utilized in the case descriptions include pseudonyms to protect the identity of the participants. While Bates designed the tactics to improve information professionals' search behaviors, Ercegovac (1989) suggested they contained potential to enhance users' interactions with online library catalogs by offering "heuristics" to facilitate search efficiency (p. 24). Gorrell et al. (2009) noted the importance of providing metacognitive support in web searching especially for assisting users in planning, monitoring, and evaluating their search. Their research focused on the development of a metacognitively aware information retrieval system that would "compensate for metacognitive weaknesses" (p. 457). Likewise, a metacognitive-based skills tutorial remains especially relevant in the digital age. Brumfield (2008) emphasized the role of an online tutorial in providing library skills instruction to novice users and those "without access to face-to-face instruction" (p. 374). Our idea tactics scaffold provides a flexible tool that can be utilized in conjunction with a learning management system or with an information literacy course delivering self-paced skills instruction on an as needed basis.

Bates and testing the tactics

Bates (1979) argued that the tactics were presented as a facilitation model of searching "of possible help to searchers in the process of tracking down information" (p. 286). She admitted that testing their effectiveness would be difficult, but suggested focusing on the impact of all of the tactics on search effectiveness and efficiency. According to Bates, determining how a person uses the tactics remains the "job of the person developing a representation model" (p. 286). Still, she outlined potential research on the "facilitation value of the tactics" utilizing control and experimental groups. She suggested that the study use information professionals or beginning library students (p. 288). Bates noted problems with using beginning students in the experiment, since "exposure to tactics at this stage of learning is confusing rather than helpful" (p. 288). Yet she maintained that the advanced skill level of information professionals could confound the results.

Bates also pointed readers who were interested in evaluating individual idea tactics to her "Testing of Information Search Tactics," which focused on an assessment of her information search tactics developed in 1978. These included 29 tactics aimed at facilitating information searching through strategies related to monitoring, file structure, search formulation, and term usage. According to Bates (1978), testing the tactics would center on novice searchers and would include three groups.

One group would perform binary searches and a second group would be instructed in binary searching, but allowed flexibility in searching. A control group would not receive any search instruction. Bates predicted that the second group would outperform the others due to their ability to combine binary search with contextual knowledge. She concluded that this test would reveal if the tactics, "as a way of thinking for human information searchers, actually improve search performance" (para. 14).

Relevance

Relevance determines search success

The retrieval of relevant materials is paramount to search success. As Saracevic (2008) reminds us, the goal of information retrieval is obtaining materials relevant to our query. Nowicki (2003) traced the growth of relevance research to the development of the information science discipline as well as information retrieval systems beginning in the 1950s. Foremost, relevance research revealed a wide range of factors that affected users' relevance decisions. Howard (1994) stated that "relevance is not a concept which can be defined neatly" (p. 172). She pointed to objective relevance that was system-based and subjective relevance that focused on the users' view of a document's pertinence. Janes (1994) proposed the term was multi-dimensional and dynamic, and was related to topicality, satisfaction, pertinence, and utility. Saracevic (1975) concluded that there was no "*one specific* view of relevance" and he urged attention to the "elements and the nature of relations between elements that are being considered" (p. 339).

Research highlighted the role of the individual in determining relevance (Nowicki 2003). Harter (1992) suggested the existence of psychological relevance in information science that varied according to an individual's point in space and time. Studies also suggested an individual's perception of relevance was affected by their previous knowledge, their awareness of the information need, the task, the goal, and the time restraints (Park, 1994). Vakkari (2001a, 2001b) found a relationship between a student's stage in their research and their assessment of relevance in materials. He maintained that beginning research students lacked a mental model of the problem, and this contributed to their difficulty in distinguishing between relevant and irrelevant materials. Saracevic (2008) found the consistency of judgments of relevance differed according to the level of expertise of the user and the number of judges.

Information retrieval systems center on matching the keywords utilized in search strings to database indexes to deliver relevant results. Barry (1994) noted that the match depended on three assumptions: that users subject terms describe the information need, that the subject terms utilized to describe the document are accurate, and that the subject matching produced relevant results. Researchers point to measures of system effectiveness as agreements between system defined relevance and what the user assessed as relevant (Saracevic, 2008). Harter (1992) identified recall and precision as measuring information retrieval success in delivering relevant materials. According to Harter, recall was the "proportion of relevant documents" retrieved and precision equaled the "proportion of retrieved documents that are relevant" to the search. Brophy and Bawden (2005) used three levels to gauge documents' relevance in their study that compared items retrieved from various library systems and Google. These three levels included: topical, or the document's similarity to the subject matter; pertinent, or the material's degree of information provided; and utility, or the item's usefulness in fulfilling the information need.

Studies suggest students employ various strategies for gauging relevance. Korobili et al.'s (2011) research on graduate students' search behaviors revealed a variety of criteria students used to determine relevance in results. According to the authors, these included the source title, the title of the journal, and the descriptors respectively. Currie et al. (2010) observed similar results in their study of undergraduate students' information-seeking behavior. Participants pointed to the importance of "relevant terminology or keywords, most often in the title" (p. 119). One student "noted the relevancy indicator symbol" in Academic Search Premier and another commented on Google's display of the most relevant articles first (p. 120).

Relevance Index

The Relevance Index in the idea tactics tutorial was designed to improve the relevance of individuals' search results. The Main Index prompts users to access the Relevance Index if they require assistance in selecting search terms. This Index contains three tactics: Think, Catch, and Notice, and these offer metacognitive strategies to readers. The Think tactic encourages students to "identify search goals or what you wish to accomplish," and it supports the role of planning in information search. The Catch tactic promotes self-regulation by reminding students to "recognize an unproductive search and institute a new approach." The Notice tactic encourages students to monitor their search by considering "the appearance of any clues that may affect your interpretation of the question and how to answer it."

Embedded within each idea tactic in the Relevance Index is information on Ebsco database search features. This includes advice on selecting databases, choosing relevant keywords, evaluating results, using subject terms, using Boolean operators, identifying synonyms, truncating words, and excluding terms.

The Index also contains information on how Ebsco databases employ relevance ranking. In this instance, the database utilized algorithms that consider the degree of match of search terms, the density of terms, and the frequency of terms in the database, as well as the recency of the article. Moreover, some Ebsco databases also consider the document type in determining relevance ranking. For example, a database consisting primarily of serials would display a journal article before a book review.

Impact of Relevance Index on participants' problem solving

Although the Relevance Index was only utilized by three participants during the problem-solving activity, each participant accessed the intervention multiple times. Moreover, an examination of their immediate problem-solving efforts revealed improvements compared to their search prior to viewing the Relevance Index.

Mary

The biggest impact of the Relevance Index on Mary's problem solving centered on her development of a search strategy. Mary's topic centered on theories of reading and she experimented with a variety of keywords prior to exposure to the Relevance Index. These efforts yielded results that were often irrelevant or too few or too numerous. Following access to the Relevance Index, Mary revised her search plan, stating, "I'm just typing in theories of reading instead of specifying each." This search yielded nearly 3,000 hits and prompted Mary to revise her strategy, including "phonological processing" in the search string. She appeared happy with the five results, commenting, "Okay great. These seem interesting." At this point, she opted to search for "models of reading." In her subsequent search efforts, she experimented with various combinations of theoretical models of reading incorporating "maotts." Following these searches, Mary adopted a new search strategy that centered on locating articles from prominent authors on her topic. In subsequent searches, she also reviewed records for theorist names and relevant keywords that she employed in new queries such as "Shaywitz," "Lyon," "Standovich," and "cognitive." The Relevance Index may have also influenced her decision to focus on educational rather than psychological databases. In addition to incorporating new search terms, Mary changed her databases, substituting ERIC for PsycINFO, to focus on educational material.

In her post-search interview, Mary stated that she was satisfied with her search results, noting she received her goal of ten as well as "a few more." Still, she said the tutorial "slowed her down," since she was very familiar with the computer. A comparison of the ratings between Mary's searches before and after exposure to the tutorial showed no improvement as all categories ranked below average. However, some of her searches (she conducted 19 in total) did yield above-average results, especially after she changed her databases to focus on educational materials. She did spend a significant amount of time reviewing her results as well as examining records during her problem-solving activity. Although Mary did not appear to gain many database search techniques from the tutorial, the focus of her topic improved during the problem-solving activity, particularly with the development of new search strategies as well as the selection of new databases.

Daemon

Daemon accessed the Relevance Index in his first encounter with the tutorial and it seemingly enhanced his problem solving. At this time he reviewed the Notice tactic example and the Number Index and its Create tactic. These sources highlight the importance of utilizing appropriate databases and keywords to enhance the relevance of the results. He revised his search following his initial review of the tutorial incorporating a new keyword as well as selecting additional databases. In his first revised search, he expanded his database selection to include Education Research Complete, ERIC, Primary Research, PsycARTICLES, and PsycINFO. The search "Jean piaget AND Cognitive development AND theor*" yielded 436 hits, and led him to narrow the results utilizing Ebsco's Subject Thesaurus term "piaget theory."

In addition to facilitating Daemon's selection of appropriate databases and keywords, the Relevance Index and particularly the Think tactic (which focused on goal setting) supported his search efforts. At this time he also clarified his search goal, noting, "I'm trying to look I'm looking for more like a biography more like a concentration of this theories. His actual theories. I need to get definitely more specific."

It is difficult to gauge the impact of the Relevance Index on Daemon's overall problem solving, since he also viewed the Evaluation and Strategy indexes. Still, the tutorial had a positive impact on his problem-solving activity. Although his initial topic was broad, exposure to the tutorial helped Daemon narrow his search using terms from relevant records. In addition, the tutorial triggered his previous knowledge, and that fostered his ability to conduct a more focused search by truncating terms and using keywords from relevant records. He also made improvements in the rating of his search scores from his first to his last search in every category. In addition, following exposure to the tutorial, he increased the amount of time he spent reviewing results. For example, a comparison of his time spent reviewing results from his first search to his last search was 13 seconds to 1 minute 33 seconds. Daemon said that he was satisfied with the results and would "be able to use this for my research topic." He indicated the tutorial helped improve his search activity. "Yeah it was good." However, he admitted he knew a lot of the techniques, but reading it "kinda like hit me. I know I should do that."

Shelly

Shelly's topic was the difference between extrinsic and intrinsic motivation for students, especially their ability to navigate the curriculum goals of elementary school. Her initial search resulted in nearly 5,000 hits and she noted that many of them didn't deal with elementary students. Although she was able to limit these results to items published in 2010, she still had too many hits and many of them did not focus on American schools. Shelly, like Daemon, read the Relevance Index in her first encounter with the tutorial. She focused on the Catch and Think tactic examples, and employed some of their suggestions into her revised searches. These examples offered information on selecting a database, choosing keywords, selecting synonyms, evaluating results, and using subject terms. At this point she stated, "So what I'm finding that possibly I'm not putting things in. I maybe am using too big a phrase as opposed to a couple of words in quotes." In her subsequent revised search, she spent more time devising search strategy and reviewing results than she had in her initial search. The Index also underscored the value of synonyms to Shelly and she experimented with various search terms throughout her activity.

Shelly also appeared to benefit from the planning, monitoring, and self-regulating focus of the tactics. The Think tactic advised users to identify search goals and the Catch tactic highlighted the need to recognize an unproductive search and instigate a new approach. Shelly applied some of these tactics in her revised search by focusing on the selection of keywords. This search – "intrinsic" "extrinsic" "motivation" – yielded 36 results. After reviewing the hits, Shelly incorporated the term "elementary." The lack of results from this search led her back to her initial 36 hits. She commented, "I like these, I hadn't seen these before. There is quite a few here that I would actually take the time to really look at." The improvement in relevance of the search results was also evident in the search ratings for this search that contained above-average scores in all categories.

She opted to return to the tutorial to obtain more strategies for increasing relevance. In revisiting the tutorial and especially the Relevance Index and Notice example, she said, "One of the biggest things I believe is talking about specific using subject terms." At this point she conducted two searches utilizing subject terms and Boolean operators to incorporate terms and synonyms. Shelly then instituted an advanced search using subject terms as well as the AND/OR Boolean operators. The search strategy included "Grades" (SU) AND "intrinsic or extrinsic" AND "motivation" elementary yielded no results. Shelly continued to experiment with various keywords, including substituting "elementary education" as a subject term for "grades" and deleting "elementary." She spent nearly two minutes reviewing the results from a relevant record.

Like Daemon, Shelly also viewed other Indexes and tactics in the tutorial, and consequently we cannot attribute her learning gains to any one component of the intervention. Foremost, she gained some database search skills following exposure to the tutorial, and these were demonstrated in her searches. In addition, Shelly searched more efficiently following access to the tutorial; she spent less time devising search strategies and more time reviewing results. For example, she typically spent two minutes reviewing results and less than a minute devising search strategies. She also examined records in the post-tutorial phase of the problem-solving activity. The tutorial also underscored the value of synonyms to Shelly, and she experimented with various search terms throughout her activity. Comparisons between the scores for Shelly's first search and last search reveal increases from average to above average in all categories.

In her post-activity interview, she emphasized her lack of experience in searching, which she said stemmed from her extended hiatus between college and graduate school. "When I went to college we had electric typewriters and you went into the library and found microfiche and microform. So it was a very different way of searching. It was pretty one dimensional. Now learning this it's certainly not one dimensional. It's a matter of remembering where I was and how to navigate it and getting back again." She also stated that she located relevant material in the activity and found the tutorial helpful. "Yeah before I did not understand about this stuff, putting that in and the subject terms and refining the field. I didn't understand that so I wasn't doing it. So now when I go home this will be an easier thing for me to do."

Summary of the Relevance Index's impact on participants' problem solving

These three participants improved their search results through the use of the Relevance Index. The Index's metacognitive tactics offered strategies that enhanced the focus of individuals' queries and therefore the retrieval of relevant results. Some of these improvements were efforts directed at planning search strategies, the use of advanced search techniques such as Boolean operators, and an increased effort to review results. In addition, participants' experimentations with keywords could reflect more monitoring and self-regulating activities. Ultimately these strategies fostered better problem-solving outcomes for two of the participants.

Narrowing and broadening search strategies

Narrowing and broadening strategies linked to query formation

Chowdhury et al. (2011) described information seeking as a challenging task due to the "exponential growth of the web and electronic information channels and sources" (p. 171). As Moulaison (2008) stated, the "number of hits returned in a web search can be staggering" (p. 232). Klein (2009) highlighted the importance of keywords in online searching. As he reminds us, "finding the right balance between terms that may be too broad and others that are overly restrictive is crucial to assure good retrieval performance" (p. 298). Klein linked query formation to an art that required knowledge of the syntax and database peculiarities.

Likewise, studies of end users' search experience illustrated the problem that users encounter during information retrieval, especially in locating too many or too few hits. A survey of Aligarh Muslim University's staff and students' Internet use identified information overload as a common problem when searching (Nazim, 2008). Forty percent of respondents described it as an obstacle in searching (p. 80). In a similar study, Chowdhury et al. (2011) queried academic staff, research staff, and research students from a national academic mailing list service on search situations that produced uncertainty among users. The authors found "too much information or information overload" and "search output is not exhaustive" as causing uncertainty among more than 20 percent of users under 61 years of age (p. 171). In addition, Korobili et al. (2011) surveyed graduate students on their search behaviors and found the main barrier to information retrieval was "retriev[ing] records with high recall and low precision" (p. 159).

Qualitative studies also pointed to problems with students' searches that yielded too few or too many results. Mansourian (2008) utilized learning diaries in her study of Tarbiat Moallem University's students' search behaviors. One student observed that "the main problem that I have in web searching is dealing with too many results" that she complained could be "confusing and time-consuming" (p. 694). The research led to Mansourian's creation of a model of web searching that listed some of the problems students encountered as too much information, too little results, or no hits. Holman (2011) observed students' interactions with search engines and databases, and found individuals were "haphazard in their strategy to focus their searches or to expand or narrow their set of results" (p. 22). She also noted that students were unclear on why a search failed and preferred to employ simple searches "even if they retrieved larger lists of results" (p. 24).

The availability of numerous bibliographic search guides from academic library websites that outline efforts to improve results that yield too many or too few hits underscore the extent of this difficulty among students (University of Washington, 2013). Cahill (2008) encouraged information professionals to consider the opportunities Google presents for teaching "users about authority, about optimizing searchers, and about the areas where Google is not the be all-and end-all" (p. 70). Moreover, Markey's (2007) examination of research on end users' searching found that Boolean operator use was more prevalent among those individuals who had received training. Siegfried et al. (1983) suggested that end users would benefit from periodic training in Boolean and other database search techniques.

Research supports the use of narrowing and broadening strategies in improving search results. Sutcliffe et al.'s (2000) study of novice and expert users of MedLine found that experts utilized more complex queries, instigated more searches, and employed more broadening and narrowing strategies (including the use of diverse Boolean operators) than novices. The authors pointed to the importance of broadening and narrowing strategies as well as evaluation for success. Still, Marchionini and Liebscher's (1991) research suggested that end users searching electronic systems "seek the path of least cognitive resistance" and utilize "minimal system features" (p. 48). Markey's (2007) review of end user searching studies confirmed Marchionini and Liebscher's findings. She characterized end user search in information retrieval systems as including a few terms, and lacking Boolean operators. She also noted that individuals only employed advanced database features infrequently. Holman (2011) observed that students rarely used Boolean operators, and those who did used them incorrectly. Moreover, she stated that they "gave up quickly if it did not provide the expected results" (p. 24).

Number Index

Consequently, we designed the Number Index to assist participants in retrieving a manageable number of results. The idea tactics tutorial's Main Index notes that the Number Index is aimed at users who are "dissatisfied with the number" of their hits. It contains three idea tactics – Mediate, Change and Create – aimed at promoting students' use of monitoring, self-regulating, and planning metacognitive strategies respectively. Meditate encourages students to "analyze the search strategy." Change advises students to "instigate a new search behavior." Create suggests that students "develop a search strategy by identifying relevant keywords, search fields and databases."

In addition to metacognitive strategies, the Index offers Ebsco database search tips for selecting databases, choosing keywords, broadening and narrowing searches, truncating, using subject terms, evaluating results, and limiting to peer-reviewed materials. Expert modeling traces the reader through various searches, and in these instances, the searcher identifies their target number of results while providing guidance on how to attain them.

Impact of Number Index on participants' problem solving

The Number Index was the most popular component of the tutorial. Nearly every participant (five out of six) accessed it, and their access was illustrated in improved search results. We first discuss those participants whose problem solving focused on the use of the Number Index.

Dwaine

Dwaine's use of the Number Index offers a dramatic illustration of its power in enhancing participants' problem solving. He sought to locate information on the types of classroom observation tools for technology integration in the classroom. His initial search string included classroom observation tool technology integration, which produced 13, 151 results. After reading the Main Index, he explained he was "going to click on the link for dissatisfied with the number of hits because 13,000 is too much."

Dwaine focused on the Number Index's Change tactic. Following his review of the Change tactic, he revised his search, utilizing the advanced search mode and the same terms as his initial search, with the exception of "tool." He reduced the number of his hits to 20 items. Dwaine devoted over a minute to reviewing these results and appeared dissatisfied with the hits, noting: "What I am really looking for is information on tools used to evaluate technology integration in the classroom and I'm still not finding that. Actually here is one." He examined a record for "Assessing technology use in the classroom" and explained his intention to use "one of these keywords as subjects since this article is relevant." He noted that the "tutorial told me I could look at keywords in an article that actually looked relevant and use that in my search. Now I am going to try to change the wording of my search." After reviewing the record for subject terms, he modified his search, substituting the phrase "technology assessment" for "technology integration." He received four results that he indicated were useful. "Okay, out of these four results I would say three of them would be exactly what I was looking for."

Dwaine's search strategies following access to the tutorial suggested he had gained search skills from the intervention. In his revised searches, he demonstrated knowledge and use of the advanced search mode and the Boolean operator AND. He did not use these techniques in his initial search. In the post-interview component of the think-aloud, he noted the tutorial's emphasis on using keywords from an article that was relevant in affecting his strategy. To this end, his revised search incorporated a new keyword from a relevant hit. Dwaine observed: "I didn't know exactly what was good to solicit in the results I wanted."

A comparison of the ratings between Dwaine's first search with his final search illustrated increases in relevancy, the ability to answer the problem, and the quality of the response from average and below average to above average in all categories. In addition, he searched more efficiently after exposure to the tutorial. He spent less time devising search strategy in his two revised searches, but his final search results had higher relevancy scores compared to his initial search outcome. In addition, Dwaine spent more time reviewing results following access to the tutorial. As he revealed during the think-aloud component of the search, he was seeking relevant keywords to apply in his revised strategy.

Lesley

The tutorial's Number Index also improved the outcome of Lesley's problem-solving activity. She needed materials on mindfulness in young children. Her initial problem-solving attempt was a basic search in Ebsco using the default database Academic Search Premier and the phrase "mindfulness and young children." The search yielded four results.

In her initial encounter with the tutorial, she read the Main Index and noted she was going to start by trying to increase the number of her hits, despite her earlier remark that she was interested in "quality not quantity." To this end she accessed the Number Index and spent a significant amount of time reading the page, as well as the Mediate, Change and Create tactics and their examples.

In her first revised search, Lesley maintained the keyword "mindfulness" but substituted "early childhood education" for "young children." In this instance, Ebsco defaulted to phrase searching and utilized smart text searching to provide 231 results. Following this effort, Lesley went to the advanced search screen and performed the identical search but narrowed her results to peer-reviewed materials. This did little to improve her search results, which exceeded 200 hits. She spent the remainder of her problem-solving activity experimenting with efforts to reduce these hits, substituting various keywords, including "kindergarten," "public," "teach," and "class." She also employed narrowing options such as specifying dates, limiting to scholarly peer-reviewed materials, and expanding her database selection to include Education Research Complete. During her problem solving, she returned to the tutorial twice to re-read the meditate example. Following her last review of the tutorial, she performed her most successful strategies during her problem solving that included an advanced search using Boolean operators and truncating terms. The first search "mindfulness" AND "teach*" AND "class*" yielded 24 results of average and above-average ratings. Her last search, "mindfulness" AND "teach*" AND "elementary*," yielded seven results that also had average and above-average scores.

Lesley initially appeared to view the tutorial as a learning tool to expand the number of her initial hits. However, as her problem-solving activity progressed, she depended on the tutorial as a reference source to obtain additional ideas to improve her search. Although she accessed the tutorial three times during the activity, she remained within the Number Index and read all of its tactic examples. Lesley employed many of the suggestions described in the tactics and the examples.

In her post-search interview, Lesley said she liked the tutorial because "it has enough information to actually help someone thinking, but it wouldn't take too long to get through." Lesley included many of the tutorial's tactic suggestions in her revised searches, such as: experimenting with keywords, adopting new search strategies, and utilizing educational databases. She also incorporated many of the database search techniques described in the tutorial in her these searches, such as using the advanced search mode and Boolean logic, and employing truncation, as well as limiting to peer-reviewed materials and specifying dates. Lesley had previous exposure to some of these search techniques in a library skills instructional class at the university, but she stated that it was "still new" to her. She also followed the tutorial's advice to examine records for relevant search terms, pointing out, "I know I could probably go into one of those better articles and see what terms they use." In another instance she commented, "I'll look at one article just to see what terms are listed there." She did not review any records for relevant keywords, but she did examine the titles carefully for appropriate search terms to include in her revised searches. During the activity, she noted she was getting some relevant materials from the search experience: "A few really good ones, gems." In commenting on the quality of her final search, she remarked, "These are the kind of articles I would probably be looking for." A comparison of her first search with her last search revealed the impact of the tutorial on her problem-solving activity. Her results improved in relevance, the ability to answer the problem, and the quality of the response. In addition, comparisons between the time she spent devising search strategies and reviewing results increased following her exposure to the tutorial for some of her searches.

Other participants' use of the tool

Other participants' access to the Number Index, while brief, also impacted their problem solving. Daemon's review of the Create tactic and its example may have influenced his decision to add additional sources to his search. The Create tactic emphasized the value of utilizing a search strategy with relevant keywords, search fields, and databases. His first revised search included ebooks, Education Research Complete, ERIC, Primary Search, PsycARTICLES, and PsycINFO. Shelly too reviewed the Number Index and its Change example. The Change tactic urged readers to "instigate a new search behavior, a different keyword or source or strategy," and the example highlighted the importance of relevant keywords. In her revised search, Shelly employed different terms for "motivation" that included initially "grading" and later "grades."

Summary of the Number Index's impact on participants' problem solving

The Number Index had a dramatic effect on participants' problem solving. In addition to assisting participants in reducing the numbers of their hits or expanding their search results, exposure to the Index also enhanced the relevance of their results. Participants appeared to adopt the Index's planning, monitoring, and self-regulating strategies as well as the database search techniques embedded in the examples. This was illustrated in their review of results to inform subsequent searches. Evidence of their planning efforts was revealed in participants' selection of new keywords and databases.

Evaluation

Evaluation supports subsequent searches

Evaluation remains an important component of online search. While librarians emphasize the importance of evaluating search results for relevancy, authority, and currency, evaluating results also supports subsequent search strategies (University of Bristol Library, 2012). Allan (2000) observed that the availabilities of new technologies highlighted the importance of librarians teaching students the art of database searching. However, he maintained that the artistry of searching was not focused on the database features, but rather search technique. For example, Allan seemingly suggested that librarians instruct students in the value of evaluating information retrieved to inform subsequent searches. According to him, "the negative answer always points toward a new selection of what question we should ask or of what to ask it" (p. 10). Likewise, Brand-Gruwel et al. (2005) found that expert information problem solvers elaborated more frequently on the content, including judging the information, its quality, its relevance and the reliability of the sources, than novices did. They stated that if "inadequate information is located within the selected sources," then "the search strategy for searching and finding information is adapted" (p. 490). Their problem-solving model equated scanning to evaluation. The authors describe scanning as determining the relevance and quality of the information to the problem.

Comparisons of expert and novice online search behaviors highlight the importance of evaluation in search success. Sutcliffe et al.'s (2000) study of novices' and experts' searching behaviors noted that novices employed more evaluation strategies than experts, and the authors maintained this compensated for the novices' lack of search strategies for their performance on some of the tasks. The article linked participants' use of broadening and narrowing strategies and/or longer evaluation to search success rather than forming complex queries. In their conclusion, they advised the development of information retrieval systems that provided "advice to encourage optimal search strategies, providing results representations to assist efficient evaluation, and active thesaurus facilities to help query articulation" (p. 1229).

Tabatabai and Shore's (1998) research on experts' and novices' web search behaviors also pointed to the importance of evaluation in information retrieval. The authors noted that experts used different criteria to evaluate web content, including: authorship, the accuracy of content, and currency. On the other hand, the research revealed that novices evaluated sources according to "surface features such as title, organization, and content" (p. 391). Moreover, Tabatabai and Shore (2005) found similar results in their review of experts', intermediaries', and novices' web searching. The authors linked evaluation as well as monitoring and reflecting strategies to search success. Likewise, Brand-Gruwel et al. (2005) found that expert information problem solvers elaborated more frequently on the content, including judging the information, its quality, its relevance and the reliability of the sources, than novices did.

Users' evaluation of results in database searching remains especially important. Instruction librarians highlight the importance of identifying a relevant hit and utilizing the record's keywords and subject terms in subsequent searches. Still, user studies that examined students' search behaviors illustrate their limited use of evaluation in information retrieval, especially to inform subsequent searches. Holman (2010) observed students' search in the web and online databases, and concluded that they "rarely took the time to look at the materials for relevance or stopped to consider an appropriate keyword" (p. 25). Similarly, Debowski's (2001) study of student search behaviors noted that students "worked industriously on the task," but their efforts were "undermined by poor search process" (p. 376). The author pointed to a lack of strategy, repetitive searches, and a failure to learn from failed searches to inform their subsequent information retrieval efforts.

Sutcliffe et al.'s (2000) study of end user information searching revealed the majority of poor performers employed "inappropriate terms, or incorrect terms and query syntax" (p. 1224). Walraven et al. (2009) stated that secondary students did not evaluate sources and information "explicitly" when searching for information on the web (p. 241). Their study found that students focused on the title and summary in the search results in their evaluation process. The most popular criteria students employed in their evaluation of information on a site centered on "connection to task" (p. 241).

Evaluation Index

The Evaluation Index promotes participants' evaluation of search results to inform their strategy in revising the search. The idea tactics tutorial's Main Index urges readers to learn tactics that center on evaluating "search results to improve subsequent search outcomes." Three idea tactics are described: Wander, Jolt, and Identify. These tactics support students' use of monitoring and self-regulating metacognitive strategies to enhance search outcomes. Wander suggests that students "examine the sources for indicators of new search opportunities and avenues."

Jolt instructs students to "move out of conventional thought patterns." Identify asks students to "determine personal and system knowledge that may improve search results."

Ebsco database search tips are included in the tactic examples. Information is provided on using Ebsco's cited references and related records features, selecting databases, evaluating results, using subject terms, keyword searching identifying synonyms, expanding the number of hits with the Boolean operator OR, and using the Academic Search Premier's Times Cited in this Database. Detailed explanations of sample searches outline the use of these features while problem solving.

Impact of Evaluation Index on participants' problem solving

Half of the participants accessed the Evaluation Index during their problem-solving activity. Within this group, two individuals only read the Index page, and the remaining two participants focused on the Jolt tactic. Still, with one exception, access to the Index appeared to improve the search results of participants' problem solving, despite the lack of time they spent in this component of the tutorial.

Kathy

The Evaluation Index seemingly did not improve Kathy's problem solving, since the ratings of her initial and final search scores did not increase. Additionally, she was an experienced searcher and she did not gain any additional database search techniques from the activity. Her topic centered on the impact of moving from a one-dimensional discussion board in a higher education environment to a two- or three-dimensional discussion board on adult learners. She spent nearly three minutes devising her initial search strategy. This search yielded 32 hits. Upon reviewing her results for two and a half minutes, she observed, "At this stage I am just looking for keywords really."

She looked at the Main, Number, and Evaluate Indexes, and also spent nearly two minutes reading the Jolt tactic example. Despite her comprehensive examination of the tutorial, she focused on the Evaluation Index. She accessed it three times and read the Jolt tactic twice. Following her review of the tutorial, she described her new search strategy, which centered on the Jolt tactic. "I got this idea of adding keywords to my search to either expand or [get a] more focused search. So I'm going to head over to this one in there. Well I hadn't thought about, okay I hadn't thought about educational psychology. I hadn't thought about delivery systems. So I'm going to add delivery systems here."

Although, Kathy did not gain any database search skills from the tutorial, her problem solving was affected by her access to the Jolt tactic. This tactic suggested that readers "move out of conventional thought patterns to view the search in an unconventional way." The example highlighted the use of subject terms from relevant articles to improve search results. It also discussed the importance of keywords and phrase searching as well as Boolean operators. Kathy spent nearly two minutes devising the search strategy for her first revised search. In this instance, she employed the Boolean OR operator with keywords she obtained from relevant articles. After reviewing the record of one of her hits, she remarked, "I hadn't thought about delivery systems. So I'm going to add delivery systems here." Her search using all Ebsco databases for "Adult ed*" AND "Multimedia" AND "Distance" OR "Delivery systems" received over 77,000 hits. Kathy devoted about one minute reviewing these hits before opting to remove databases to narrow her results. "With a list this big the next step that I would do is head over to my databases and takes a look at some of the databases that are pulling because some of these are not going to be education related."

However, Kathy inadvertently selected rather than removed databases. When this effort yielded another large results set, she again focused on her choice of databases. "So maybe we'll put in 'not medical.' Go back to these databases and see. I'm keeping most of the soft science stuff unless it's computer science." Her revised search utilized the same keywords, with the new database selection. This search attempt also produced an excessive number of hits and led Kathy to limit to academic audiences with the keywords "higher ed*." She spent about half a minute devising a strategy to narrow her results further; this included using the NOT operator to eliminate topics that were not relevant, such as "test*" and "assess*." When this attempt produced over 600 hits, she focused on the search limits available from Ebsco's thesaurus, selecting "higher education," "distance education," "education technology," and "online courses," as well as "universities and colleges." This final search reduced her number of hits from 627 to 47.

Although Kathy's final search scores did not improve compared to her initial search, the activity did offer her new knowledge of information retrieval techniques. In her post-search interview, she stated that the tutorial taught her about incorporating additional terms in her search.

According to Kathy, "I had logged out completely and just kept a list of the keywords I liked. I hadn't thought about adding it on to expand my search." She said the tutorial would be especially beneficial to freshmen, especially after they received face-to-face instruction. She remarked, "This is almost like the next step, which I like." She described the obstacles she encountered in her problem solving as identifying relevant search terms.

Other participants' use of the tool

Daemon spent a brief time in the Evaluation Index and he did not read any of the tactic examples. He accessed the Index twice and, following his second access, he stated, "It says to look at the sources. I'm going to go back to my folder." After reviewing his saved records, he explained, "Actually I want to go back and see what the search terms are here. I see general is used. I'm going to go back and add that to my search terms. I also see introduction is used." His revised search included "Jean Piaget" AND "developmental psychology" AND "introduction." The search yielded 27 results. Following a review of the results, he remarked, "OK, this is probably the best search terms I used so far. Yeah, introduction was a good word to use. Mainly because I'm reading my topic is going to be a survey which is kind of an overview of the basics. My audience has no prior knowledge of Jean Piaget to begin with." This search remained his last effort and it had the highest scores compared to his other searches.

Shelly's final review of the tutorial included access to the Evaluation Index's Wander and Jolt tactic examples. These pages provided similar database search instruction to the tactics she accessed earlier in her problem-solving activity, with one exception. The Wander tactic example contained information on the Ebsco's cited references and related records features. Shelly did not include these advanced features in her subsequent searches, but she did maintain the advanced search mode with the Boolean operators in her search incorporating additional terms. For example, one of her last search strategies centered on "elementary education" (SU) AND "intrinsic or extrinsic" OR "grades and motivation." In Shelly's final search, she narrowed the publication dates to 2009 to the present and limited to materials published in the United States. This search yielded 33 results, which she indicated contained material applicable to her topic. Moreover, her final search scores were all in the above-average range and represented a major improvement from her initial search. Still, her problem-solving gains may have stemmed from her access to the Strategy Index that she reviewed following her examination of the Evaluation Index.

Summary of the Evaluation Index's impact on participants' problem solving

Foremost, the Evaluation Index enhanced participants' monitoring activities, including evaluating records and self-regulating to improve subsequent results. Comments by participants reflected an increased awareness of the importance of evaluation during problem solving. The Index also highlighted planning strategies and participants' efforts to incorporate new search terms as well as database search techniques, suggesting they adopted the Index's suggestions especially for moving "out of conventional thought patterns." Ultimately, participants who accessed this component, with one exception, improved their problem solving.

Strategy

Significance of a search strategy

Information retrieval research highlights the importance of identifying a search strategy for success. Allan (2000) seemingly linked the presence of a search strategy to search results, commenting, "garbage in garbage out" (p. 9). He urged librarians to critique students' search activities. For example, he suggested asking students what "tools they used needlessly or forgot to use," "data they think likely to be worth gathering," data that they didn't include but should have, how they decided relevance, and how they may have been more "efficient or effective" (p. 15). Stronge et al. (2006) linked strategy formulation to users' evaluation of the task that encompassed assessing the information need and considering different paths to obtain it. The authors highlighted the importance of evaluating the success of strategies used and selecting alternative strategies if needed. Likewise, Brand-Gruwel et al. (2005) argued that "the formulated search strategy facilitates the search for information" (p. 490).

Comparisons of expert and novice search behaviors illustrate the importance of search strategies. Tabatabai and Luconi's (1998) research focused on web-based problem solving, and they concluded that experts "started with a search plan" but novices "did not articulate a plan"

(p. 391). Moreover, the authors characterized the latter's strategies as primarily trial and error, and included a large number of return moves. Brand-Gruwel et al. (2005) observed that the "main difference between the experts and the novices" was the experts' "attention to (re) formulation of the problem" while novices ignored this activity (p. 503). Sutcliffe et al. (2000) found that experts adopted consistent search strategies that included cycles of narrowing and broadening while novices searches were trial and error. The authors concluded "individuals can be successful by following a single good strategy even though their approach may be flawed" (p. 1228). Tabatabai and Shore (2005) found experts changed their strategies more frequently and "understood the rationale behind what they wanted to do next" (p. 233). On the other hand, they reported novices "relied more on trial and error" rather than "spending time exploring or planning" (p. 238).

Research reveals students often fail to develop a search strategy prior to searching or do not modify ineffective search strategies. Simon's (1995) study of graduate students' search behaviors revealed these individuals failed to appreciate the importance of developing a search strategy for search success. According to the author, "strategies appeared to have developed as the searches progressed" (p. 78). Currie et al. (2010) observed undergraduate students' information-seeking behavior and concluded that most of the participants "did not begin the search process identifying the major keywords and they did not connect key concepts with Boolean search terms" (p. 119). Korobili et al. (2011) surveyed students on their search behaviors and found that over one-third of searchers reported never or seldom modifying their search strategy. According to the authors, participants indicated they typically "change the keyword or keywords" or "choose another source" (p. 158).

Holman (2011) characterized undergraduate students as haphazard in their search strategies. She stated that they employed simple searches "using names or short phrases" (p. 21) and narrowed searches by expanding keywords, although this was not used consistently. Holman maintained that students search suffered from the lack of a mental model of the search system. Likewise, Chu and Law (2008) characterized beginning graduate students as novice searchers who employed "plain English phrases" and lacked an understanding of the need to use a search statement that "combined key search terms and search operators" (p. 171). Similarly Korobili et al.'s (2011) survey of graduate students' information-seeking behavior revealed that the majority employed phrases for locating information and seldom or never used Boolean operators.

Strategy Index

The Strategy Index is aimed at supporting participants' efforts to devise an effective search strategy to obtain relevant results. The idea tactics tutorial's Main Index describes this component of the tutorial as focusing attention on devising a search strategy. The Strategy Index provides three idea tactics: Break, Regulate, and Skip. These tactics support students' use of planning, monitoring, and self-regulating metacognitive strategies to improve search results. Break advises students to "change standard search habits." Regulate reminds students to "pay attention to your thought processes as well as how you structure the search." Skip encourages students to "explore the topic from a different perspective."

The Strategy Index also offers Ebsco database search tips. These include advice on selecting databases, specifying the research method, evaluating results, truncating terms, narrowing the search, identifying synonyms, using subject terms, excluding terms, using subject terms, keyword searching, and broadening the search. Screen captures and detailed explanations of example searches provide additional instruction in using these database features to optimize search results.

Impact of Strategy Index on participants' problem solving

The Strategy Index was not an especially popular component of the tutorial. Only three participants accessed it and only one of these individuals accessed a tactic example. This may have stemmed from its position at the bottom of the list of idea tactics on the Main Index page.

Daemon

Daemon accessed the Strategy Index twice during his problem solving. Although he did not read any of the index's tactic examples, he did incorporate some of the tactic suggestions in his revised searches. For example, after reviewing the Break, Regulate, and Skip tactics described on the Strategy Index, he remarked, "I'm going to clear out these search terms and try something new." His subsequent search included the terms "Piagetian theory" AND "overview." After he incorporated "cognitive" into his search string, he commented, "I'm starting to get articles I can use, some are ebooks, some are them overview of a lot of the psychological theories." He continued to experiment with various keywords and evaluating the results for relevancy. At one point he noted, "I'm going to take out overview 'cause that is not the term to use."

Mary

Mary was the only participant who read the Strategy Index in her first review of the tutorial. Although she did not read any of the tactic examples, her revised search did appear to incorporate some of the tactic's suggestions on changing search habits, focusing on thought processes, and exploring the topic from a different perspective. After reviewing the tutorial she commented, "Okay, so now we are going to searching trying to find something really that I hadn't thought about." In her revised search she changed her keywords from "Neurobiological theories of reading" to "Neurobiological theories models of reading."

Shelly

Shelly's exposure to Strategy Index was brief. She spent a mere ten seconds reviewing the Index and 23 seconds reading the Break tactic. Her revised search did incorporate new terms as well as the Boolean OR operator. However, this may have stemmed from her attention to the Evaluate Index's Wander and Jolt example, since she spent the majority of her time in that Index.

Summary of the Strategy Index's impact on participants' problem solving

It is difficult to gauge the impact of the Strategy Index on participants' problem solving, since only a few individuals accessed this component of the tutorial. In addition, their time with the Strategy Index remained limited and only one individual viewed a tactic example. Two individuals also read the Evaluation Index immediately before or after reading the Strategy Index. However, comments by one of the participants suggested her problem solving was enhanced by the planning strategies promoted in the Strategy Index. Likewise, the participants who accessed this component of the tutorial may have benefited from the reinforcement opportunities it offered on planning, monitoring and self-regulating problem solving.

Summary of the impact of the Indexes on participants' problem solving

Bates (1979) suggested measures of the idea tactics' performance centered on whether individuals searched more effectively and effectively. This chapter included some of the findings from Blummer's (2012) unpublished dissertation research, titled *Evaluating the Effectiveness of a Metacognitive Tool on Education Graduate Students' Information Search Behavior in Digital Libraries*. A comparison of six participants' search behaviors before and after exposure to the tutorial suggests that it did improve individuals' problem solving. Four out of six participants increased their search scores in a comparison of their initial and final searches. Many participants, including those who did not gain search scores, expressed satisfaction with their results. An analysis of participants' database search behaviors suggest they gained knowledge of search techniques as well. Moreover, participants' comments in their post-activity interview indicated their satisfaction with the results of the problem-solving activity. Research suggests a wide variety of factors influence information retrieval, such as task, user domain and system knowledge, search goals, and time restraints. The idea tactics tutorial offers an intervention designed to enhance individuals' thought processes and database search skills to improve their problem solving in research databases.

14

Overall effect of tutorial on search outcomes

Abstract: This chapter discusses the overall effect of the tutorial on participants' search outcomes. The findings are organized around the four research questions. First, what search techniques did participants demonstrate in their initial search? Second what general attributes were common among participants in their use of the tutorial? Third, what search techniques did participants demonstrate in their final searches? Fourth, how did the tutorial affect the outcome of the problem solving? We focus on the impact of the tutorial on participants' search scores and their database search techniques. We also detail obstacles that participants encountered during their problem solving, and their satisfaction level with the results. Lastly, we identify additional issues that surfaced during the activity.

Key words: search techniques, problem solving, outcome, relevance, ability to answer the question, authoritativeness, quality of the response, records examined, satisfaction level.

Introduction

Our book is based on an unpublished dissertation study that sought to examine the impact of a metacognitive intervention on participants' problem solving in research databases. This chapter stems from the dissertation findings. Eight education graduate students performed an initial search in an Ebsco database utilizing a think-aloud protocol to gather material for an information problem. The idea tactics tutorial was presented as a scaffold to support students' subsequent search efforts. Comparisons between six of the eight participants' initial search, such as their search skills and strategies, and their revised searches illustrate the role of the intervention on students' problem solving. In this chapter we focus on the results of six participants' problem solving. The organization of the chapter around the four research questions highlight the study's findings, especially the effect of the scaffold on participants' search behaviors. Ultimately the study's outcomes facilitated the design of a protocol to guide students in applying relevant metacognitive strategies during online search. These are discussed in latter chapters.

Research questions

The study's four research questions, which were outlined in Chapter 1, are as follows.

1. *What search techniques did participants demonstrate in their initial search?* This question considers what strategies and skills participants utilized in their pre-tutorial search such as selecting additional databases, employing Boolean operators, truncating terms, accessing the advanced search mode, conducting subject searches, and locating terms from relevant articles.

2. *What general attributes were common among participants in their use of the tutorial?* This question tracks the number of seconds individuals spent in the tutorial and the number of accesses to the various components of the tutorial. It explores how participants used the tutorial. Did participants refer back to the tutorial during their searches or merely utilize it as a one-shot learning tool? How many tactics did participants read and did they access a variety of tactics or stay in one category? Were some tactics used more often than others? How much time did participants spend accessing the various tactics in the tutorial? How frequently did participants access the tutorial?

3. *What search techniques did participants demonstrate in their final searches?* This question compares the search techniques participants demonstrated in their revised searches after exposure to the tutorial. These techniques were not revealed in participants' initial search.

4. *How did the tutorial affect the outcome of the problem-solving activity?* This question compared participants' initial search skills with those demonstrated in subsequent searches. It also compares participants' initial search scores with their final search scores for relevance, ability to answer the question, authoritativeness, and the quality of the response. In addition, it considers the number of revised searches participants conducted, the number of records they examined,

and the time they spent devising search strategies and reviewing results. Were there relationships among the time spent in the tutorial, the number of tutorial accesses, the number of revised searches, and the time spent devising search strategies and reviewing results? In addition, how did the amount of time spent in the tutorial and the number of accesses to the tutorial, and the number of revised searches affect participants' final search scores? The question also examines participants' satisfaction level with the results. Lastly, the question noted any issues that affected participants' problem-solving activities.

Research question 1: What search techniques did participants demonstrate in their initial search?

In their initial search, all six participants demonstrated some familiarity with advanced search techniques. These included tactics to narrow search results such as setting publication dates, limiting to peer-reviewed materials, or utilizing the subject thesaurus and location features of the results page. Likewise, during their first search, more than half of the participants had an awareness of the importance of selecting appropriate databases to enhance their search results. Advanced search techniques remain especially important in maximizing the power of database searching by allowing users to include additional databases, limit to specific fields, incorporate various versions of a term, narrow to specific dates and article types, as well as employ Boolean logic.

Databases

The majority of participants recognized the role of the databases in returning material relevant to their topic. However, only three individuals expanded the default database, Academic Search Premier, to include additional sources. Some individuals' failure to expand the databases may have stemmed from a lack of knowledge on how to choose databases in Ebsco. Lesley opted not to choose any databases for the initial search "because I just wanted to see what I can get."

On the other hand, Dwaine and Mary immediately selected additional databases to include in their search. Kathy utilized the "all database" option in Academic Search Premier, explaining, "with adult education a lot of things exist in databases other than just the generic education ones." She indicated a desire to "cast a wider net first and then narrow down."

Still, for the initial search activity, fewer than half of the participants appeared knowledgeable of the availability of Ebsco's advanced search mode, the value of truncating, and the benefits of Boolean operators. The majority of participants performed a basic search in the Ebsco database with a few keywords or a phrase rather than accessing the advanced search page. Their query length was short and ranged from two to five terms.

Research question 2: What general attributes were common among participants in their use of the tutorial?

The majority (n=5) of the participants referred back to the tutorial during the problem-solving session, but the number of and motive for their accesses varied. For example, Dwaine read the tutorial's Change example and opted to follow the example's advice to utilize the keywords from a relevant record to improve search results. However, his inability to locate keywords in the record led him back to the Change example for additional information.

On the other hand, Lesley, Mary, and Shelly accessed various components of the tutorial numerous times during the activity. They scanned it to obtain ideas for improving their search results. For example, as Daemon remarked after reviewing one of his revised searches, "I'm going to go back to the tutorial 'cause I'm not getting much results." Kathy remained the only participant to read the tutorial once. She utilized the tutorial as a one-shot learning tool.

Popularity of components

The Number Index remained the most popular component of the tutorial (n=5), followed by the Evaluation and Relevance Indexes. The popularity of these pages mirrored the problems that participants encountered in their problem-solving activity. All participants sought methods to broaden or narrow their search results due to too many or too few hits. For example, Lesley received only four results in her initial search, while Mary obtained over 13,000 hits for this component of the activity.

In addition, participants (n=3) sought information on how to evaluate their results to improve subsequent searches. Kathy applied the Evaluation Indexes' Jolt tactic to "get a more focused search." In this instance, she examined a relevant record in her initial search results to obtain keywords to include in her revised search. Shelly also read this tactic example and in her revised search she incorporated Boolean operators and substituted synonyms for the terms used in her initial search.

Some participants expressed concern about the relevance of their results that did not support their topic, and this led several (n=3) to the Relevance Index. Shelly stated that the articles did not "deal with elementary it deals with college and... I've seen a lot of stuff dealing with schools in Turkey and schools in Korea or China." Moreover, Lesley noted that "the third one is about parenting, which I'm not sure would be really relevant."

Participants accessed the Main Index frequently, but only as an avenue to the tutorial's other pages. Only Dwaine, Lesley, and Kathy spent more than 30 seconds reading the Main Index initially. Participants spent the least amount of time in the Strategy Index, although it was reviewed by Daemon, Mary, and Shelly.

Those participants that demonstrated knowledge of advanced search skills in their initial search and appeared comfortable in the search environment, including Daemon and Mary, relied on the Indexes, rather than the examples, for ideas to improve their search. The Indexes focused on descriptions of the metacognitive idea tactics, rather than applying specific database search strategies.

Table 14.1 illustrates that Daemon used all of the Indexes and Mary reviewed three out of four. These individuals appeared very confident in their search abilities throughout their problem-solving activities, and they did not express uncertainty or nervousness while searching. Daemon said he was a full-time student and had received library instruction in several of his classes early in the semester.

On the other hand, Table 14.1 shows that Dwaine and Lesley focused on the Number Index in their use of the tutorial. While Kathy examined the Number Index as well, she only accessed it once compared to the Evaluation Index that she viewed in three separate instances. The table reveals that Shelly, like Daemon, examined all of the Indexes. However, unlike Daemon, Shelly did not appear confident in her search abilities, but both participants utilized the tutorial to gather ideas to improve the outcome of their problem-solving activities.

Table 14.1	Total number of seconds participants spent reading Index pages				
Name	Main	Relevance	Number	Evaluation	Strategy
Daemon	27, (5)	25, (2)	26, (2)	33, (2)	48, (2)
Dwaine	38, (1)		69, (1)		
Kathy	38, (2)		39	32, (3)	
Lesley	31, (1)		111, (5)		
Mary	29, (3)	51, (2)	27, (1)		33, (1)
Shelly	33, (4)	45, (4)	30, (1)	67, (3)	10, (2)

Note: includes the number of accesses to the Indexes.

Participants also spent a significant amount of time in the Jolt example. This example was available under the Evaluation Index and it aimed at helping users to evaluate search results, to improve outcomes. Although it was accessed by only two out of six participants, these individuals devoted a significant amount of time to reading the example. For instance, Kathy spent nearly half of her total time in the tutorial reviewing the Jolt example and Shelly devoted a minute and a half to the page. An identical number of individuals accessed the Notice example, but they did not spend much time on the page.

Three of the tactic examples were not used at all. Two appeared under the Strategy Index and included the Regulate and Skip examples. In addition, the Identify example that was available from the Evaluation Index was not accessed. The lack of use of these tactics may have stemmed from their location. Two were listed on the Strategy Index, the last Index on the Main Index page. Moreover, the Identify example was listed at the bottom of the Evaluation Index page. Participants sought to access links as quickly as possible and often did not click on links at the bottom of the pages.

Only Shelly moved around the tutorial, reviewing every Index and nearly all of the examples. Daemon utilized all of the Indexes as well, but he only viewed two tactic examples.

The remaining participants stayed within the Number or the Evaluation Indexes. Within these indexes, with the exception of Lesley, individuals accessed only one tactic example or none.

Time in tutorial

The amount of time that individuals spent reading the Index pages and the tactic examples varied. Participants' number of accesses to these tutorial components also ranged during the problem-solving activities, as Table 14.1 reveals.

Research question 3: What search techniques did participants demonstrate in their final searches?

The tutorial and database search skills

All participants gained search skills following exposure to the tutorial. Table 14.2 lists the search techniques performed by participants during the activity in their revised searches and the number of times they performed these strategies. The list does not reflect all of the techniques that participants employed during the activity, only those that were not displayed in their initial search. Participants may have had familiarity with a technique, but failed to demonstrate it during their initial search.

All of the database techniques presented in the tactic examples were reflected in at least one of the participants' revised searches, with one

| **Table 14.2** | Search strategies participants demonstrated in their revised searches |

Name	Locate terms from relevant articles	Use subject terms	Employ Boolean operators	Change search terms	Change databases	Apply limits	Truncate
Lesley	1		7	7	1	4	5
Daemon	3			8	1		3
Shelly		7	7	4			
Mary	4			16			
Kathy				3			
Dwaine	1		2	2			

Note: includes the number of instances of search strategies.

exception. Although Shelly read the Wander example, which contained information on the cited reference feature, she failed to utilize this strategy in her revised search. However, several techniques were presented in tactics that were not accessed by any of the participants. These included the related records feature and the option to specify methodology. Their lack of use suggests participants were unaware of these more advanced database features.

Attention to keywords

The most common strategy that participants gleaned from the tutorial centered on utilizing more relevant keywords. All participants experimented with employing various concepts for their search terms. Lesley explained, "I'm thinking of keywords." Kathy stated, "Distance or delivery is kind of what I'm looking for." Daemon said, "I am going to take out overview 'cause that is not the term to use." Following another unsuccessful search, he noted, "I'm going to clear out these search terms and try something new."

Attention to keywords also led to participants' use of the Boolean operators. Kathy was the only participant to use the NOT operator to exclude items from her results set. On the other hand, Shelly incorporated the OR operator within a field to expand the number of relevant results.

The think-aloud protocol revealed that many participants focused on the age of their students in selecting keywords for their search. As Kathy remarked, "Age is definitely one I would look at. I want to make sure these are all adults." Lesley explained her use of the term kindergarten: "that is my age group." Likewise Shelly sought studies involving elementary students. In these ways, participants sought to increase the relevancy of their results.

Some participants incorporated subject terms from relevant records in their new strategy. However, subject terms were typically used as keywords and not as a fielded search. Daemon obtained search terms for a revised search from the subject source terms in a catalog record he deemed relevant. He stated that he was "culling subject terms for more specific terms. I'm using subject terms of articles I find useful."

Lack of subject term usage

Only Shelly conducted searches utilizing the subject terms field in her revised strategy. She also had difficulty using the subject search in Ebsco.

This is surprising considering the emphasis of the tutorial on incorporating subject terms to improve search results. Nearly all of the tactic examples pointed to the use of subject terms to improve relevance. Participants' focus on keywords in their revised searches may have stemmed from time constraints. Many of the tactics listed on the Index pages point to the simple changes that impact searches, such as the importance of selecting appropriate keywords. Using a variety of keywords in a search remained an easy strategy to improve results.

The tutorial also highlighted the importance of databases to participants. Although, the majority of participants remained familiar with education-related sources, the tutorial reminds participants of databases' significance in returning relevant results. Lesley stated, "I know Education Research Complete is one I think I can use." She admitted, "I could... separate articles written about education from articles about patients, subjects, and psychological studies." Likewise, following a review of the Create tactic's suggestion to identify relevant databases, Daemon selected the eBook collection, Education Research Complete, ERIC, Primary Search, PsycARTICLES, and PsycINFO. Mary also changed her databases in the middle of her problem-solving activity, replacing PsycINFO with ERIC.

Truncation was another strategy participants gleaned from the tutorial. Several participants truncated terms in their revised searches. Although Lesley said she learned this strategy from an instructional class, the tutorial may have triggered her knowledge of its value in information search.

Review for relevant keywords

The tutorial also increased participants' tendencies to review records for relevant keywords. Dwaine insisted, "The tutorial told me to look at keywords in an article that looked relevant and use that in my search. I am going to use one of these keywords as subject since this article is relevant." Kathy explained, "I got about Jolt, which is this idea of adding keywords to my search to either expand or [get a] more focused search. So I'm going to head over to this one and look at their keywords and hopefully there is one in there." Similarly Shelly examined the record of a relevant article for more keywords. "Ah here is some more words reinforcement, personal choice." While reviewing a relevant search result, Daemon stated, "I want to go back and see what the search terms are here."

Change in search modes

In addition, the tutorial impacted participants' use of search modes in their revised searches. Following access to the tutorial, two out of three participants went from Ebsco's basic to the advanced search mode in their revised searches using the Boolean AND operator. The remaining three participants had utilized this search technique in their initial search. Although the mechanics for accessing the advanced search mode were not described in the tutorial, the tactic examples contained screen captures of this feature and the accompanying text described the advantages of using Boolean operators.

Research question 4: How did the tutorial affect the outcome of the problem-solving activity?

Access to the tutorial did not affect the number of revised searches that participants performed. Figure B1 in Appendix B represents a scatter plot of the total time participants spent in the tutorial compared to their number of revised searches. The illustration revealed a random scatter of points. This distribution indicates there was no relationship between the total time in the tutorial and the number of revised searches individuals performed.

There was an association between the amount of time participants spent in the tutorial and their examination of records (Appendix B, Figure B2). The line of points that runs from the upper left to the lower right indicates that the relationship between the two variables was negative. This distribution suggests that for some individuals, the more time they spent in the tutorial, the fewer records they examined. Still, there was no association between the number of records viewed and participants' final search scores. A scatter plot of those variables illustrated a random scatter of points. There was a relationship between the time spent in the tutorial and the time devoted to revising search strategy (Appendix B, Figure B3). The line of points in this instance clustered from the lower left to the upper right, indicating a positive relationship for some individuals. The distribution reveals that participants spent more time revising their search strategy as their time in the tutorial increased.

This affected the outcome of their searches indirectly. As Figures B4–B6 in Appendix B illustrate, there was a negative distribution between the time spent devising search strategy and half of the participants' scores for relevance and the ability to answer the problem, and the quality of their last search. The scatter plot in these diagrams reveal a cluster of points from the upper left to the lower right, demonstrating an inverse relationship.

Exposure to the tutorial appeared to have an inverse effect on the amount of time participants devoted to reviewing results (Appendix B, Figure B7). This scatter plot displays a cluster line from the upper left to the lower right, indicating an inverse or negative relationship. Participants spent less time reviewing results as their time in the tutorial increased. There was also a negative relationship between time spent in reviewing results and some (n=3) of the participants' scores for relevance, ability to answer the problem, and the quality of their last search. This is displayed in Appendix B, Figures B8–B10.

As Table 14.3 displays, the time participants spent devising search strategies and reviewing results before and after exposure to the tutorial varied. In addition, the number of records participants examined in the post-tutorial phase of the activity ranged from zero to 12, and was tied to the number of seconds spent in the tutorial, but not on participants' scores on their final searches. The more time in the tutorial, the fewer records participants opened.

Table 14.3	Total seconds participants spent devising search strategy and reviewing results					
Name	Devising search strategy initial	Reviewing results initial	Initial records viewed	Devising search strategy post	Reviewing results post	Records viewed post
Daemon	55	23	0	213	695	2
Dwaine	87	56	0	55	101	1
Kathy	157	105	1	441	275	1
Lesley	18	57	0	192	255	0
Mary	43	102	1	353	887	12
Shelly	34	30	0	375	643	4

Note: zero records reviewed indicates only titles were reviewed and no records were opened.

Tutorial accesses and final search scores

Scatter plots displaying participants' total minutes in the tutorial with their final search ratings for relevance, authoritativeness, ability to answer the problem, or quality of the last search reveal a random scatter of points. This distribution suggests there was no relationship between time spent in the tutorial and participants' final search scores. However, for half of the participants, increased accesses to the tutorial led to higher scores for the relevance and quality of the last search as well as its ability to answer the question. In these instances, the line of cluster points ran from the lower left to the upper right (Appendix B, Figures B11–B13).

Of the six participants problem solving, four made gains in their search scores following access to the tutorial. Figures B14 to B19 in Appendix B illustrate the improvements in search scores for relevance, the ability to answer the question, and the quality of the response for all but Mary and Kathy. Gains were made for the authoritativeness of the responses between the first search and the last search as well for most participants. These bar charts reveal the impact of the tutorial on participants' final search scores. The relevance of the results for Daemon, Dwaine, and Shelly increased from 3.0 to 4.0 respectively. In addition, Lesley increased the relevance of her results from 2.0 to 3.0. Similar gains were witnessed by these participants in the other score categories.

Mary's lack of search improvement following access to the tutorial could be attributed to the 19 revised searches she performed. Figures B20–B22 in Appendix B reveal an inverse relationship between the number of revised searches and the relevance of the last search and the ability to answer the problem, as well as the quality of the last search for some participants. The distribution depicts a line that runs from the upper left to the lower right for five participants, which suggests that the relationship between the two variables was negative.

Search obstacles and participants' satisfaction level

Broad results

Several obstacles were revealed from the think-aloud problem-solving activities. For example, all participants obtained results that were too broad and required efforts to narrow the search during their problem-solving activities. Dwaine described his use of the subjects as being "to narrow down my actual search." Likewise, Kathy eliminated databases that were not education-related to narrow down her number of hits. Shelly focused on peer-reviewed journals, setting dates and limiting the geography to the United States. Narrowing down individuals' search results was not limited to an excessive number of hits. In one of her revised searches, Lesley obtained 24 results, which she admitted was better than previous searches, but she explained, "I would probably want to narrow this down."

Number of results

Only Mary and Shelly had a clear idea of how many items they wanted. They aimed to meet the requirements for their paper: ten articles. Other participants neglected to note how many materials they wanted. Overall participants sought fewer results, rather than large numbers of hits. Kathy considered 32 items "pretty good." When Dwaine's revised search yielded 20 results, he noted, "that's much closer." Shelly indicated her 32 results were "much less to look through." However, Lesley indicated a desire to narrow down the 24 results she received from searching "mindfulness" AND "teach" AND "class." Still, she noted that she wanted "a good one, quality not quantity. I don't know what she is requiring for the project." Many reached a point in the search where they were satisfied with the number and the quality of their results. After placing a number of articles in his folder, Daemon stated, "I would probably stop here 'cause I've got enough."

Time

Time represented another concern for participants in searching. Lesley pointed out, "I got fewer hits with this. I still have 170 – I mean, I would be willing to go through these, but I know it's not very efficient." Shelly remarked, "There is quite a few here that I would actually take the time and really look at."

Uncertainty and errors

Participants' feelings of uncertainty and errors were revealed in the activities. Several participants appeared to lack confidence in their search strategies and results. Comments such as "I have got 32 results which is pretty good I think," "I am going to stop here I think," and I don't understand" suggest participants remained uneasy in the search environment. Shelly readily admitted she did not have search experience, describing herself as a "novice." Dwaine concluded: "The obstacles were my own in that I didn't know exactly what was good to solicit in the results I wanted."

Spelling errors and other mistakes were also common during the problem-solving activities, particularly during the initial search and with the use of surnames. In one instance, Kathy inadvertently selected numerous medical related databases she had intended to delete. Moreover, Lesley limited her search to materials published in recent years, but forgot to update her date selection. Likewise, Dwaine and Mary misspelled surnames in their searches.

Other problems that participants encountered stemmed from their lack of awareness of search techniques and the peculiarities of databases. Dwaine appeared confused about the difference between locating keywords and subject headings in a record, as well as about how to obtain Boolean operators. "The tutorial talked about using keywords from the article that was relevant, but I don't see a page that has keywords, just subjects." In his post-activity interview he noted, "I did notice that in the screenshot of the tutorial it used AND – it didn't tell you how to get those."

The biggest error, though, centered on participants' use of keywords without Boolean operators. In this case, Ebsco treated the words as a phrase and reverted to smart text searching, yielding large result sets that were typically not relevant to the topic. The note "Your initial search did not yield any results" preceded the results set.

Think-aloud

Half of the participants (n=3) did not view the think-aloud protocol as a hindrance to their information seeking in the activity. Mary stated, "Well to be honest no, 'cause I always talk to myself anyway." Some participants experienced problems with the think-aloud protocol. Dwaine admitted that it was difficult to explain his actions while searching. He said, "It's not like me. I'm always thinking, but thinking out loud I'm not." Lesley suggested, "I wasn't sure if I was to be talking to you [or] to no one." Kathy noted that it was hard to keep remembering to explain her actions. Still, these participants sought to emphasize an awareness of their search strategies. Lesley pointed out, "I do think about what I'm doing most of the time. I'm not just putting things in and seeing what happens."

Satisfaction

All participants expressed satisfaction with the results obtained from their problem-solving activities. Mary appeared pleased, suggesting, "After some time you find exactly what you need. Well I aimed to get ten. The big ones I really wanted and I got those ten plus a few more." Daemon concluded, "I will be able to use this for my research." Lesley suggested she found "a few really good ones, gems." Shelly admitted she was seeing things she hadn't seen in earlier searches: "I've seen ones that I have not seen." Kathy's comments related to her initial search results. "I really like the first ones and second ones. I want to save these."

Additional issues revealed in the post-search interview and during the think-aloud

Research skills

The problem-solving activity highlighted the importance of research skills to participants. In their post-activity interview, participants discussed the value of research skills. According to Daemon, "Research is something that you kind of need. It's a skill almost. Having tutorials and being taught a specific strategy is very helpful, especially at the graduate level." Lesley pointed to a recent instructional session she had attended, noting, "It was the first time anyone had even mentioned to me things like using an asterisk." Shelly observed, "For me it's learning this because I've never been exposed to this kind of stuff. For me it's learning how to do this. When I went to college it was one-dimensional kind of stuff in card catalogs." Kathy believed the "biggest stumbling block is trying to figure out what terms you need to search for in order to get the information you are looking at."

Librarians and libraries

The problem-solving activity also increased participants' appreciation of librarians and libraries. Daemon noted he had learned a lot of strategies from the university's librarians who provided instruction in several of his classes early in the semester. Kathy applauded the value of librarians to graduate students. She described them as the experts in searching library databases and admitted she sought advice from them following a search. "I always try to search on my own first and if I get too much or too little or not what I am looking for I always go to a librarian. Here's what I am looking for – do you have any suggestions, can you help me get any closer." Lesley discussed her recent experience with an instructional class at the university that was very helpful "because before I would go through page after page of articles trying to find ones." Mary expressed her use of libraries, explaining, "I wouldn't go into Google automatically; I would go into the library and find those scholarly databases first."

Summary of the tutorial's impact on participants' problem solving

Participants benefited from the problem-solving activity and especially its intervention on two levels. First, the tutorial highlighted individuals' awareness of the metacognition concept and encouraged them to apply planning, monitoring, and self-regulating strategies in their searches to improve outcomes. The idea tactics provided participants with suggestions aimed at changing their thought processes to improve search strategies and results. Many participants seemingly adopted these ideas especially as Bates (1979) intended them to be used, including when searchers were "stumped" (p. 280). Second, the provision of various search techniques in the tactic example pages served as a how-to guide for applying advanced search skills. All participants demonstrated some gains in database search techniques following exposure to the tactic examples. In two instances, participants noted the tactic examples triggered prior knowledge, which they employed in subsequent searches. Consequently the tutorial remained an effective intervention for supporting education graduate students' search in research databases.

15

The tutorial and idea generation and mental pattern breaking

Abstract: This chapter discusses the role of the tutorial in fostering idea generation, as well as mental pattern breaking among participants. Bates (1979) arranged her tactics into two groups: idea generation and pattern breaking. In pattern breaking, Bates suggested that some of the tactics were designed to "break patterns of thought," while others aimed to change aspects of a search to alter individuals' perspectives (p. 289). In the dissertation study, participants' abilities to consider new ideas and adopt new search patterns helped them overcome obstacles and led to improved outcomes. Participants also benefited from the database search techniques that were embedded in the idea tactics. A comparison of participants' search scores for their initial and final scores illustrates the impact of the tutorial on individuals' problem solving.

Key words: tutorial, metacognition, metacognitive, problem solving, obstacles, mental pattern breaking, idea generation, idea tactics.

Introduction

Land and Greene (2000) wrote that system and domain knowledge remained especially important for information seeking in open-ended environments. However, they reported that metacognitive knowledge compensated for individuals' lack of familiarity with various subjects and technologies during information search. Our study contributed to the research on information problem solving by illustrating the effectiveness of a metacognitive scaffold for improving search outcomes, especially in research databases. It also supported findings that linked metacognitive knowledge to idea generation and organization (Englert and Raphael, 1988; Englert et al., 1988). Following an initial search on a topic, participants selected tutorial tactics aimed at enhancing their search outcomes. These tactics promoted idea generation as well as mental pattern breaking, and they enhanced participants' problem solving particularly by helping individuals overcome obstacles in their search. Participants also benefited from the database search techniques that were embedded in the tactics. These techniques remind users of the importance of selecting appropriate databases, keywords, and search fields to optimize results. Ultimately the combination of metacognitive strategies and database search techniques enhanced participants' problem solving.

Bates' idea tactics

Bates (1979) described the purpose of her idea tactics as "generating new ideas or solutions" to problems in information searching (p. 280). She suggested that these ideas may help "professional information specialists" in searching print or electronic databases, and should be used primarily for situations when the searcher is "stumped" (p. 280). Bates advocated utilizing these tactics at the "beginning of a search" or "when ordinary means have failed" (p. 280). The article described the tactics as part of a "facilitation model of searching" directed at improving search efficiency and effectiveness (p. 280).

Bates (1979) arranged her tactics into two groups: idea generation and pattern breaking. She listed idea generation tactics as Think, Meditate, and Wander. She viewed pattern-breaking tactics as Catch, Break, Notice, Jolt, Change, and Skip. In pattern breaking, Bates suggested some of the tactics were designed to "break patterns of thought" while others aimed to change aspects of a search to alter individuals' perspectives (p. 289).

Idea tactics tutorial

On the other hand, in this study the tactics were grouped to facilitate participants' efforts to devise solutions to problems that users encounter during information search, such as the relevance of the results and the number of hits. Two additional categories, evaluation and strategy, provided tactics to promote evaluating and strategizing participants' problem solving.

Three tactics utilized in the tutorial did not appear on Bates' list. These tactics were based on metacognitive strategies including Create, Identify, and Regulate. In the study, two of these tactics examples, Regulate and Identify, were not accessed during participants' problem-solving activities. This may have stemmed from the location of the examples in the tutorial. Identify appeared as the last link in the Evaluation Index. Regulate and Skip – the latter comprised another tactic example not accessed during the study – were available in the Strategy Index, the last index on the Main Index page. Participants sought those tactics examples most easily accessible and these were typically from the Relevance and Number Indexes, links that appeared at the top of the Main Index page. Participants' failure to access the Regulate, Skip, and Identify tactics did not necessarily impact their search outcomes, since the tactics contained material that was often described in other tactics such as Boolean operators and subject terms.

In the study, the idea tactics were utilized by students with some search experience, not professional information specialists. Participants performed an initial search on a topic and utilized the idea tactics for strategies aimed at improving their search outcomes. Dwaine focused on the Change Tactic and the Number Index to obtain ideas to revise his search strategies and improve his results. Kathy visited the tutorial once and read two Indexes and one tactic during her problem solving. The remaining four participants referred back to the tutorial throughout their problem solving, reviewing Indexes or tactic examples for various strategies to enhance their search outcomes.

Idea generation and mental pattern breaking

The study confirmed Bates' suggestions that the tactics helped "generate new ideas or solutions to problems" in searching and that their use is applicable in print and online databases (p. 280). Following access to the tactics, all participants experimented with keywords, and some (n=2) changed databases, (n=3) accessed Boolean operators, and (n=1) utilized subject terms. Lesley and Daemon also truncated terms and some participants (n=4) examined relevant records for keywords to include in subsequent searches.

The idea tactics fostered, as Bates maintained (p. 281), "mental pattern breaking" for the six participants. This was especially apparent during Mary's problem-solving activity and it improved her search outcome. For instance, she began her search using PsychInfo and the default Academic Search Premier Database. Following numerous unsuccessful searches, she viewed the tutorial's Relevance Index. This page contained two of Bates' "mental pattern breaking" tactics, Catch and Notice. Bates described these tactics as of the "introspective sort," suggesting the individual "introspects and analyzes the problem" and "breaks one's accustomed ways of thinking" (p. 281).

Upon revising her search, Mary changed her search terms several times using variations on "models of reading," and also switched from PsycINFO to ERIC. At this point, the relevance of some of her subsequent search results increased. She also opted to seek "four key writers that subscribe to that [neurobiological] "theory" rather than search on "neurobiological." Bates distinguished the Change, Focus, and Skip mental pattern-breaking tactics from the others. According to her, these strategies facilitated "arbitrary" changes to provide a "different perspective to help solve the problem" (p. 281).

In addition, Bates promoted the idea tactics as facilitating "idea generation" in searches, and this too was revealed in the present study (p. 281). Following access to the Relevance and Number Indexes' "idea generation's" Think and Meditate tactics, Daemon experimented with various keywords in his search. For example, in subsequent searches, he substituted "Piagetian theory" for "jean piaget" and "cognitive learning theory" for "cognitive development." The tutorial also helped him hone his search strategy to obtain summaries of Jean Piaget's work through the inclusion of terms such as "overview" and "introduction." Kathy's problem solving also offered evidence of the "idea generation" role of the tactics. Following a review of the tutorial that included reading the Evaluate and Relevance Indexes, which contained the "idea generation's" Think and Wander tactics, Kathy examined a record to locate additional terms (or ideas) to incorporate in her revised search. In addition, Shelly demonstrated idea generation following review of the Wander tactic in her inclusion of the Boolean OR operator to add "grades or motivation" to her search.

Database search strategies

The inclusion of database search strategies with the idea tactics provided users with additional techniques designed to enhance search results.

Participants who focused on tactic examples, such as Dwaine and Lesley, demonstrated "idea generation" and "mental pattern breaking," as well as improved database search techniques during their problem-solving activities. Dwaine read the Change tactic example and this enabled him to break his "mental pattern" by adopting the advanced search mode and new search terms in his revised strategy. In his subsequent search, Dwaine employed the Boolean AND operator to link "classroom observation" with "technology integration," and he reduced his number of hits from over 13,000 to 20. After he consulted the tutorial again, he changed "technology integration" to "technology assessment" and obtained his desired results. Dwaine did not demonstrate knowledge of the advanced search mode or subject terms in his initial search. He improved his final search scores for relevancy, the ability to answer the question, and the quality of the response from his initial search (Appendix A, Tables A1a and A1b).

Overcoming obstacles

Participants used the idea tactics as Bates (1979) suggested to overcome obstacles they encountered during their problem solving. Taylor (1962) identified problems that users encountered in search environment, which he attributed to the organization of the system, the question, and its complexity, as well as the individual's "state of mind" (p. 394). He believed the latter was especially important since it could affect users' abilities to receive the appropriate information (p. 394). Other authors emphasized the role of users in facilitating the search process. Kuhlthau (1993) described stages that users progress through in their information seeking, including feelings of uncertainty. According to the author, "information seeking was a process of construction where users progress from uncertainty to understanding" (1993, p. 345). This progression was also witnessed during participants' problem-solving activities as they obtained relevant materials to support their topic. Following Lesley's search on "mindfulness and early childhood education" and "teach*" and "class," she examined the results and commented, "I think this is better." In her post-activity interview, she alluded to the importance of understanding to her search. "I want as broad, as many thing to choose from as possible. With this topic, I'm not exactly sure exactly how I feel about it, or how I would use it. I just want to learn about it and see if the things I am interested in are connected in other people's minds."

Likewise, upon reviewing his results, Daemon noted, "All right, now I'm culling subject terms. I'm finding more specific terms for John Piaget." Moreover, after reading the tutorial, Kathy commented, "So what I'm finding [is] that possibly I'm not putting things in. I maybe am using too big a phrase as opposed to a couple of words in quotes. I'm going back."

Moreover, the organization of the tutorial using the themes of Relevance, Number, Evaluation, and Strategy was designed to support participants during their problem solving. These themes represented common search obstacles that users experience and therefore facilitated participants' access to tactics designed to enhance outcomes. After an unsuccessful search that yielded one result, Lesley said, "So I'm stuck." She returned to the tutorial and read the Number Indexes' Meditate tactic example for additional search ideas. Likewise, Daemon stated, "I'm going to go back to the tutorial because I'm not getting many results." At this point he examined the Strategy and Evaluate Indexes.

The most popular tutorial components were the Number and Evaluation Indexes, and this may have stemmed from the difficulties that participants experienced in their problem solving. Participants accessed information aimed at alleviating search obstacles such as too many or too few results, a common problem for most individuals during the activity. For example, as Dwaine noted, "I'm going to click on the link for dissatisfied with the number of hits 'cause 13,000 is too much."

Participants spent the most time in the Change and Meditate tactic examples located in the Number Index. Participants also sought advice on how to evaluate their search strategies as well as their results. Kathy selected the Evaluation Indexes' Jolt tactic example and noted her intention to "add keywords to either expand or [get a] more focused search."

Likewise, participants' behaviors during the present study were in agreement with the information-seeking research in their depiction of the obstacles that searchers face as well as the uncertainty they experience in this environment. In her post-search interview, Kathy described a search obstacle as the "lack of consistency in search terms at all ever." For other participants, a lack of system knowledge and inefficient search skills produced uncertainty during their problem solving. Shelly emphasized her inexperience with database searching throughout her problem-solving activity and in the post-search interview. During one attempt to revise her search, she asked, "Now do I change fields?" Moreover, Lesley's comments during her think-aloud hinted at her uncertainty as well during the activity. "Well, it looks like not all of these are from the types of journals that I would want, probably. There are still too many, I think."

Some participants' uncertainty was manifested in nervousness. In her think-aloud, Shelly commented, "The words I'm typing in are extrinsic vs. intrinsic motivation elementary students spelled wrong because I'm nervous."

The findings of the present study remain in agreement with some of the results from Moore's (1995) information problem-solving research in identifying problems that users experience when formulating search strategies. Although the author focused on 11-year-old students' information problem solving, the present study shared similar conclusions. Moore observed that students were aware of their difficulties in identifying "questions to drive information retrieval" (p. 20). This too was a complaint of some (n=2) of the problem solving participants in the present study. As Lesley commented, "It's hard for me... sometimes to put my ideas into words. It's hard to choose relevant search terms that get me to go where I want to go without boxing me in." Mary stated, "The main thing is finding which words will actually get the meat of what you need." However, while Moore observed that the youngsters experienced difficulties delineating "fragments of information" from concepts to create more focused "information seeking," this was not the case for the graduate students (p. 22). Participants in the present study were typically able to develop better strategies to improve their outcomes. After reviewing his results, Daemon stated, "Cognitive learning theories... I'm going to add cognitive to the search." When Lesley's search on "mindfulness in young children" proved unsuccessful, she substituted the phrase "early childhood education."

Tutorial enhances search outcomes

A comparison of participants' search results before and after exposure to the tutorial revealed that four out of six individuals ranked higher in the relevance, the authoritativeness, the ability to answer the problem, and the quality of the response in the scores for their final efforts (Appendix A, Tables A1–6). Moreover, in subsequent searches following exposure to the tutorial, all students demonstrated some use of database techniques presented in the intervention, including: using a variety of search terms, reviewing records for keywords, accessing the advanced search mode, selecting additional databases, and employing subject terms. In addition, participants' comments in their post-search interviews on the tutorial remained favorable. Some individuals, especially Lesley and Daemon, noted that the tutorial triggered their prior knowledge of search techniques. Other participants such as Kathy, Dwaine, and Shelly likened the tutorial to a tool and suggested it offered new strategies for searching. Kathy stated it would be especially beneficial to undergraduates. Lesley described it as "having enough information to help without taking too long to get through." Shelly said the knowledge was especially helpful to her due to her inexperience with searching. She pointed to learning about subject terms and refining fields. According to Shelly, "Now when I go home, this [search] will be easier for me."

An analysis of participants' interaction with the tutorial highlighted the value of the tool in improving search outcomes. Scatter plot diagrams in Figures 11, 12, and 13 (available in Appendix B) illustrate a parallel relationship between the number of accesses to the tutorial and higher search scores for participants' final search for the relevance, the ability to answer the problem, and the quality of the response in their final search efforts.

Impact of metacognitive scaffolds

The present study confirms previous research on the role of metacognitive scaffolds in improving individuals' problem solving. Wolf et al. (2003) maintained that their Information Problem Solving model, by supporting students in task analyses, strategy selection, and self-monitoring, helped individuals to overcome their lack of writing experience. Likewise, in the present study, the tutorial, by promoting participants' planning, monitoring, and self-regulating efforts, facilitated individuals' search activities regardless of their subject knowledge or database skills. Dwaine appeared to have scant knowledge of his topic. In his first revised search, he said, "What I am really looking for is information on tools used to evaluate technology integration in the classroom and I'm still not finding that." Upon reviewing his results further, he stated, "Actually here is one." Dwaine opened this record and utilized one of its subject terms, "technology assessment," in a subsequent search. This yielded him four results that he noted were very relevant.

Land and Greene's (2000) research on pre-service teachers' information seeking attributed differences in outcomes to participants' domain, system, and metacognitive knowledge. Still, in the present study, differences existed only for the outcome of participants' initial searches. The tutorial served to minimize differences among participant' skill levels. For example, Kathy and Daemon exhibited system and domain knowledge, and it was reflected in the advanced search strategies they utilized in their initial search as well as their initial search scores. On the other hand, Lesley, Shelly, and Dwaine lacked extensive domain and/or system knowledge. Their exposure to the tutorial led them to overcome these deficiencies, as their final search scores reflected. Shelly, a self-described novice searcher, stated, "Well, I'm finding different things, which is important for the paper." Lesley noted she found "a few really good ones, gems." The tutorial assisted participants' abilities to modify their search behaviors by refining topics, developing new search strategies, assessing results, and performing additional searches.

Summary of the idea tactics' role in idea generation and mental pattern breaking

This study supports research by Taft (2010) that found metacognitive strategy instruction supports idea generation. In this study, participants received instruction in planning, monitoring, and self-regulating their problem solving. This instruction centered on idea tactics and fostered individuals' idea generation as well as their mental pattern breaking that helped them overcome common obstacles in online search. Comparisons between participants' search results before and after exposure to the tutorial revealed that four out of six individuals ranked higher in the relevance, the authoritativeness, the ability to answer the problem, and the quality of the response in the scores for their final efforts. In addition, all participants demonstrated improved search skills following access to the tutorial. Ultimately the research demonstrates the effectiveness of an idea tactics tutorial as a scaffold for improving participants' problem solving.

16

The impact of the tutorial on participants' metacognitive behaviors in problem solving

Abstract: We trace the impact of the tutorial on participants' use of metacognition in problem solving. We were able to document evidence of metacognitive changes in participants' search strategies as a result of the tutorial. During the activity, individuals referred to their prior knowledge, and demonstrated self-reflecting and monitoring techniques. The study also found relationships between individuals' use of metacognitive strategies in their information problem solving. For example, the tutorial helped individuals who received too many or too few results, as well as irrelevant hits, to clarify their thought processes, and this promoted strategy development. We consider participants' adoption of the metacognitive strategies proposed in the idea tactics as well as their increased awareness of their metacognition. We also compare our findings with research on metacognition instruction and problem solving.

Key words: metacognition, metacognitive, search techniques, tutorial, monitoring, problem solving, obstacles, outcome, prior knowledge, idea tactics.

Introduction

Instructing students in planning, monitoring, and self-regulating strategies remains especially effective in imparting these behaviors in individuals. In this study, participants seemingly adopted the metacognitive strategies promoted by the idea tactics tutorial. Foremost, participants implemented the suggestions contained in the tactics in devising search strategies or examining results. Participants also appeared more aware of their metacognition following exposure to the tutorial. For example, during the activity, individuals referred to their prior knowledge and also demonstrated self-reflecting and monitoring techniques. In addition, participants utilized the database search strategies outlined in the tactic examples. In this chapter we explore the impact of the tutorial on enhancing participants' metacognitive behaviors while problem solving. We also compare our findings with research on metacognition instruction and problem solving. Ultimately, individuals' adoption of the metacognitive strategies proposed in the tutorial, coupled with their increased awareness of their metacognition, enhanced participants' search results.

Metacognitive instruction

Research confirms the role of metacognitive instruction in enhancing individuals' metacognition, particularly their adoption of metacognitive strategies. Shen and Liu (2011) demonstrated the influence of metacognitive training on enhancing college students' self-planning and self-monitoring behaviors. Kauffman et al. (2008) illustrated the role of prompts in supporting college students' self-monitoring and problem-solving skills. The authors surmised that the "problem solving prompts helped to clarify the assignment goals and encouraged student to self-monitor and self-regulate" their behavior (p. 130).

Nash-Ditzel (2010) traced the effect of metacognitive instruction on college students modeling these strategies in reading exercises. She noted that students initially doubted the effectiveness of these strategies in improving their reading, but individuals "came to acknowledge the value of the reading strategy" (p. 55). She concluded the "reading behavior changed substantially for all five participants" (p. 57). Moreover, Nash-Ditzel observed that over time, the strategies became "comfortable, and internalized" (p. 58).

Participants' adoption of idea tactic's metacognitive behaviors in problem solving

Similarly, we were able to document evidence of metacognitive changes in participants' search strategies as a result of the tutorial. Mary focused on the Indexes rather than the tactic examples. The Indexes highlighted the importance of metacognitive strategies and especially the use of appropriate keywords, plans, and sources rather than specific database search techniques. After Mary's review of the Relevance Index, she used different search terms. For example, she changed "theories of reading phonological processing" to "theoretical models of reading." In a later search, she utilized ERIC rather than PsycINFO. This decreased the number of her results but increased the relevancy, the quality of the response, and the ability to answer the problem for these searches that increased from below average in relevance, ability to answer the problem, and increased the quality of the response to average and above average respectively. Moreover, in subsequent searches Mary opted to search for "four key writers that subscribe" to the neurobiological theories of learning. She obtained these names from careful review of records in her results.

On the other hand, individuals who implemented strategies described in the tactic examples improved their search outcomes as well. Participants also demonstrated use of database search techniques presented in the examples. For example, Dwaine accessed the Change example tactic and adopted its advice to solicit keywords from relevant records for his revised search. In his subsequent search, he included the term "technology assessment," which he located from examining a relevant title. This strategy increased the relevancy of his hits and improved his scores to above average in all categories (Appendix A, Tables A1a and A1b). According to Dwaine, "Out of four results, I would say three of them would be exactly what I am looking for."

Lesley's searches improved in relevancy after she accessed the Number Index's Meditate example. This tactic example promoted the use of various keywords, broadening the search, and truncating words. Following review of the tutorial, she incorporated numerous terms in her search string and also truncated terms. For example, she substituted "early childhood education" for "young children" and experimented with various terms to capture the instructional aspect of her topic, such as "kindergarten," "public school," "class," and "teach." Lesley's revised strategy helped reduce the number of her hits while increasing her scores in all categories for her final search results (Appendix A, Tables A2a and A3b).

Kathy's adoption of the search strategy, promoted by the Jolt tactic, including adding keywords to expand the focus and number of results, did not improve her final search results for the relevancy, ability to answer the problem, and quality of the response (Appendix A, Tables A3a and A3b). Her selection of Ebsco's all database option, coupled with her incorrect placement of the Boolean OR operator, produced a number of false hits. However, Kathy indicated that she gained new search techniques from the tutorial, particularly in using the Boolean operators to expand a search with multiple keywords.

Shelly's problem-solving activity illustrates the impact of the tactics as well as the search techniques on outcomes. She accessed the tutorial three times, examining all of the Indexes and the majority (nine out of twelve) of tactic examples. She changed her strategy in subsequent searches, employing many of the techniques described in the examples. For example, after reviewing the Relevance Indexes' Catch and Notice tactic examples, she focused on using subject terms and synonyms in her search. Her review of the Jolt tactic with its emphasis on the Boolean OR operator prompted her to incorporate additional terms in her search (Appendix A, Tables A6a and A6b).

Participants' increased awareness of metacognitive abilities while problem solving

Triggered previous knowledge

The present study shares outcomes similar to Chen and Ge's (2006) findings on the benefits that learners received from prompting and expert modeling. In the present study, the tutorial, like the cognitive modeling system in Chen and Ge's research, helped participants to trigger their prior knowledge as well as supporting them during their problem solving. Both Lesley and Daemon observed that the tutorial facilitated their abilities to remember search techniques presented in previous library instructional classes. However, Lesley noted that her earlier instruction focused on a "predefined search," but the problem solving allowed her to "do it on my own." According to Daemon, "I knew a lot of it. When I was reading it, it kinda like hit me. I know I should do [it] that way, it just kinda triggered." In addition, one of the participant's comments about the tutorial in the present study remained similar to those voiced by the graduate students in Chen and Ge's research, concerning the helpfulness of the cognitive modeling system in facilitating individuals' thought processes. Lesley described the tutorial as having "enough information to actually help someone thinking."

Promoted self-reflection

Participants' think-aloud also offered evidence of self-reflecting in their problem solving. Kathy noted, "I'll go to the advanced search page. It's easier for me to start here because I know off the bat there [are] a lot of things I don't want." While explaining her initial search strategy, she remarked, "I'm going to go ahead and [select] all publication types for now and all document types. So I will probably eliminate some of these later on. So the other place that I'm going to go is [to] choose my databases. I have learned with at least adult education a lot of things exist in databases other than just generic education ones." Similarly, Lesley maintained, "I know I could probably go into one of those better articles and see what terms they use." Daemon explained his use of Ebsco's folder feature. "I would add it to a folder so I could find it later." In reviewing the results of her initial search, Shelly explained her previous difficulties in narrowing the hits. "There is no field I can find or understand or limit it to elementary school."

Use of metacognitive knowledge

Mary also demonstrated metacognitive knowledge while outlining her information-seeking behavior. "I wouldn't go into Google automatically. I would go into the library and find those scholarly databases first." Dwaine highlighted the importance of citation tracing to his information-seeking strategies. "I would want to see what the references are. I would look at specific articles based on citations. One of these is from a book so I have a feeling there would be quite a few citations named."

Evidence of planning and evaluating

The present study also found relationships between individuals' use of metacognitive strategies in their information problem solving. For example, in his think-aloud protocol, Daemon revealed planning and evaluating search efforts. After reviewing one of his results, he explained, "I'm looking for more like a biography, more like a concentration of his theories. This is just for instance an elementary teacher's application of John [sic] Piaget theories... I need to get definitely more specific." To this end, in his revised search he incorporated the term "overview" with "Piagetian theory."

Supports previous research

The illustration of participants' use of metacognitive strategies while problem solving supports previous research on the topic by Salomon and Perkin (1989), Flavell (1978), Sternberg and Frensch (1989, 1990), and Brown (1977, 1982). These authors maintained that individuals use metacognition in problem solving for monitoring, regulating, and coordinating the process. Likewise, Marchionini (1989) highlighted the role of metacognition in information seeking. Marchionini observed that metacognition instigated individuals' "information need," facilitated the creation of "mental models for systems and domains," and promoted the monitoring of the search's "progress" (p. 14).

Moore (1995) concluded that all students in her study demonstrated incidences of metacognitive activity, but she noted differences in the quality of their knowledge as well as the complexity of the strategies they exercised. This also proved true for the graduate students in the present study. All participants employed metacognitive behaviors, but the extent of their use and their effectiveness differed among individuals. For example, Lesley demonstrated planning in her search, explaining, "I think I'll narrow down by getting peer-reviewed journals. I'm not going to get full text yet 'cause I'm still looking to see what I can get." Likewise, Kathy revealed extensive planning in her initial search with her use of specific keywords, selection of databases and document types, and specification of publication dates. Similarly, Mary offered evidence of self-reflecting strategies when reviewing an article's relevance. Upon reading the title aloud, "Towards a neurobiological model," Mary commented, "possibly, I need to check it out."

The present study also supports much of Huttenlock's (2008) findings on the role of a scaffold in facilitating metacognitive strategies during information search. Huttenlock highlighted users' efforts to identify relevant keywords through revised search efforts and this too was observed in participants' problem-solving activities. She also noted that all participants, even those in the control group, employed metacognitive strategies during search that she believed stemmed in part from their responses to the information displayed on the search screen. This was revealed in the present study during participants' initial search (pre-tutorial) when individuals demonstrated planning, self-reflecting, and evaluating strategies. For example, in his initial search, Dwaine noted, "I'm going to type in classroom observation and choose my databases first." Upon reviewing the results from her first search, Mary observed, "Not exactly what I want. I want to find a more specific study of research." In addition, Huttenlock found that the advance organizer that was used differently by participants helped enhance their metacognitive questioning, which was more deliberate and focused. Likewise, participants in the present study used the tutorial differently. In this instance, Dwaine and Kathy relied on the intervention to improve their basic search strategy that they changed only slightly during their problem-solving activity. These participants accessed the tutorial infrequently, largely to clarify information on search techniques. On the other hand, Mary, Shelly, Lesley, and Daemon utilized the tutorial as a reference source for search strategies and skills.

Monitoring

The present study verified Tabatabai and Shore's (2005) research on the role of monitoring as a characteristic of expert searching. This was illustrated during Mary's problem-solving activity. In selecting search terms, Mary, a self-described skilled searcher, noted words she "had previously used."

However, monitoring was observed among novice searchers as well in the present study. During her think-aloud, Shelly explained, "Well, I'm finding different things, which is important for the paper." Similarly, Dwaine noted, "Out of these four results I would say three of them would be exactly what I am looking for, so I would at this point take those three, print them and read them." Moreover, following a search that yielded 170 results, Lesley noted, "So I got fewer hits with this."

Education students' use of metacognitive skills

In addition, the present study supports previous research on the importance of metacognitive skills in facilitating education students' information seeking. It confirms Hill and Hannafin's (1997) findings on the relationship between metacognition and system orientation, but in the present study, disorientation did not affect search outcomes.

For example, Shelly alluded to a lack of orientation in searching during her post-activity interview. "It's a matter of remembering where I was and how to navigate it and getting back there again. I do remember... most times where I've been; it's just a longer haul for me." Still, Shelly's disorientation did not hinder her development of appropriate search strategies for her topic. Her final search scores increased in all categories from her initial effort (Appendix A, Tables A6a and A6b). Lesley suggested that the selection of keywords remained especially important in minimizing problems with orientation in search. "It's hard to choose relevant search terms that get me where I want to go without boxing me in."

The present study also extends Huttenlock's (2008) findings on the role of a metacognitive scaffold in stimulating education students' metacognitive behaviors that also fostered their information seeking. In our study, the tutorial helped individuals who received too many or too few results, as well as irrelevant hits, to clarify their thought processes, and this promoted strategy development. The idea tactics utilized by the participants offered suggestions such as "Change, Meditate, Create, Jolt, Notice, Think, Notice, Wander, and Break," which facilitated problem solving through the generation of new strategies as well as the explanation of database search techniques. After reading the Jolt tactic example, Kathy explained, "So I got about Jolt, which is this idea of adding keywords to my search to either expand or [get a] more focused search. So I'm going to head over to this one intersection of training and podcasts in adult education and look at their keywords. Well, I hadn't thought about educational psychology." Dwaine demonstrated similar use of the tutorial's Change tactic with his review of a relevant record and his incorporation of the phrase "technology assessment" in his search terms. This provided him with a result set that contained four items, three of which he believed were "exactly what I was looking for."

Summary of the role of the tutorial in fostering metacognitive behaviors

The present study confirms previous research on the effectiveness of metacognitive scaffolds in enhancing these behaviors in students (Wolf et al., 2003). In the present study, the tutorial, by promoting participants' planning, monitoring, and self-regulating strategies, imparted these behaviors to students. In addition, the activity also fostered participants' reflecting and evaluating efforts. These strategies served to facilitate individuals' search activities regardless of their subject knowledge or database skills. Overall, four out of six participants improved their search outcomes compared to their initial search due to the availability of the tutorial. In addition, all participants gained search skills following exposure to the tutorial.

17

Metacognition and information literacy

Abstract: This chapter explores research on metacognition and information literacy. Mutch (1997) was one of the earliest writers to link information literacy to metacognition. Similarly, school librarians recognized the significance of metacognitive strategies to students' information literacy. Moreover, information-seeking research highlights the importance of metacognition in information literacy. Research reveals a wide variety of efforts aimed at incorporating metacognitive strategies into information literacy instruction. One of the earliest included Wolf et al.'s (2003) use of Eisenberg and Berkowitz's information problem-solving model as a metacognitive and information literacy scaffold. Recent efforts to incorporate metacognition in information literacy instruction include problem-based learning and interactive games, as well as utilizing web 2.0 technologies, action research efforts and the Reflective Judgement Model.

Key words: information literacy, metacognition, problem-based learning, reflection, strategies, ACRL information literacy competency standards in higher education.

Introduction

The study extends the research on metacognition as a component of information literacy and underscores the value of instructing students in using metacognitive skills. The Association of College & Research Libraries' (ACRL) Information Literacy Competency Standards for Higher Education defines information literacy as recognizing an information need and employing strategies to locate relevant information to fulfill the need. Our study demonstrated the importance of metacognition in facilitating participants' information literacy while problem solving in research databases. The idea tactics, which included metacognitive strategies as well as database search techniques, helped education graduate students of all skill levels improve their search outcomes. Blummer et al.'s (2012) survey of the research skills of education graduate students pointed to some individuals' dissatisfaction with the content of their previous library instruction. Some respondents described the instruction as "very basic" and two individuals suggested it was not helpful. Research in the European Union showed that individuals' use of metacognitive strategies, such as planning, monitoring, and self-regulating while web and database searching, enhanced their information problem-solving skills. As Thelwall (2004) reminds us, future scholars will require a different set of search skills. Consequently, the idea tactics tutorial offers librarians and educators a new perspective on the instruction of information literacy.

Early support

Mutch (1997) was one of the earliest writers to link information literacy to metacognition. The author, a professor at Nottingham Trent University's Department of Finance and Business Information Systems, highlighted the importance of reflective processes that support knowledge production.

School librarians

Within the next few years, school librarians also touted the benefits of metacognitive strategies to enhance students' information literacy. Langford (2001) likened metacognition to critical literacy. She characterized it as a subset of information literacy that focused on thinking beyond reflection to "analysis and a determined a course of action" (para. 9). She maintained that critical literacy promoted the development of "critical and creative thinking within the information process" (para. 6). Three years later, Goodin urged library media teachers to "practice" metacognition in their reading strategies. The author observed, "once you become aware of your own expert reading processes, you are prepared to use that proficiency to help" teachers (p. 13). Similarly, Farmer (2007) promoted a learner-centered assessment of information literacy for the school community that included students' metacognitive skills. According to the author, "the ability to self-identify and monitor learning helps learners determine their strengths and direct their efforts to improve their information literacy skills" (p. 82).

Hamilton (2010), a school librarian in Georgia, reported on her use of blogs to encourage high school students to "reflect and think about their information literacy skills and research processes" (para. 1). She observed that the research reflections offered students "an opportunity to engage in metacognition," and provided information on their "perspectives on information sources" and evaluation processes, and helped her identify individuals' difficulties with the project (para. 5).

Academic librarians

Recently, academic librarians joined school librarians in their efforts to support the incorporation of metacognition in information literacy instruction. In 2011, Stephen Bell, the ACRL's president, appointed a task force to revise their Information Literacy Competency Standards for Higher Education (Bell, 2011). According to Bell, the task force was charged with expanding the definition of information literacy to consider the importance of other literacies as well as students' development of metacognitive abilities.

Martin's (2013) *Learning from Recent British Information Literacy Models: A Report to ACRL's Information Literacy Competency Standards for Higher Education Task Force* identified metacognitive learning as a component in A New Curriculum for Information Literacy (ANCL) and the Society of College, National and University Libraries (SCONUL) Seven Pillars models. The author stressed the learning outcomes of these models that supported students' self-assessment and reflection, and that underscored the "reiterative" and "holistic" nature of information literacy (p. 16).

Research on metacognition and information literacy

Information-seeking research highlights the importance of metacognition in information literacy. Lee and Wu (2013) traced the effect of information-seeking activities and social entertainment reading activities on students' reading literacy, especially their development of metacognitive reading strategies. The authors found a link between students' frequency of information seeking and knowledge of metacognitive strategies. According to the article, "when people more frequently engage in information seeking reading activities, they obtain a more positive perception of the usefulness of metacognitive strategies" and this produces "better reading scores" (p. 174). Students utilized these strategies when they searched online. The authors surmised that this pointed to the importance of incorporating instruction of metacognitive strategies for "online and offline reading" (p. 175).

Rastgoo et al. (2011) also linked information literacy to metacognition. The authors focused on Internet information literacy, and their study centered on the provision of Internet search skills and individuals' use of metacognitive strategies. The authors found that participants who received Internet information literacy skills training exhibited differences in "metacognitive components such as (procedural knowledge, declarative knowledge, conditional knowledge, information management strategies, dubbing strategies and evaluation)" (p. 966). The article's conclusion stated that Internet information literacy represented a "valuable means" to develop students' metacognition and promote lifelong learning (p. 966).

Additionally, Madden et al.'s (2012) study of postgraduate students' evaluation practices on the web illustrated the relationship between information literacy and metacognition. The authors sought to identify criteria that individuals employed to assess the trustworthiness of websites and participants' use of metacognitive strategies, as well as their awareness of the appropriateness of their assessment strategies. The qualitative research revealed that participants employed a wide range of criteria to evaluate websites, such as first impressions, website appearance, and website contents. Madden et al. concluded that the participants had not received website evaluation training and instead had "developed their own guidelines" that "give the clearest evidence of metacognition" (p. 682). The authors observed that the findings suggested against providing "students with a set of rules" for assessing the credibility of websites. Instead, they recommended that information literacy training incorporate metacognitive practices in evaluating websites, such as reflection and self-questioning.

Gross's (2005) thesis linked metacognition to information literacy as well. She utilized competency theory to suggest that individuals with low-level information-literacy skills lacked the cognitive ability to self-identify their training needs. She observed that "one of the greatest challenges for information professionals may be in developing out-reach efforts" for "individuals who think they are performing well, but who are not" (p. 160).

To this end, she encouraged educating students on competency theory, conducting skills assessments, and providing students with "the skills they lack" (p. 160). According to Gross, "interventions that build skills also increase an individual's ability to assess his or her own performance" (p. 161).

Kiliç-Çakmak (2010) stressed that information literacy self-efficacy remained especially important for e-learners to support self-directed learning. She examined distance education students' information literacy self-efficacy, utilizing the Information Literacy Self efficacy Scale and the Motivated Strategies for Learning Questionnaire. Kiliç-Çakmak stated that "information literacy self-efficacy of students increases when they frequently use metacognitive strategies and highly believe that they have control over the learning processes" (p. 201). To enhance students' information literacy self-efficacy, she advised providing learning environments that offered students planning, monitoring, and regulating opportunities, as well as incorporating interactive media such as wikis and blogs.

Westby (2010) suggested that new definitions of literacy highlighted the need to understand how students make meaning in various modes. She pointed to the New London's Group promotion of teaching multiliteracies through situated practices, overt instruction, critical framing, and application. Moreover, she described Australian speech language pathologists' efforts to promote phonological awareness and language skills among children with language impairments by fostering their metalinguistic skills.

Information literacy metacognition instruction

Research reveals a wide variety of efforts aimed at incorporating metacognitive strategies into information literacy instruction. One of the earliest included Wolf et al.'s (2003) use of Eisenberg and Berkowitz's information problem-solving model as a metacognitive and information literacy scaffold for eighth-grade students' research efforts. The authors recommended that future efforts incorporate "scaffolding directly into the multimedia environments" and infuse "information problem-solving vocabulary throughout the school day" (p. 339). Likewise, the literature illustrates a diversity of information literacy instructional efforts that incorporate metacognitive strategies. Many of these are directed at university students and capitalize on the availability of online resources and tools.

Problem-based learning

Researchers at the University of Strathcylde utilized groupware in a shared workspace to support a collaborative problem-based learning environment in a design engineering class (McGill et al., 2005). The authors underscored the importance of the learning technologist who provided information literacy instruction to the students. According to McGill et al. students received education in the use of team concept maps to support planning and conducting searches, evaluating results, as well as "organizing information, and assimilating found information into their own design concepts" (p. 633). The availability of wiki pages allowed students to "reflect on their progress with the design and to link to resources" (p. 633). The authors surmised that the concept map and wiki pages facilitated the students' abilities to "collaboratively construct their own 'knowledge structures' in the design problem domain" (p. 633). This use represented what Jonassen and Carr (1998) termed Mindtools, whereby technologies support learners' engagement in critical thinking.

Problem-based learning also remained a component of an information literacy module in a distance education school library media program that enhanced students' metacognitive behaviors as well (Diekema et al., 2011). The authors found that some students "displayed metacognitive strategies that enabled them to conduct a more extensive research process" (p. 264). The article described these strategies as pausing and evaluating progress, reflecting on what they found, as well as redefining questions and search strategies. Diekema et al. suggested that the study supported the use of authentic learning environments to focus "the learner's attention in new ways" and shift the "conception of information literacy from finding sources to using information to learn" (p. 267).

Interactive game

Santamaria and Petrik's (2012) development of an interactive game to introduce freshmen students to the academic library centered on metacognition. The librarians observed that incoming students suffered from a lack of metacognitive awareness, which hindered their ability to ask relevant questions to support their research efforts. To remedy this, the librarians developed Miller-opoly, which "provided students with basic facts about the library that could help them formulate questions on the spot" (p. 266). According to Santamaria and Petrik, the game offered students a metacognitive perspective to "recognize what they do and do not know by building off of a pre-existing framework" (p. 266). Although the article stated that the project did not include an assessment component, the authors suggested using the game as a measure to train new student workers in the library.

Web 2.0

King (2011) proposed utilizing Web 2.0 for incorporating metacognition into information literacy instruction. According to her, "Web 2.0 can shape the most fundamental of learning outcomes: metacognition, the higher level of thinking and processing information" (p. 23). King maintained that metacognitive development remains especially "effective when students are motivated by information that interests them" or within a familiar learning environment (p. 24). To that end, she linked Web 2.0 tool capabilities to Bloom's digital taxonomy in her advocacy of a Web 2.0 pedagogy. According to her, teachers' incorporation of Web 2.0 pedagogies in the classroom fostered a "student-centered approach to developing students' information literacy and metacognitive skills" (p. 28).

Action research

Jeffrey et al. (2011) reported on action research aimed at enhancing university students' digital information literacy through weekly workshops. The study centered on promoting individuals' reflective skills through the use of blogs and the Three Step Reflective Framework. This model represented a cyclical process whereby students identified an issue, devised an action, and engaged in "monitoring-reflection, learning, and new planning" and evaluation (p. 391). The article reported that one of the study's outcomes included students' control over their learning through monitoring strategies that revealed "unknown gaps in skills and knowledge" (p. 401). In addition, Jeffrey et al. observed "a growing self-awareness of how [the participants] approached learning and what worked for them" (p. 403). The article's conclusion emphasized the value of learning environments that provided collaboration and a "supportive community" for fostering experimentation (p. 406).

Similarly, a faculty–librarian collaboration in a political studies course at the Augustana Campus of the University of Alberta led to an action research project aimed at enhancing students' information literacy, research, and reflective skills (Polkinghorne and Wilton, 2010). Course assignments supported the ACRL information literacy outcomes and also included a reflective component to "encourage self-awareness" (p. 462). In addition, students developed "skills résumés" in the beginning and at the end of the course, which outlined their competencies (p. 464). According to Polkinghorne and Wilton, students' final skills résumés were "richer, more thorough, and more precise" than their initial self-assessments (p. 467).

Reflective Judgement Model

An innovative information literacy effort at Oregon State University centered on the Reflective Judgement Model, which depicts an individual's mental model of knowledge construction in seven stages. The model, developed by Kitchener and King in 1981, maintains that beginning college students typically score in the middle on the Reflective Judgement Interview, and move toward more reflective thinking through their academic career. The model promotes a variety of learning experiences to foster students' reflective thinking. Consequently Deitering and Gronemyer (2011) developed an information literacy unit for an English composition class based on the model. For the assignment, students followed scholarly and public research on a topic through blog postings and created "public writing" that expanded the conversation (p. 500). Deitering and Gronemyer stated that the assignment fostered students' abilities to use a variety of sources to construct their own meaning on topics.

Summary of information literacy and metacognition

Nesset (2013) noted the importance of reflection in information seeking and learning. According to her, "reflecting on past behaviors" allowed students to identify and correct mistakes (p. 104). Still, she admitted that "reflection does not always occur" and she underscored the need for metacognitive instructional efforts (p. 104). Bowler (2007) referred to metacognitive knowledge as "a critical piece in the information literacy puzzle" (p. 1). Šauperl et al. (2006) observed that when information is used to support individuals' efforts to solve problems, students "learn problem solving, learning strategies and research procedures" (p. 298). They equated the process to metacognition, and they believed that it enabled students to "evaluate and select information critically" to satisfy various information needs (p. 298). The idea tactics provided participants with instruction in metacognitive strategies as well as database search skills to foster their problem solving in research databases. The research revealed that students employed metacognitive strategies and also improved their database search skills. Ultimately the study demonstrated the importance of metacognition as a component of information literacy instruction.

18

Utilizing the tutorial

Abstract: This chapter offers guidelines for maximizing the use of the tutorial. First, the chapter highlights the role of the tutorial as a reference tool. The tutorial remained most beneficial to participants when it was utilized briefly for reference purposes rather than as a one-shot learning tool. Second, the chapter offers suggestions on how to modify the tool to support users in diverse disciples and for students of various age groups. Modification would focus on the tactic's examples to support information search in diverse databases, the web and print resources. These examples could be directed at helping elementary, middle, high school and undergraduate students' information problem solving, as well as helping graduate students in other disciplines. Third, the chapter includes ideas for improving the tool. The tutorial requires instructions aimed at maximizing students' use of the tool.

Key words: tutorial, prompts, adapting, user groups, elementary, middle, high school, undergraduate students, content, library training, instruction.

Introduction

The idea tactics tutorial proved to be an effective intervention for promoting participants' metacognitive strategies while problem solving. Participants also benefited from the tutorial's database search techniques, which fostered better search outcomes. The tool remained most effective when used in short intervals to provide participants with ideas to overcome obstacles in the search environment. This research focused on education graduate students' use of the tutorial for problem solving with Ebsco databases. However, the tutorial contains potential for assisting other user groups in information search. This requires modification of the idea tactics' examples to support search in different resources and for various student groups.

Importance of the tutorial as a reference tool

The tutorial remained most beneficial to participants when it was utilized briefly for reference purposes rather than as a one-shot learning tool. Dwaine's problem-solving activity illustrates this use. Although he did not spend an excessive amount of time in the tutorial, he adopted its suggestions and referred back to the tool for additional ideas or to clarify information accessed earlier. Dwaine noted his effort to adopt the tutorial's suggestion to use "keywords from an article that was relevant." He obtained better results compared to his initial search following review of the tutorial and he did not have to perform an excessive number of revised searches to obtain an improved outcome (Appendix A, Tables A1a and A1b). Kathy, on the other hand, employed the tutorial as a one-shot learning tool. After her initial search, she examined the tutorial, viewing two indexes and one tactic example. She applied the strategies presented in the example in her revised searches. These strategies increased the number of her results, but she did not increase the relevance of her results (Appendix A, Tables A3a and A3b). Revisiting the tutorial may have provided Kathy with tips on methods to reduce her number of hits as well as the relevancy of her results.

Participants who appeared comfortable in the search environment, such as Mary and Daemon, typically read the Indexes rather than the tactic examples. Their problem solving suggested these individuals utilized the tutorial as a reference source to gather ideas from the tactics to improve search outcomes. The Indexes promoted the use of metacognitive strategies and did not include database search techniques. An examination of their searches illustrates the use of new strategies and keywords during these participants' problem solving. After Mary read the Strategy Index, which contained the Skip tactic that urges readers to "explore the topic from a different perspective," she added the term "models" to her search string. Likewise, Daemon's review of this Index led him to incorporate "overview" into his search terms.

However, Lesley and Shelly also moved in and out of the tutorial during their problem-solving activity, using it as a reference source for search tips and database search techniques as well as metacognitive strategies aimed at improving their results. These participants obtained more relevant results following access to the tutorial (Appendix A, Tables A2a, A2b, A6a, and A6b). Following Lesley's examination of the Number Indexes' Meditate, Change, and Create examples, she incorporated Boolean search operators in her search. Shelly's application of the Notice tactic example also led to her use of Boolean operators and to utilizing the subject field.

Use of tutorial to combat problems

The value of the tutorial as a reference source during problem solving may stem from the variety of difficulties participants encountered while problem solving that required review of the tutorial for search tips in reducing results, expanding the number of hits, or increasing the relevancy of results. Likewise, the time participants spent in the tutorial for each access, which ranged from 6 to 210 seconds, suggests that individuals scanned the Indexes and the examples to obtain strategies to improve their search results as quickly as possible to resume their problem solving.

Tutorial addresses variation among individuals' search skills

A variation in the problem-solving skills of the participants also suggests the tutorial would be effective as a reference source for some individuals. Thornes (2012) reminds us that "an online learning environment has the capacity to support the needs of students with varied levels of IL skills" (p. 83). Likewise, Tabatabai and Luconi (1998) found differences between problem-solving strategies among expert and novice education graduate students. Experts were identified by the number of hours they spent on the web each week. Tabatabai and Luconi reported that experts devoted more time to planning search strategies, setting goals, and reflecting on the task compared to the novices. The latter, the authors reported, overlooked relevant sources and suffered from information overload, unlike experts.

Our study found similar differences between those participants with varying levels of search skills, such as Daemon and Shelly. However, both participants' search outcomes improved following access to the tutorial. For example, Daemon demonstrated his knowledge of advanced search skills in his initial search and he also revealed planning as well as goal setting during his problem-solving activity. When his search returned irrelevant results, Daemon decided that "I'm going to start choosing more databases." On the other hand, following Shelly's initial search, which yielded nearly 5,000 results, she appeared overwhelmed and remarked, "I have to figure out how to get it down." However, both individuals utilized the tutorial as a reference tool. Both individuals accessed the tool four times during their problem-solving activity and made gains in the relevance of their results as well as their ability to answer the question, and the quality of the response from the first to the final search (Appendix A, Tables A5a, A5b, A6a, and A6b).

Participants' comments on tutorial support its use for reference

Comments related to the tutorial in the post-search interviews remained favorable and also underscored its usefulness as a reference tool. The majority of participants (five out of six) believed that the tool improved the outcomes of their problem-solving activities. Dwaine observed the tutorial taught him the value of reviewing results. He admitted, "I guess I didn't really think [of] looking at the keywords. That's what helped me narrow down my search." Daemon and Lesley suggested that the intervention triggered their prior knowledge of search techniques they had learned in previous library instructional classes. Shelly believed the tutorial was particularly beneficial for her, a non-traditional student who required instruction in database search techniques.

Optimizing use of the tutorial

As the paragraphs above illustrate, participants benefited most from the tutorial when it was used as a reference source to support information retrieval. In this manner the idea tactics provided users metacognitive strategies and database search skills to enhance their search results. Foremost, the tutorial worked best when individuals employed it to support their information problem solving. As noted in Chapter 5, information problems require individuals' abilities to identify an information need, locate relevant sources, and organize and synthesize the information from various sources.

On the other hand, our tool is not designed to support search for reference questions. These are questions with known answers, such as: What is the long-term temperature of Charleston, South Carolina for the month of December? Individuals should also avoid employing the tutorial to conduct a literature review on a topic or a cited author search. Utilizing the tutorial for these purposes would not produce an exhaustive search, since the tutorial focuses on search of online resources and not print materials.

Adapting the tutorial

The tutorial remains a flexible tool that can be adapted to different learning environments as well as diverse user groups. The idea tactics and their examples are aimed at supporting education graduate students' search activities. However, by revising the tool's content, librarians and educators can provide metacognitive and information-seeking assistance to students in other disciplines as well as individuals of various ages. In this event, modification would focus on the tactic's examples to support information search in diverse databases, the web, and print resources. Moreover, these examples could be directed at helping elementary, middle, high school, and undergraduate students' information problem solving, as well as graduate students in other disciplines.

Identify users' information-seeking behaviors

Prior to adapting the tutorial for other user groups, it is critical to understand their research preferences and behaviors. This can be accomplished by identifying users' information-seeking habits and any obstacles they encounter while researching. Our research included a pilot study that adapted Earp's (2008) questionnaire on education graduate students' information sources preferences, to reveal the research habits of a similar group of students enrolled in a mid-Atlantic university. We also interviewed education graduate students at that university to identify their research needs, search skills, and optimal instructional environments. In addition, we conducted an extensive literature review on the information-seeking habits and research skills representative of our participants, to supplement our quantitative and qualitative research. The information gleaned from these sources guided the development of the idea tactics tutorial.

Readers interested in modifying the idea tactics tutorial for various audiences should employ similar strategies to identify the research needs of their audience. The literature contains a wide range of studies that track information-seeking behaviors of user groups in different disciplines.

Many of these articles contain the survey instruments utilized in the research. Similarly focus group interviews could and should be employed to supplement information gleaned from the literature.

Idea tactics for elementary students

De Vries et al. (2008) maintained that reflective web searching was especially important for elementary students to support their abilities to utilize computers to locate relevant information. The authors assessed the success of a portal and a worksheet in helping students employ reflective thinking. Consequently, the idea tactics could be utilized to support elementary students' thinking through their incorporation in a portal and worksheet. In this instance, the idea tactics would foster students' reflective thinking while guiding their information seeking.

Idea tactics for middle school students

Research by Davis (2003) on the usefulness of generic prompts in helping middle school students develop an understanding of science concepts suggests that the type of intervention offered by the idea tactics would also enhance their web search. Davis employed the Knowledge Integration Environment that "uses sentence-starter prompts to foster both metacognitive and sensemaking activities" (p. 94). The author concluded that generic prompts led to "productive reflection that in turn helps students expand their repertoires of ideas and identify weaknesses in their knowledge" (p. 116). Similarly, the idea tactics present sentence fragments that encourage reflection as well as monitoring and planning. These concepts could also be used in a web page or portal learning environment to provoke reflective thought and support understanding for middle school students.

Idea tactics for high school students

Research by Brand-Gruwel et al. (2009) that revealed teenagers' search difficulties suggest this user group would benefit from the idea tactics tutorial too. The authors compared the information problem solving of various groups and found secondary students were engaged in less orientation to the process of information seeking than other participants. Chung and Neuman's (2007) study of high school students' information searching revealed they did not initially plan their information search activities. These individuals would also benefit from the idea tactics' emphasis on planning, monitoring, and self-regulating information search. Librarians and educators could present the tactics in a variety of formats including an online tutorial, a print handout, a link on a learning management system, or in a face-to-face instructional session.

Idea tactics for undergraduate students

A few of the participants in our study were younger individuals new to the graduate program. The characteristics of their information seeking remained similar to undergraduates described in the literature, in failing to plan searches, using few keywords, and spending minimal time reviewing results. The success of the tutorial in improving these participants' search results suggests that it would perform similarly with undergraduate students.

Tutorial modification mechanics for diverse user groups

In addition to adapting the idea tactics and problem-solving examples to suit the user group, modification would also encompass search tactics to support database, web, or print inquiries. Teaching younger students how to use the library print collection would include information on searching the library catalog as well as the classification system utilized in the collection. Moreover, the terminology as well as the graphics will need to be altered to support younger audiences. Christensen et al. (2013) reported on their use of the comic strip format for their Hemingway Library Information Online skills tutorial to "catch the attention of high school students" (p. 8).

Employing the tutorial in different learning environments

Embedded instruction

Wopereis et al.'s (2008) research illustrated the effect of embedded instruction on solving information problems. The authors concluded that embedded instruction produced a positive effect on individual's regulation of the IPS process, which they attributed to the reflective questions. The tutorial seemingly resembled embedded instruction in its use of suggestions that served as reflective questions and prompts to guide participants in seeking new strategies for their problem solving. This remained particularly apparent for the Change tactic, the most popular tactic in the tutorial. The Change tactic urged readers "to instigate a new search behavior, keyword or source or strategy." Upon reading this tactic, many participants such as Dwaine and Lesley adopted these suggestions and altered their search behaviors. Dwaine's comment upon reading the tactic remains illustrative of its impact on participants' search strategy: "Now I'm going to try to change the wording of my search by using classroom observation and technology integration." On the other hand, Lesley incorporated new keywords in her revised search after reading the Change tactic, substituting "early childhood education" for "young children." This expanded the number of her results from four to 231. It also led her to employ advanced search techniques to narrow her results by specifying dates and peer-reviewed materials. Consequently, we propose that the idea tactics could be employed to offer embedded instruction to novice learners.

Point-of-need instruction

Mestre (2012) highlighted the importance of online tutorials for point-of-need instruction. Likewise, our study suggested the idea tactics tutorial would remain effective incorporated in a course management system or on a class web page. In this capacity, the tutorial would be utilized as a self-directed tool as it was employed in the study. Our research suggested that education students sought flexible training such as a tutorial. Moreover, the literature highlighted millennial students' desire for experiential learning opportunities and points to the potential popularity of the tool with these individuals as well (Bowen et al., 2011).

Cooke (2010) noted the importance of librarians supporting adult learners who may experience high levels of anxiety when researching. Badke (2008) suggested that we can help adult learns by "providing them with a research model along with strategies that model and use the digital tools they need" (p. 50). Consequently, these users might also benefit from the idea tactics, especially since research suggests they are typically self-directed learners.

Face-to-face instruction

The idea tactics could also be presented in a traditional learning environment. School media specialists and academic librarians could incorporate the idea tactics in bibliographic training through a lecture format. This may be preferable for younger students. The tutorial contains potential for incorporation in face-to-face library training sessions. In Kathy's post-activity interview, she suggested it could be used to supplement database training opportunities offered to undergraduate students. She observed, "We teach freshmen about Boolean operators and stuff and this [is] almost like the next step, which I like." Similarly, Thornes (2012) described the importance of the information literacy tutorial designed for the School of Geography at the University of Leeds as a post-workshop activity. According to her, the tutorial was used as a "follow-up resource" that provided students with "more information, practice, or just to go over something in their own time [as] a source for this additional help and support" (p. 91). Thornes suggested that program leaders' intention to use the scaffold as a pre-activity workshop proved unrealistic due to time constraints in planning the face-to-face sessions. However, the flexibility of the idea tactics tutorial's content supports its use prior to or following traditional library training opportunities.

Tutorial improvements

Posting user guidelines

The present study underscored the value of the metacognitive tutorial as a stand-alone instructional tool for students. Several improvements to the tutorial would enhance its ability to provide search support for education graduate students' problem solving. Foremost the tutorial should contain instructions aimed at maximizing students' use of the tool. Information should be provided on the various ways to navigate through the tutorial, such as a linear format or by topic. User guidelines should also highlight the value of focusing on one or two tactics, as well as to encourage individuals to balance their time in devising strategy, reviewing results, and examining records. Too much time spent on any of these activities can negatively affect search outcomes. In addition, Somaza-Fernández, and Abadal (2009) suggested that tutorials should include information on time needed to complete the tool to support "autonomous learning" (p. 130). In this case, users of the idea tactics would be informed that the tool's completion type varies according to user needs.

Improving visual appearance

Additional changes focus on the visual appearance of the tool. The links to the practice database that appear on the Index pages should be removed. While research suggests that tutorials should contain practice opportunities, our research contradicted these findings. Participants sought to delve into their information problem solving without practicing, and these links proved confusing to individuals. Moreover, when the tutorial was demonstrated at the 2011 Georgia Conference on Information Literacy, one of the audience members suggested replacing the tutorial's clip art with photographs, to increase participants' engagement with the content. Studies reveal that photos have a greater impact and are more entertaining than clip art.

Inclusion of new content

Furthermore, the tutorial would benefit from inclusion of some new content. For example, one participant remained unclear on how to access the Boolean AND operator. Providing a screen capture of the advanced search mode with a description of Boolean operators would underscore the value of this search strategy. Likewise, additional search examples should highlight the differences between keywords and subject terms in search. While some participants employed subject terms in their revised strategies, these were typically used as keywords rather than subject searches. The tutorial should also stress that the optimal number of search results varies according to the user needs. Several participants appeared confused over what constituted a sufficient results set. This remains especially important, since there was reluctance among individuals to view many titles.

In addition, including a section on the Main Index page that describes how Ebsco treats phrase searching in the basic search may enhance search results. One frequent error participants made during the problem-solving activities included the use of the basic search mode like Google by typing in a phrase. This produced a Smart Search results set that yielded a large number of hits or no hits.

Urging readers to review their search terms, database selections, and limits before and after the search may decrease the number of errors. The problem-solving activity illustrated participants' carelessness in entering search terms, selecting databases, and limiting results. Although some of these mistakes centered on mistyped words that the system identified, others included more serious errors that affected search results. Unfortunately, few participants attributed the irrelevance of their search results to user error in conducting the search.

Summary of utilizing the tutorial

Mestre (2010, 2012) identified strategies for the effectiveness of library instructional tutorials, and the idea tactics tutorial incorporates many of these features. The tool supports various learning styles and highlights important information, as well as providing clear navigation and images that support the text. Information is presented in chunks, text is kept to a minimum, and the experience remains "personal and relevant" (p. 273). The idea tactics tutorial can be employed as a self-directed tool posted in a learning management system. It would also provide reinforcement and practice when used in conjunction with a traditional information literacy training session. The flexibility of the tutorial fosters its modification to support students' information problem solving in other disciplines and age groups. Incorporating improvements to the tutorial would enhance its effectiveness in facilitating students' use of metacognitive strategies and advanced database search techniques while problem solving. Still, as Thornes (2012) reminds us, librarians and educators should develop marketing strategies to ensure the use of online resources such as library training tutorials.

19

Conclusion and recommendations for future studies

Abstract: Our research highlighted the role of metacognitive skills in problem solving and information search, and especially online search. The study was based on the first author's unpublished doctoral dissertation, and in this book it has been expanded and updated. We offered evidence of education students' lack of research skills and individuals' need for skills. Our review of metacognitive scaffolds underscores their success in enhancing students' learning outcomes. Future studies that aim to evaluate the impact of the idea tactics tutorial on individuals' problem solving should consider efforts to minimize differences among the complexity of participants' search topics. This would facilitate an accurate evaluation of the tutorial's impact on problem-solving behaviors.

Key words: search topics, variation, topic development, future, research.

Our research highlighted the importance of providing metacognitive strategies as well as database search skills to education graduate students while problem solving. The study was based on the first author's unpublished doctoral dissertation, and in this book it has been expanded and updated. The study contributes to the research on the use of a metacognitive scaffold to enhance students' problem solving. Providing teacher educators skills that enhances learning increases the likelihood they will impart similar skills to their students.

Throughout this book, we have sought to illustrate the relationship between metacognition and information problem solving. Our research highlighted the role of metacognitive skills in problem solving and information search, and especially online search. Moreover, we offered evidence of education students' lack of research skills and individuals' need for skills. Our review of metacognitive scaffolds underscores their success in enhancing students' learning outcomes. An analysis of students' information problem solving before and after exposure to the idea tactics points to its importance in enhancing individuals' search results.

One of the weaknesses of the present study centered on the variation among participants' search topics in the problem-solving activity. This variation, which included a lack of topic development for some participants, produced search outcomes that differed in the number as well as the relevance of the hits. These differences hindered an accurate assessment of the tutorial's impact on individuals' problem-solving activities. For example, conducting a Boolean search in education-related databases would support topics such as Dwaine's "classroom observation tools for technology integration." On the other hand, topics such as Lesley's "mindfulness and young children," Shelly's "extrinsic versus intrinsic motivation in elementary students," and Kathy's "adult ed and multimedia in distance education" remained more specific and required the development of complex search strategies to yield relevant results. Likewise, Mary's "neurobiological theories of reading" search was broad and seemingly would have benefited from efforts to narrow the topic.

Future studies that aim to evaluate the impact of the idea tactics tutorial on individuals' problem solving should consider efforts to minimize differences among the complexity of participants' search topics. Controlling the search environment by providing all of the participants with an identical topic for the activity and limiting the available databases would reduce the variability of search outcomes. This would facilitate an accurate evaluation of the tutorial's impact on problem-solving behaviors. Still, researchers must weigh the advantages and disadvantages of measuring the tutorial's effectiveness in utilizing identical search topics.

Appendix A: Search ratings

Table A1a Dwaine's first search

Category	Failed	Below average	Average	Above average	Excellent
Relevant			3		
Authoritative				4	
Answered problem			3		
Quality of response		2			

Note: Dwaine's first search: classroom observation tool technology integration (included Education Research Complete). This search produced 13,151 hits.

Table A1b Dwaine's last search

Category	Failed	Below average	Average	Above average	Excellent
Relevant				4	
Authoritative				4	
Answered problem				4	
Quality of response				4	

Note: This search: classroom observation AND technology assessment yielded four results.

Table A2a Lesley's first search

Category	Failed	Below average	Average	Above average	Excellent
Relevant		2			
Authoritative				4	
Answered problem		2			
Quality of response		2			

Note: Mindfulness and young children. She obtained four results.

Table A2b   Lesley's last search

Category	Failed	Below average	Average	Above average	Excellent
Relevant			3		
Authoritative				4	
Answered problem			3		
Quality of response			3		

Note: Mindfulness AND teach* AND elementary*. This search produced seven results.

Table A3a   Kathy's first search

Category	Failed	Below average	Average	Above average	Excellent
Relevant		2			
Authoritative				4	
Answered problem		2			
Quality of response			3		

Note: Adult ed* AND multimedia AND distance (all databases).

Table A3b   Kathy's last search

Category	Failed	Below average	Average	Above average	Excellent
Relevant	1				
Authoritative			3		
Answered problem	1				
Quality of response		2			

Note: Adult ed* AND multimedia AND distance OR delivery systems AND Higher ed* NOT test* NOT Assess* publication date 2001–11, narrowed search with Thesaurus higher ed, distance ed, education technology. This search produced 47 hits. Databases included: Academic Search Premier, Business Source complete, CINAHL, ERIC, PsycINFO, Regional Business News, Education Research Complete, Military & Government Collection, MAS Ultra, Socioindex, Psychology and Behavioral Sciences Collection, Computer Science Index, Professional Development Collection, Library & Information Science and Technology Abstracts, Social Science Abstracts, Women's Studies International, Econlit, Music Index, Communication and Mass Media, Teacher Reference Center, Abstracts in Social Gerontology, International Bibliography of Theatre & Dance, Art Abstracts, PsycARTICLES, Ebook Collection, Human Resources Abstracts, American History and Life, Historical Abstracts, Humanities Abstracts, Philosophers Index.

Table A4a Mary's first searches

Category	Failed	Below average	Average	Above average	Excellent
Relevant		2			
Authoritative			3		
Answered problem		2			
Quality of response		2			

Note: Neurobiological (included PsycINFO). She obtained 13,119 results. Her second search was neurobiological define and it produced nine results. These scores were averaged.

Table A4b Mary's last search

Category	Failed	Below average	Average	Above average	Excellent
Relevant		2			
Authoritative			3		
Answered problem		2			
Quality of response		2			

Note: Theoretical models of reading cognitive (included ERIC). The search yielded 809 hits.

Table A5a Daemon's first searches

Category	Failed	Below average	Average	Above average	Excellent
Relevant			3		
Authoritative			3.5		
Answered problem		2.5			
Quality of response			3		

Note: Jean pieget and learning theories. This search yielded no results. However the database responded with "Did you mean Jean Piaget?" which contained 323 hits. His second pre-tutorial search, jean piaget and cognitive development, produced 88 results. These scores were averaged.

Table A5b Daemon's last search

Category	Failed	Below average	Average	Above average	Excellent
Relevant				4	
Authoritative				4	
Answered problem				4	
Quality of response				4	

Note: Jean piaget AND "developmental psychology" AND introduction (includes Education Research Complete, ERIC, Primary Research, PsycARTICLES, PsycINFO). This search produced 27 hits.

Table A6a Shelly's first search

Category	Failed	Below average	Average	Above average	Excellent
Relevant			3		
Authoritative			3		
Answered problem			3		
Quality of response			3		

Note: Extrinsic vs intrinsic motivation in elementary students. This search produced 4,912 results.

Table A6b Shelly's last search

Category	Failed	Below average	Average	Above average	Excellent
Relevant				4	
Authoritative				4	
Answered problem				4	
Quality of response				4	

Note: Elementary education (SU) AND intrinsic or extrinsic OR grades and motivation (limited to US and publication dates 2009 to 2011). She obtained 33 results.

Appendix B: Scatter plot diagrams and bar graphs

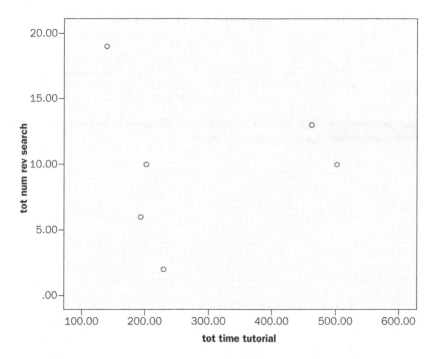

Figure B1 Total time in tutorial had little impact on the number of revised searches performed

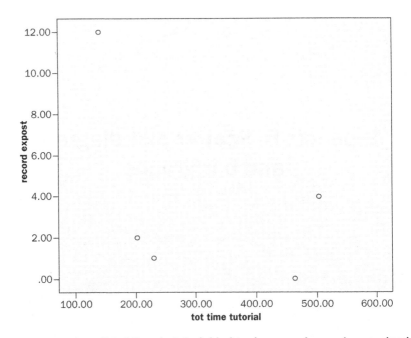

Figure B2   Total time in tutorial led to decreased records examined for most participants

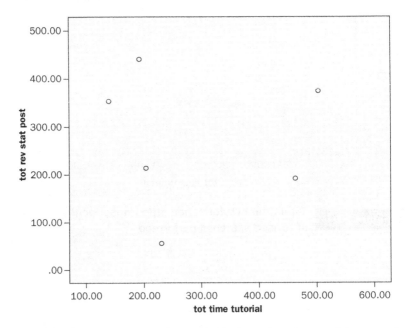

Figure B3   Time spent in tutorial led to more time revising search strategy for half of the participants

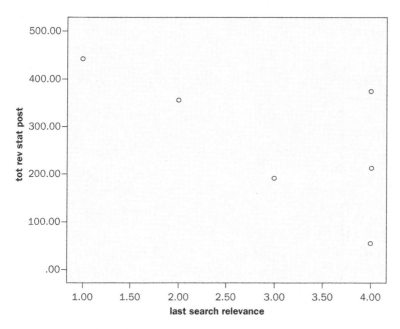

Time spent devising search strategy decreased the relevance of the last search for some participants

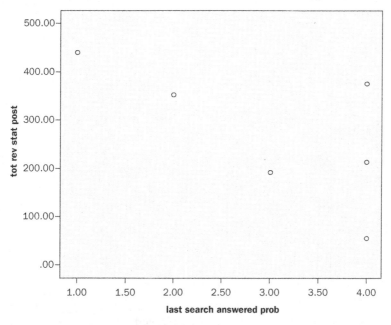

Figure B5 Time spent devising search strategy decreased ability of the last search to answer the problem for half of the participants

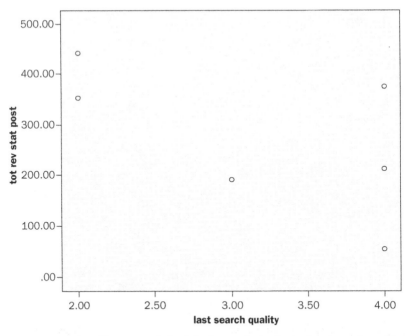

Figure B6 Time spent devising search strategy decreased quality of the last search for half of the participants

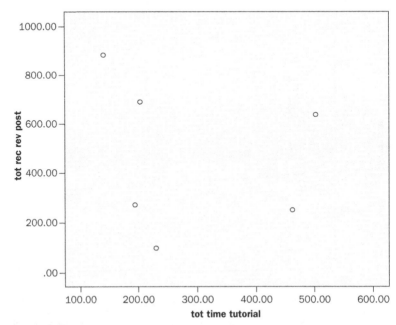

Figure B7 Time in tutorial led to less time reviewing records for half of the participants

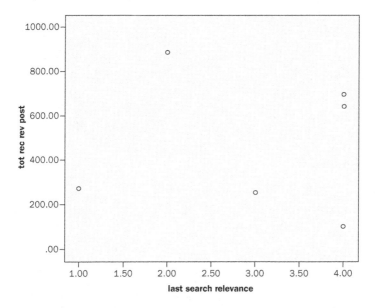

Figure B8   Time spent reviewing results decreased the relevance of the last search for half of the participants

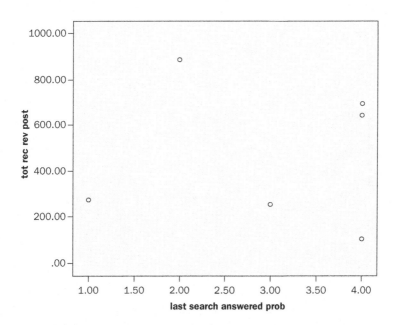

Figure B9   Time spent reviewing results decreased the ability of the last search to answer the problem for half of the participants

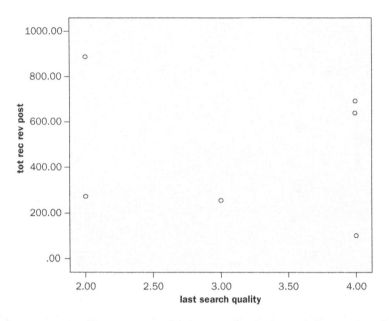

Figure B10 Time spent reviewing results decreased the quality of the last search for half of the participants

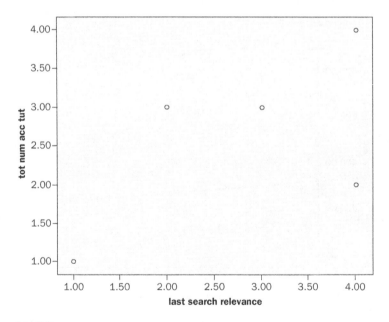

Figure B11 Increased accesses to the tutorial led to higher scores for the relevance of the results for half of the participants

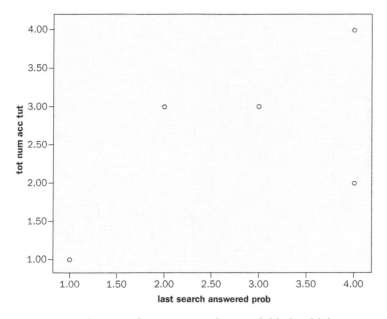

Figure B12 Increased accesses to the tutorial led to higher scores for the ability of the last search to answer the problem for half of the participants

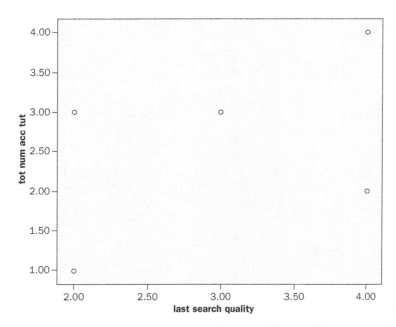

Figure B13 Increased accesses to the tutorial led to higher scores for the quality of the last search for some participants

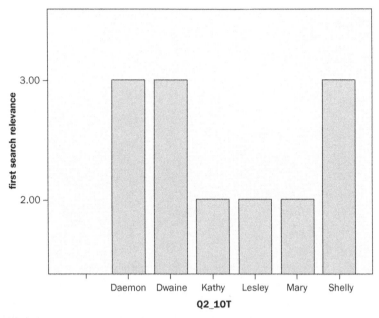

Figure B14 Participants' first search rating for relevance of the results

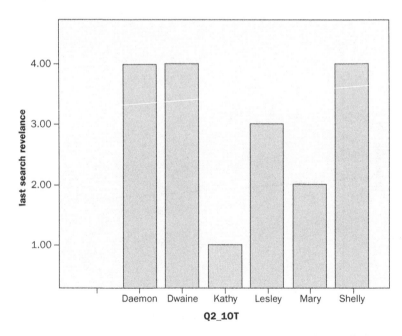

Figure B15 Participants' last search rating for relevance of the results

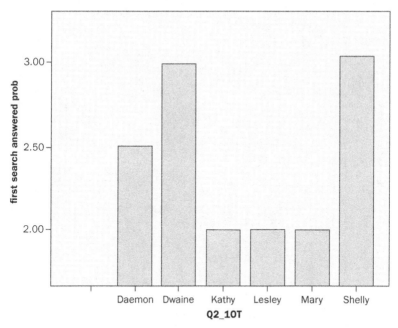

Figure B16 Participants' first search rating for results' ability to answer the problem

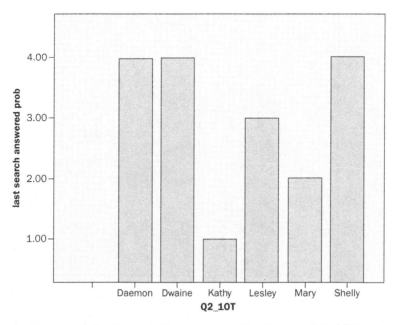

Figure B17 Participants' last search rating for results' ability to answer the problem

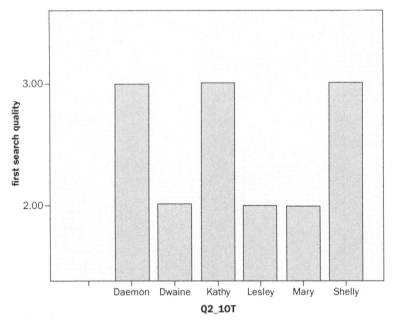

Figure B18 Participants' first search rating for results' quality of the response

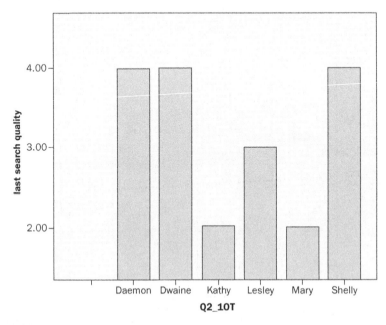

Figure B19 Participants' last search rating for quality of the response

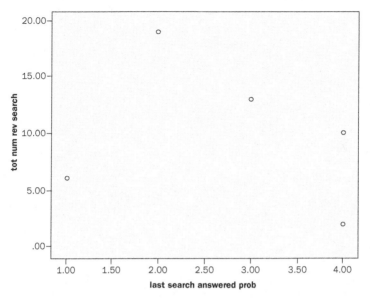

Figure B20 The inverse relationship between the number of revised searches and the ability of the search to answer the problem for some participants

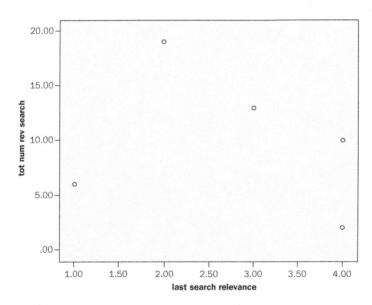

Figure B21 The inverse relationship between the number of revised searches and the relevance of the last search for some participants

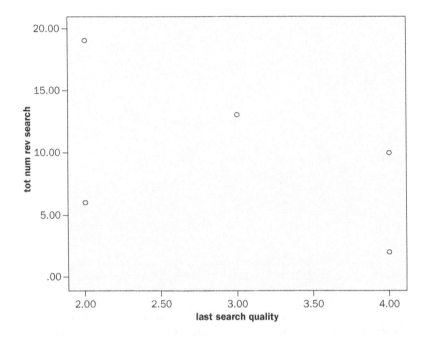

Figure B22 The inverse relationship between the number of revised searches and the quality of the response of the last search for some participants

References

Ahmed, S. M. Z., McKnight, C., & Oppenheim, C. (2006). A user-centred design and evaluation of IR interfaces. *Journal of Librarianship and Information Science, 38*(3), 157–72.

Ahmed, S. M. Z., McKnight, C., & Oppenheim, C. (2009). A review of research on human-computer interfaces for online information retrieval systems. *Electronic Library, 27*(1), 96–116.

Akama, K. & Yamauchi, H. (2004). Task performance and metacognitive experiences in problem-solving. *Psychological Reports, 94*(2), 715–22.

Albion, P. R. (2007). *Student teachers' conference and competence for finding information on the internet.* Paper presented at the 18th International Conference of the Society for Information Technology & Teacher Education (SITE 2007), March 26–30 2007, San Antonio, TX.

Allan, G. (2000). The art of learning with difficulty. *College & Undergraduate Libraries, 6*(2), 5–25.

Annevirta, T. & Vauras, M. (2006). Developmental changes of metacognitive skill in elementary school children. *Journal of Experimental Education, 74*(3), 197–225.

Argelagós, E. & Pifarré, M. (2012). Improving information problem solving skills in secondary education through embedded instruction. *Computers in Human Behavior, 28*(2), 515–26.

Armbruster, B. B., Echols, C. H., & Brown, A. L. (1983). *The Role of Metacognition in Reading to Learn: A Developmental Perspective.* (Reading Education Report No. 40). Illinois University, Urbana Center for the Study of Reading. Cambridge, MA: Bolt, Beranek and Newman, Inc.

Association of College & Research Libraries (1996). *Information literacy competency standards for higher education.* Retrieved November 12, 2013, from *http://www.ala.org/acrl/standards/informationliteracycompetency.*

Avdic, A. & Eklund, A. (2010). Searching reference databases: what students experience and what teachers believe that students experience. *Journal of Librarianship and Information Science, 42*(4), 224–35.

Azevedo, R. (2002). Beyond intelligent tutoring systems: using computers as METAcognitive tools to enhance learning? *Instructional Science, 30*(1), 31–45.

Azevedo, R. (2005). Using hypermedia as a metacognitive tool for enhancing student learning? the role of self-regulated learning. *Educational Psychologist, 40*(4), 199–209.

Azevedo, R., Cromley, J. G., & Seibert, D. (2004). Does adaptive scaffolding facilitate students' ability to regulate their learning with hypermedia? *Contemporary Educational Psychology, 29*(3), 344–70.

Azevedo, R. & Hadwin, A. (2005). Scaffolding self-regulated learning and metacognition – implications for the design of computer-based scaffolds. *Instructional Science, 33*(5), 367–79.

Azevedo, R., Moos, D. C., Johnson, A. M., & Chauncey, A. D. (2010). Measuring cognitive and metacognitive regulatory processes during hypermedia learning: issues and challenges. *Educational Psychologist, 45*(4), 210–23.

Badke, W. (2008). Information literacy meets adult learners. *Online, 32*(4), 48–50.

Bannert, M. (2006). Effects of reflection prompts when learning with hypermedia. *Journal of Educational Computing Research, 35*(4), 359–75.

Bannert, M., Hildebrand, M., & Mengelkamp, C. (2009). Effects of a metacognitive support device in learning environments. *Computers in Human Behavior, 25*(4), 829–35.

Bannert, M. & Reimann, P. (2012). Supporting self-regulated hypermedia learning through prompts. *Instructional Science, 40*(1), 193–211.

Barry, C. L. (1994). User-defined relevance criteria: an exploratory study. *Journal of the American Society for Information Science, 45*(3), 149–59.

Bates, M. J. (1978). The testing of information search tactics. *Proceedings of the ASIS Annual Meeting. 15,* 25–7.

Bates, M. J. (1979). Idea tactics. *Journal of the American Society for Information Science, 30*(5), 280–9.

Bates, M. J. (1979). Information search tactics. *Journal of the American Society for Information Science, 30*(4), 205–14.

Baumann, J. F., Jones, L. A., & Seifert-Kessell, N. (1993). Using think alouds to enhance children's comprehension monitoring abilities. *Reading Teacher, 47*(3), 184.

Bazeley, P. (2006). The contribution of computer software to integrating qualitative and quantitative data and analyses. *Research in the Schools, 13*(1), 64–74.

Beile, P. (2002). *The effect of library instruction learning environments on self-efficacy levels and learning outcomes of graduate students in education.*

Bell, S. J. (2013, June 4th 2013). Rethinking ACRL's information literacy standards: the process begins. Message posted to *http://www.acrl.ala. org/acrlinsider/archives/7329.*

Berardi-Coletta, B., Dominowski, R. L., Buyer, L. S. & Rellinger, E. (1995). Metacognition and problem solving: a process-oriented approach. *Journal of Experimental Psychology. Learning, Memory & Cognition, 21*(1), 205.

Bertland, L. H. (1986). An overview of research on metacognition: implications for information skills instruction. *School Library Media Quarterly, 14*, 96–9.

Bhavnagri, N. P. & Bielat, V. (2005). *Faculty-librarian Collaboration to Teach Research Skills: Electronic Symbiosis*, Taylor & Francis Ltd.

Blummer, B. (2009). Providing library instruction to graduate students: a review of the literature. *Public Services Quarterly, 5*(1), 15–39.

Blummer, B. (2012). *Evaluating the effectiveness of a metacognitive tool on education graduate students' information search behavior in digital libraries* (Unpublished doctoral dissertation). Towson University, Towson, MD.

Blummer, B., Kenton, J. & Song, L. (2010). The design and assessment of a proposed library training unit for education graduate students. *Internet Reference Services Quarterly, 15*(4), 227–42.

Blummer, B., Lohnes, S., & Kenton, J. M. (2012). The research experience for education graduate students: a phenomenographic study. *Internet Reference Services Quarterly, 17*(3–4), 117–46.

Borgman, C. L. (1996). Why are online catalogs still hard to use? *Journal of the American Society for Information Science, 47*(7), 493–503.

Borgman, C. L. (2003). Designing digital libraries for usability. In A. P. Bishop, N. A. Van House & B. P. Buttenfield (eds), *Digital library use* (pp. 85–118). Cambridge, MA: MIT Press.

Bowen, G., Burton, C., Cooper, C., Cruz, L., McFadden, A., Reich, C., & Wargo, M. (2011). Listening to the voices of today's undergraduates: implications for teaching and learning. *Journal of the Scholarship of Teaching & Learning, 11*(3), 21–33.

Bowler, L. (2007). *Methods for Revealing the Metacognitive Knowledge of Adolescent Information Seekers During Information Search Process.*

Unpublished manuscript. Retrieved from *http://www.cais-acsi.ca/proceedings/2007/bowler_2007.pdf*.

Bowler, L. (2010a). The self-regulation of curiosity and interest during the information search process of adolescent students. *Journal of the American Society for Information Science & Technology, 61*(7), 1332–44.

Bowler, L. (2010b). A taxonomy of adolescent metacognitive knowledge during the information search process. *Library & Information Science Research, 32*(1), 27–42.

Brand-Gruwel, S. & Wopereis, I. (2006). Integration of the information problem-solving skill in an educational programme: the effects of learning with authentic tasks-preprint. *Technology, Instruction, Cognition & Learning, 4*(3), 243–63.

Brand-Gruwel, S., Wopereis, I., & Vermetten, Y. (2005). Information problem solving by experts and novices: analysis of a complex cognitive skill. *Computers in Human Behavior, 21*(3), 487–508.

Brand-Gruwel, S., Wopereis, I., & Walraven, A. (2009). A descriptive model of information problem solving while using internet. *Computers & Education, 53*(4), 1207–17.

Bransford, J. D. & Stein, B. S. (1993). *The ideal problem solver*. New York: W. H. Freeman and Company.

Brem, S. K. & Boyes, A. J. (2000). Using Critical Thinking To Conduct Effective Searches of Online Resources. *ERIC Digest* Retrieved from *http://www.eric.ed.gov.proxy-tu.researchport.umd.edu/contentdelivery/servlet/ERICServlet?accno=ED447199*.

Brophy, J. & Bawden, D. (2005). Is google enough? comparison of an internet search engine with academic library resources. *Aslib Proceedings, 57*(6), 498–512.

Brown, A. L. (1977). *Knowing When, Where, and How to Remember: A Problem of Metacognition* (Technical report No. 47). Illinois University, Urbana Center for the Study of Reading. Cambridge, MA: Bolt, Beranek and Newman, Inc.

Brown, A. L. (1987). Metacognition, executive, self-regulation and other more mysterious mechanisms. In F. E. Weinert & R. H. Kluwe (eds), *Metacognition, motivation, and understanding* (pp. 65–116). Hillsdale, NJ: Lawrence Erlbaum Associates.

Brown, A. L. (1997). Transforming schools into communities of thinking and learning about serious matters. *American Psychologist, 52*(4), 399–413.

Brown, A. L. & Bransford, J. (1982). *Learning, Remembering, and Understanding* (Technical report No. 244). Illinois University, Urbana

Center for the Study of Reading. Cambridge, MA: Bolt, Beranek and Newman, Inc.

Brown, A. L. & DeLoache, J. S. (1977). *Skills, plans, and self-regulation.* (Technical report No. 48). Illinois Univ, Urbana Center for the Study of Reading. Cambridge, MA: Bolt, Beranek and Newman, Inc.

Brown, B. & University of Montana. (January 2012). *Improving bibliographic database search results.* Retrieved from *http://www.lib. umt.edu/files/ImprovingBibliDatabSearchRes.pdf.*

Brumfield, E. J. (2008). Using online tutorials to reduce uncertainty in information seeking behavior. *Journal of Library Administration, 48*(3), 365–77.

Bullock, S. M. (2013). Using digital technologies to support self-directed learning for preservice teacher education. *Curriculum Journal, 24*(1), 103–20.

Cahill, K. (2008). An opportunity, not a crisis: How google is changing the individual and the information profession. *Journal of Library Administration, 47*(1), 67–75.

Campbell, D. T. & Fiske, D. W. (1959). Convergent and discriminant validation by the multitrait-multimethod matrix. *Psychological Bulletin, 56*(2), 81–105.

Campione, J. C. (1987). Metacognition and problem learners. In F. E. Weinert & R. H. Kluwe (eds), *Metacognition, motivation, and understanding* (pp. 117–40). Hillsdale, NJ: Lawrence Erlbaum Associates.

Campione, J. C. & Armbruster, B. B. (1983). *An Analysis of the Outcomes and Implications of Intervention Research* (Technical report no. 283). Illinois University, Urbana Center for the Study of Reading. Cambridge, MA: Bolt, Beranek and Newman, Inc.

Case, D. (2002). *Looking for Information A Survey of Research on Information Seeking, Needs, and Behavior.* New York: Academic Press.

Case, J. & Gunstone, R. (2002). Metacognitive development as a shift in approach to learning: an in-depth study. *Studies in Higher Education, 27*(4), 459–70.

Catalano, A. J. (2010). Using ACRL standards to assess the information literacy of graduate students in an education program. *Evidence Based Library & Information Practice, 5*(4), 21–38.

Chase, W. G. & Ericsson, K. A. (1981). Skilled memory. In J. R. Anderson (ed.), *Cognitive Skills and their Acquisition* (pp. 141–89). Hillsdale, NJ: Lawrence Erlbaum Associates.

Chase, W. G. & Simon, H. A. (1973). Perception in chess. *Cognitive Psychology, 4*(1), 55–81.

Chen, C. (2010). Promoting college students' knowledge acquisition and ill-structured problem solving: web-based integration and procedure prompts. *Computers & Education, 55*(1), 292–303.

Chen, C. & Ge, X. (2006). The design of a web-based cognitive modeling system to support ill-structured problem solving. *British Journal of Educational Technology, 37*(2), 299–302.

Chi, M. T., Bassok, M., Lewis, M. W., Reimann, P., & Glaser, R. (1989). Self-explanations: How students study and use examples in learning to solve problems. *Cognitive Science, 13*(2), 145–82.

Chi, M. T. H. (1978). Knowledge structures and memory development. In R. S. Siegler (ed.) (pp. 73–96). Hillsdale, NJ England: Lawrence Erlbaum Associates, Inc.

Chi, M. T. H., Glaser, R., & Res, E. (1982). Expertise in problem solving. In R. J. Sternberg (ed.), *Advances in the psychology of human intelligence vol. 1* (pp. 7–73). Hillsdale, NJ: Erlbaum.

Chowdhury, S., Gibb, F., & Landoni, M. (2011). Uncertainty in information seeking and retrieval: a study in an academic environment. *Information Processing & Management, 47*(2), 157–75.

Christensen, J., Morgan, F., & Kinikin, J. (2013). An online information skills tutorial. *School Library Monthly, 29*(5), 8–10.

Chu, S. K. & Law, N. (2007). Development of information search expertise: postgraduates' knowledge of searching skills. *Portal: Libraries and the Academy, 7*(3), 295–316.

Chu, S. K. & Law, N. (2007). Development of information search expertise: research students' knowledge of source types. *Journal of Librarianship and Information Science, 39*(1), 27–40.

Chung, J. S. & Neuman, D. (2007). High school students' information seeking and use for class projects. *Journal of the American Society for Information Science & Technology, 58*(10), 1503–17.

Clarebout, G., Elen, J., Johnson, W. L., & Shaw, E. (2002). Animated pedagogical agents: an opportunity to be grasped? *Journal of Educational Multimedia and Hypermedia, 11*(3), 267–86.

Clayton, V. & Nordstrom V. (1987) Bibliographic instruction for graduate students in an educational research seminar. *Education Libraries, 12*(2), 51–3.

Coiro, J. (2011). Talking about reading as thinking: modeling the hidden complexities of online reading comprehension. *Theory into Practice, 50*(2), 107–15.

Colaric, S. M., Fine, B., & Hofmann, W. (2004). *Pre-service Teachers and Search Engines: Prior Knowledge and Instructional Implications*, draft manuscript.

Cole, C. (2001). Intelligent information retrieval: Part IV. testing the timing of two information retrieval devices in a naturalistic setting. *Information Processing & Management, 37*(1), 163.

Connell, T. H. (1995). Subject searching in online catalogs: metaknowledge used by experienced searchers. *Journal of the American Society for Information Science, 46*(7), 506–18.

Cooke, N. A. (2010). Becoming an andragogical librarian: using library instruction as a tool to combat library anxiety and empower adult learners. *New Review of Academic Librarianship*, 16(2), 208–27.

Cook-Cottone, C., Dutt-Doner, K., & Schoen, D. (2005). Understanding student article retrieval behaviors: instructional implications. *Research Strategies, 20*(4), 379–88.

Cool, C. & Xie, H. How can IR help mechanisms be more helpful to users? *Proceedings of the 67th ASIS&T Annual Meeting, 41*, pp. 249–55.

Corbus, L., Dent, V. F., & Ondrusek, A. (2005). How twenty-eight users helped redesign an academic library website: a usability study. *Reference & User Services Quarterly, 44*(3), 232–46.

Cottrell, J. R. & Eisenberg, M. B. (2001). Applying an information problem-solving model to academic reference work: findings and implications. *College & Research Libraries, 62*(4), 334–47.

Coutinho, S., Wiemer-Hastings, K., Skowronski, J. J., & Britt, M. A. (2005). Metacognition, need for cognition and use of explanations during ongoing learning and problem solving. *Learning & Individual Differences, 15*(4), 321–37.

Creswell, J. W. (2007). *Qualitative Inquiry and Research Design: Choosing Among Five Approaches*. Thousand Oaks, CA: Sage Publications.

Creswell, J. W. (2009). *Research Design: Qualitative, Quantitative, and Mixed Methods Approaches* (3rd ed.). Thousand Oaks, CA: Sage Publications.

Creswell, J. W. & Miller, D. L. (2000). Determining validity in qualitative inquiry. *Theory into Practice, 39*(3), 124.

Creswell, J. W., Plano, Clark, V. L., Gutmann, M. L., & Hanson, W. E. (2003). Advanced mixed methods research designs. In A. Tashakkori & C. Teddlie (eds), *Handbook of mixed methods in social & behavioral research* (pp. 209–40). Thousand Oaks, CA: Sage Publications.

Cronbach, L. J. (1975). Beyond the two disciplines of scientific psychology. *American Psychologist, 30*(2), 116–27.

Currie, L., Devlin, F., Emde, J., & Graves, K. (2010). Undergraduate search strategies and evaluation criteria: Searching for credible sources. *New Library World, 111*(3), 113–24.

Dalrymple, P. W. (2001). A quarter century of user-centered study: the impact of Zweizig and Dervin on Library Information Science research. *Library and Information Science Research, 23*(2), 155–65.

Davis, E. A. (2000). Scaffolding students' knowledge integration: Prompts for reflection in KIE. *International Journal of Science Education, 22*(8), 819–37.

Davis, E. A. (2003). Prompting middle school science students for productive reflection: Generic and directed prompts. *Journal of the Learning Sciences, 12*(1), 91–142.

de Vries, B., van, der Meij. H, & Lazonder, A. W. (2008). Supporting reflective web searching in elementary schools. *Computers in Human Behavior, 24*(3), 649–65.

Debowski, S. (2001). Wrong way: Go back! an exploration of novice search behaviours while conducting an information search. *Electronic Library, 19*(6), 371–82.

Deitering, A. & Gronemyer, K. (2011). Beyond peer-reviewed articles: Using blogs to enrich students' understanding of scholarly work. *Portal: Libraries and the Academy, 11*(1), 489–503.

Deleo, P. A., Eichenholtz, S., & Sosin, A. A. (2009). Bridging the information literacy gap with clickers. *Journal of Academic Librarianship, 35*(5), 438–44.

Denison, D. R. & Montgomery, D. (2012). Annoyance or delight? college students' perspectives on looking for information. *Journal of Academic Librarianship, 38*(6), 380–90.

Dervin, B. (1977). Useful theory for librarianship: Communication, not information. *Drexel Library Quarterly, 13*(3), 16–32.

Dervin, B. (1983). An overview of sense-making research: concepts, methods and results. Paper presented at the Annual Meeting of the International Communication Association, Dallas, TX.

Dervin, B. (1992). From the mind's eye of the user: the sense-making methodology. In J. D. Glazier & R. Powell (eds), *Qualitative research in information management* (pp. 61–82). Englewood, CO: Libraries Unlimited.

Dervin, B. & Foreman-Wernet, L. (2013). Sense-making methodology as an approach to understanding and designing for campaign audiences: a turn to communicating communicatively. In: R. Rice & C. K. Atkin (eds), *Public communication campaigns* (pp. 147–62). Thousand Oaks, CA: Sage Publications.

Dervin, B. & Naumer, C. M. (2009). Sense-making. In S. W. Littlejohn & K. A. Foss (eds), *Encyclopedia of Communication Theory*, Volume 2 (pp. 876–80). Thousand Oaks, CA: Sage Publications, Inc.

Dervin, B. & Naumer, C. M. (2010). Sense-making. In M. Bates (ed.), *Encyclopedia of Library and Information Sciences* (3rd ed.) (pp. 4696–4707). London: Taylor & Francis.

Dervin, B. & Nilan, M. (1986). Information needs and uses. *Annual Review of Information Science and Technology 2*, 3–33.

Dervin, B. & Shields, P. (2011). Disciplining communication: invention, resistance, the dialectic struggle, and its paradoxes. In F. Deppe, W. Meixner, & G. Pallaver (eds), *Widerworte: Philosophie politik kommunikation* (pp. 51–61). Innsbruck: Innsbruck University Press.

Diekema, A. R.: Holliday, W., & Leary, H. (2011). Re-framing information literacy: problem-based learning as informed learning. *Library & Information Science Research, 33*(4), 261–8.

Doganay, A. & Demir, O. (2011). Comparison of the level of using metacognitive strategies during study between high achieving and low achieving prospective teachers. *Educational Sciences: Theory and Practice, 11*(4), 2036–43.

Doolittle, P. E., Hicks, D., Triplett, C. F., Nichols, W. D., & Young, C. A. (2006). Reciprocal teaching for reading comprehension in higher education: a strategy for fostering the deeper understanding of texts. *International Journal of Teaching and Learning in Higher Education, 17*(2), 106–18.

Du, J. T. & Evans, N. (2011). Academic users' information searching on research topics: characteristics of research tasks and search strategies. *Journal of Academic Librarianship, 37*(4), 299–306.

Dutt-Doner, K., Allen, S. M., & Corcoran, D. (2005). Transforming student learning by preparing the next generation of teachers for type II technology integration. *Computers in the Schools, 22*(3), 63–75.

Earp, V. J. (2008). Information source preferences of education graduate students. *Behavioral & Social Sciences Librarian, 27*(2), 73–91.

Efklides, A. (2001). Metacognitive experiences in problem solving: metacognition, motivation, and self-regulation. In A. Efklides, J. Kuhl, & R. M. Sorrentino (eds), Trends and prospects in motivation research (pp. 297–323). Dordrecht Netherlands: Kluwer Academic Publishers.

Eisenberg, M. & Berkowitz, B. (1988). Library and information skills curriculum scope and sequence: the big six skills. *School Library Media Activities Monthly, 5*(1), 26–8, 45, 50–1.

Eisenberg, M. B. & Berkowitz, R. E. (1993). *Curriculum Initiative: An Agenda and Strategy for Library Media Programs*. Norwood, NJ: Abex Publishing Corporation.

Eisenberg, M. B. & Berkowitz, R. E. (1990). *Information Problem Solving: The Big Six Skills Approach to Library and Information Skills Instruction*. Norwood, NJ: Ablex Pub. Corp.

Eisenberg, M. B., & Berkowitz, R. E. (1999). *Teaching Information and Technology Skills: The Big 6 in Elementary School*. Worthington, OH: Linworth Publishers.

Eisenberg, M., Johnson, D., & Berkowitz, B. (2010). Information, communications, and technology (ICT) skills curriculum based on the Big6 skills approach to information problem-solving. *Library Media Connection, 28*(6), 24–7.

Ellis, D., Cox, D., & Hall, K. (1993). A comparison of the information seeking patterns of researchers in the physical and social sciences. *Journal of Documentation, 49*(4), 356–69.

Ellis, D. (1989). A behavioural approach to information retrieval system design. *Journal of Documentation, 45*(3), 171–212.

Ellis, D. & Haugan, M. (1997). Modelling the information seeking patterns of engineers and research scientists in an industrial environment. *Journal of Documentation, 53*(4), 384–403.

Englert, C. S., Raphael, T. E., Fear, K. L., & Anderson, L. M. (1988). Students' metacognitive knowledge about how to write informational texts. *Learning Disability Quarterly, 11*(1), 18–46.

Englert, C. S. & Raphael, T. E. (1988). Constructing well-formed prose: Process, structure, and metacognitive knowledge. *Exceptional Children, 54*(6), 513–20.

Erbas, A. & Okur, S. (2012). Researching students' strategies, episodes, and metacognitions in mathematical problem solving. *Quality & Quantity, 46*(1), 89–102.

Ercegovac, Z. (1989). Augmented assistance in online catalog subject searching. *Reference Librarian, 10*(23), 21–40.

Ericsson, K. A. & Simon, H. (1984). *Protocol analysis verbal reports as data*. Cambridge, MA: MIT Press.

Evans, J. E. (1986). Information resources, perspectives and strategies for graduate educational research: a course proposal. (Report No. IR051945). East Lansing, MI: National Center for Research on Teacher Learning (ERIC Document Reproduction Service No. ED 82578).

Fabiano, E. (1996). Casting the 'net: reaching out to doctoral students in education. *Research Strategies, 14*(3), 159–68.

Farmer, L. S. J. (2007). Learner-centered assessment of information literacy. *Educational Media & Technology Yearbook, 32*, 76–87.

Fisher, D., Frey, N., & Lapp, D. (2011). Coaching middle-level teachers to think aloud improves comprehension instruction and student reading achievement. *Teacher Educator, 46*(3), 231–43.

Flavell, J. H. (1971). First discussant's comments: what is memory development the development of? *Human Development, 14*, 272–8.

Flavell, J. H. (1976). Metacognitive aspects of problem solving. In L. B. Resnick (ed.), *The Nature of Intelligence* (pp. 231–6). New York: John Wiley & Sons.

Flavell, J. H. (1977). *Cognitive Development.* Englewood Cliffs, NJ: Prentice-Hall.

Flavell, J. H. (1978). Metacognitive development. In J. M. Scandura & C. J. Brainerd (eds), *Structural/Process Models of Complex Human Behavior* (pp. 213–45). Alphen aan den Rijn, The Netherlands: Sijthoff & Noordhoff.

Flavell, J. H. (1979). Metacognition and cognitive monitoring: a new area of cognitive-developmental inquiry. *American Psychologist, 34*(10), 906–11.

Flavell, J. H. (1981). Cognitive monitoring. In W. P. Dickson (ed.), *Children's Oral Communication Skills* (pp. 35–59). New York: Academic Press.

Flavell, J. H. & Wellman, H. M. (1977). Metamemory. *Perspectives on the development of memory and cognition.* (pp. 3–34). Hillsdale, N. J.: Lawrence Erlbaum Associates.

Franklin, G. & Toifel, R. C. (1994). The effects of BI on library knowledge and skills among education students. *Research Strategies, 12*(4), 224–37.

Frensch, P. A. & Sternberg, R. A. (1989). Expertise and intelligent thinking: when is it worse to know better? In R. Sternberg (ed.), *Advances in the psychology of human intelligence* (pp. 157–88). Hillsdale, NJ: Lawrence Erlbaum.

Fukumoto, T. & Kishi, Y. (2007). Proposal of thinking process model based on putting a question to oneself for problem solving by skilled engineers. *Journal of Nuclear Science and Technology, 44*(7), 997–1006.

Gagnière, L., Betrancourt, M., & Détienne, F. (2012). When metacognitive prompts help information search in collaborative setting. *European Review of Applied Psychology / Revue Européenne De Psychologie Appliquée, 62*(2), 73–81.

Gazda, R. B. (2005). An investigation of learner navigation in an instructional hypermedia program. *Dissertation Abstracts International Section A: Humanities and Social Sciences, 66*(3).

Ge, X., Chen, C., & Davis, K. A. (2005). Scaffolding novice instructional designers' problem-solving processes using question prompts in a web-based learning environment. *Journal of Educational Computing Research, 33*(2), 219–48.

Ge, X. & Land, S. M. (2003). Scaffolding students' problem-solving processes on an ill-structured task using question prompts and peer interactions. *Educational Technology Research & Development, 51*(1), 21–38.

Ge, X. & Land, S. M. (2004). A conceptual framework for scaffolding ill-structured problem-solving processes using question prompts and peer interactions. *Educational Technology Research & Development, 52*(2), 5–22.

Georgas, H. (2013). Google vs. the library: Student preferences and perceptions when doing research using google and a federated search tool. *Portal: Libraries and the Academy, 13*(2), 165–85.

George, C. A. (2008). *Lessons learned: Usability testing a federated search product Electronic Library, 26*(1), 5–20.

George, C., Bright, A., Hurlbert, T., Linke, E. C., St. Clair, G., & Stein, J. (2006). Scholarly use of information: Graduate students' information seeking behaviour. *Information Research, 11*(4).

Gibbs, G. R. (2007). Analyzing qualitative data. In U. Flick (ed.), *The sage qualitative research kit*. London: Sage.

Glaser, B. G. & Strauss, A. L. (1967). *The discovery of grounded theory: Strategies for qualitative research*. New York: Aldine Publishing Co.

Glaser, R. (1985). *Thoughts on expertise* (Technical No. 8). University of Pittsburgh, Learning Research and Development Center. Arlington, VA: Office of Naval Research.

Glaser, R. (1976). Components of a psychology of instruction: Toward a science of design. *Review of Educational Research, 46*(1), 1–24.

Godbold, N. (2006). Beyond information seeking: towards a general model of information behaviour. *Information Research, 11*(4).

Goodin, S. (2004). Libraries and secondary literacy – the missing link. *CSLA Journal, 27*(2), 13–14.

Goodwin, S. (2005). Using screen capture software for web site usability and redesign buy-in. *Library Hi Tech, 23*(4), 610–21.

Gorrell, G., Eaglestone, B., Ford, N., Holdridge, P., & Madden, A. (2009). Towards "metacognitively" aware IR systems: an initial user study. *Journal of Documentation, 65*(3).

Grafstein, A. (2002). A discipline-based approach to information literacy. *Journal of Academic Librarianship, 28*(4), 197.

Grant, M. & Berg, M. (2003). Information literacy integration in a doctoral program. *Behavioral & Social Sciences Librarian, 22*(1), 115–28.

Green, R. & Bowser, M. (2002). Managing thesis anxiety: a faculty-librarian partnership to guide off-campus graduate education students through the thesis process. *Journal of Library Administration, 37*(3), 341.

Green, R. & Macauley, P. (2007). Doctoral students' engagement with information: an American-Australian perspective. *Portal: Libraries and the Academy, 7*(3), 317–32.

Greene, J. A. & Azevedo, R. (2009). A macro-level analysis of SRL processes and their relations to the acquisition of a sophisticated mental model of a complex system. *Contemporary Educational Psychology, 34*(1), 18–29.

Gross, M. (2005). The impact of low-level skills on information-seeking behavior. *Reference & User Services Quarterly, 45*(2), 155–62.

Guba, E. G. & Lincoln, Y. S. (1994). Competing paradigms in qualitative research. In N. K. Denzin & Y. S. Lincoln (eds), *Handbook of Qualitative Research* (pp. 105–17). Thousand Oaks, CA: Sage Publications, Inc.

Guthrie, J. T., Britten, T., & Barker, K. G. (1991). Roles of document structure, cognitive strategy, and awareness in searching for information. *Reading Research Quarterly, 26*(3), 300–24.

Hacker, D. J. & Dunlosky, J. (2003). Not all metacognition is created equal. *New Directions for Teaching & Learning, (95)*, 73–9.

Hadwin, A. F., Wozney, L., & Pontin, O. (2005). Scaffolding the appropriation of self-regulatory activity: a socio-cultural analysis of changes in teacher-student discourse about a graduate research portfolio. *Instructional Science, 33*, 413–50.

Hamilton, B. (2010, October 29). Assessment and metacognition: blogging research reflections. Retrieved from *http://theunquietlibrarian. wordpress.com/2010/10/29/assessment-and-metacognition-blogging-research-reflections.*

Hannafin, M. J., Hall, C., Land, S., & Hill, J. (1994). Learning in open-ended environments: assumptions, methods, and implications. *Educational Technology, 34*(8), 48–55.

Hannafin, M., Land, S., & Oliver, K. (1999). Open learning environments: foundation, methods, and models. In C. M. Reigeluth (ed.), *Instructional-design Theories and Models: A New Paradigm of*

Instructional Theory, volume II (pp. 115–40). Mahwah, NJ US: Lawrence Erlbaum Associates Publishers.

Harter, S. P. (1992). Psychological relevance and information science. *Journal of the American Society for Information Science, 43*(9), 602–15.

Head, A. J. & Eisenberg, M. B. (2009). *Lessons Learned: How College Students Seek Information in the Digital Age*. (Project Information Literacy Progress Report) Retrieved from *http://projectinfolit.org/pdfs/ PIL_Fall2009_Year1Report_12_2009.pdf*.

Hess, B. (1999). Graduate student cognition during information retrieval using the world wide web: a pilot study. *Computers & Education, 33*(1), 1–13.

Hilbe, J. M. (2004). A review of SPSS 12.01, part 2. *American Statistician, 58*(2), 168–71.

Hilbe, J. M. (2003). A review of current SPSS products: SPSS 12, SigmaPlot 8.02, SigmaStat 3.0, part 1. *American Statistician, 57*(4), 310.

Hill, J. R. (1995). *Cognitive Strategies and the Use of a Hypermedia System: An Exploratory Study*. Dissertation Abstracts International Section A: Humanities and Social Sciences, 56 (7-A), 2648.

Hill, J. R. (1999). A conceptual framework for understanding information seeking in open-ended information systems. *Educational Technology Research and Development, 47*(1), 5–27.

Hill, J. R. & Hannafin, M. J. (1997). Cognitive strategies and learning from the world wide web. *Educational Technology Research and Development, 45*(4), 37–64.

Hoepfl, M. C. (1997). Choosing qualitative research: a primer for technology education researchers. *Journal of Technology Education, 9*(1), 47–63.

Holman, L. (2011). Millennial students' mental models of search: implications for academic librarians and database developers. *Journal of Academic Librarianship, 37*(1), 19–27.

Hooks, J. D. & Corbett, F. (2005). Information literacy for off-campus graduate cohorts: collaboration between a university librarian and a master's of education faculty. *Library Review, 54*(4), 245–56.

Hoover, D. G. & Clayton, V. (1989). Graduate bibliographic instruction in ERIC on CD-ROM. *Behavioral & Social Sciences Librarian, 8*(1–2), 1–12.

Hoppmann, T. K. (2009). Examining the 'point of frustration': the think-aloud method applied to online search tasks. *Quality & Quantity, 43*(2), 211–24.

Howard, D. L. (1994). Pertinence as reflected in personal constructs. *Journal of the American Society for Information Science, 45*(3), 172–85.

Huttenlock, T. L. (2008). Use of an advance organizer in the ill-structured problem domain of information seeking: a comparative case study. *Dissertation Abstracts International Section A: Humanities and Social Sciences, 69* (2-A), 578.

Ifenthaler, D. (2012). Determining the effectiveness of prompts for self-regulated learning in problem-solving scenarios. *Journal of Educational Technology & Society, 15*(1), 38–52.

Israel, S. E. & Massey, D. (2005). Metacognitive think-alouds: Using a gradual release model with middle school students. In S. E. Israel, C. C. Block, K. L. Bauserman & K. Kinnucan-Welsch (eds), *Metacognition in literacy learning: Theory, assessment, instruction, and professional development* (pp. 183–98). Mahwah, NJ US: Lawrence Erlbaum Associates Publishers.

Janes, J. W. (1994). Other people's judgments: a comparison of users' and others' judgments of document relevance, topicality, and utility. *Journal of the American Society for Information Science, 45*(3), 160–71.

Jeffrey, L., Hegarty, B., Kelly, O., Penman, M., Coburn, D., & McDonald, J. (2011). Developing digital information literacy in higher education: obstacles and supports. *Journal of Information Technology Education, 10*, 383–413.

Johnson, R. B. & Onwuegbuzie, A. J. (2004). Mixed methods research: a research paradigm whose time has come. *Educational Researcher, 33*(7), 14–26.

Johnson, R. B., Onwuegbuzie, A. J., & Turner, L., A. (2007). Toward a definition of mixed method research. *Journal of Mixed Methods Research, 1*, 112–33.

Johnston, B. & Webber, S. (2003). Information literacy in higher education: a review and case study. *Studies in Higher Education, 28*(3), 335.

Jonassen, D. H., Carr, C., & Yueh, H. (1998). Computers as mindtools for engaging learners in critical thinking. *Techtrends, 43*(2), 24–32.

Katopol, P. F. (2012). Information anxiety and African-American students in a graduate education program. *Education Libraries, 35*(1–2), 5–14.

Kauffman, D. F., Ge, X., Xie, K., & Chen, C. (2008). Prompting in web-based environments: supporting self-monitoring and problem solving skills in college students. *Journal of Educational Computing Research, 38*(2), 115–37.

Kayongo, J. & Helm, C. (2010). Graduate students and the library: a survey of research practices and library use at the University of Notre Dame. *Reference & User Services Quarterly, 49*(4), 341–9.

Kiliç-Çakmak, E. (2010). Learning strategies and motivational factors predicting information literacy self-efficacy of E-learners. *Australasian Journal of Educational Technology, 26*(2), 192–208.

Kim, K. & Allen, B. (2002). Cognitive and task influences on web searching behavior. *Journal of the American Society for Information Science and Technology, 53*(2), 109–19.

King, P. M., & Kitchener, K. S. (1994). *Developing Reflective Judgement: Understanding and Promoting Intellectual Growth and Critical Thinking in Adolescents and Adults*. San Francisco: Jossey-Bass Inc., Pub.

King, R. (2011). Metacognition, information literacy, and web 2.0 as a instructional tool. *Currents in Teaching and Learning, 3*(2), 22–32.

Kitchener, K. S., & King, P. M. (1981). Reflective judgement: concepts of justification and their relationship to age and education. *Journal of Applied Developmental Psychology, 2*(2), 89–116.

Klein, S. T. (2009). On the use of negation in boolean IR queries. *Information Processing & Management, 45*(2), 298–311.

Korobili, S., Malliari, A., & Zapounidou, S. (2011). Factors that influence information-seeking behavior: the case of Greek graduate students. *Journal of Academic Librarianship, 37*(2), 155–65.

Kracker, J. (2002). Research anxiety and students' perceptions of research: an experiment. part I. effect of teaching Kuhlthau's ISP model. *Journal of the American Society for Information Science & Technology, 53*(4), 282–94.

Kramarski, B. & Michalsky, T. (2010). Preparing preservice teachers for self-regulated learning in the context of technological pedagogical content knowledge. *Learning and Instruction, 20*(5), 434–47.

Ku, K. Y. L., & Ho, I. T. (2010). Metacognitive strategies that enhance critical thinking. *Metacognition and Learning, 5*(3), 251–67.

Kuhlthau, C. C. (1991). Inside the search process: information seeking from the user's perspective. *Journal of the American Society for Information Science, 42*(5), 361–71.

Kuhlthau, C. C. (1993). A principle of uncertainty for information seeking. *Journal of Documentation, 49*(4), 339–55.

Kuhlthau, C. C. (1999). Accommodating the user's information search process: challenges for information retrieval system. *Bulletin of the American Society for Information Science & Technology, 25*(3), 12.

Kuhlthau, C. C. (2004). *Seeking Meaning: A Process Approach to Library and Information Services* (2nd ed.). Westport, CN: Libraries Unlimited.

Kuhlthau, C. C., Heinström, J., & Todd, R. J. (2008). The "information search process" revisited: is the model still useful? *Information Research, 13*(4).

Land, S. M. & Greene, B. A. (2000). Project-based learning with the world wide web: a qualitative study of resource integration. *Educational Technology Research and Development, 48*(1), 45–67.

Langford, L. (2001). CRITICAL LITERACY: a building block towards the information literate school community. *Teacher Librarian, 28*(5), 18.

Laverty, C., Reed, B., & Lee, E. (2008). The "I'm feeling lucky syndrome": teacher-candidates' knowledge of web searching strategies. *Partnership: The Canadian Journal of Library & Information Practice & Research, 3*(1), 1–19.

Laxman, K. (2010). A conceptual framework mapping the application of information search strategies to well and ill-structured problem solving. *Computers & Education, 55*(2), 513–26.

Lazonder, A. W. & Rouet, J. (2008). Information problem solving instruction: Some cognitive and metacognitive issues. *Computers in Human Behavior, 24*(3), 753–65.

LeBaron, J. F., Gibson, J. T., Burke, D. M., & Scollin, P. A. (1998). How educators find resources on the internet: a discussion of independent search behaviors by graduate education students. *Internet and Higher Education, 1*(3), 191–201.

LeCompte, M. D. & Goetz, J. P. (1982). Problems of reliability and validity in ethnographic research. *Review of Educational Research, 52*(1), 31–60.

Lee, C. B., Teo, T., & Bergin, D. (2009). Children's use of metacognition in solving everyday problems: an initial study from an Asian context. *Australian Educational Researcher, 36*(3), 89–102.

Lee, J. Y., Paik, W., & Joo, S. (2012). Information resource selection of undergraduate students in academic search tasks. *Information Research: An International Electronic Journal, 17*(1).

Lee, Y. & Wu, J. (2013). The indirect effects of online social entertainment and information seeking activities on reading literacy. *Computers & Education, 67*, 168–77.

Leech, N. L. & Onwuegbuzie, A. J. (2009). A typology of mixed methods research designs. *Quality & Quantity, 43*(2), 265–75.

Lesley, M., Watson, P., & Elliot, S. (2007). "School" reading and multiple texts: examining the metacognitive development of secondary-level preservice teachers. *Journal of Adolescent & Adult Literacy, 51*(2), 150–62.

Libutti, P. (1991). Library support for graduate education research and teaching East Lansing, MI: National Center for Research on Teacher Learning (ERIC Document Reproduction Service No. ED 349007).

Lin, X. (2001). Designing metacognitive activities. *Educational Technology Research and Development, 49*(2), 23–40.

Lin, X. & Lehman, J. D. (1999). Supporting learning of variable control in a computer-based biology environment: effects of prompting college students to reflect on their own thinking. *Journal of Research in Science Teaching, 36*(7), 838–58.

Lincoln, Y. S. & Guba, E. G. (1985). *Naturalistic inquiry.* Beverly Hills, CA: Sage Publications.

Luconi, F. & Tabatabai, D. (1999). *Searching the Web: Expert-novice Differences in a Problem Solving Context.* Paper presented at the Annual Meeting of the American Educational Research Association, Montreal, QC, Canada.

Madden, A. D., Ford, N., Gorrell, G., Eaglestone, B., & Holdridge, P. (2012). Metacognition and web credibility. *Electronic Library, 30*(5), 671–89.

Maier, N. R. F. (1933). An aspect of human reasoning. *British Journal of Psychology, 24,* 144–55.

Malliari, A., Korobili, S., & Zapounidou, S. (2011). Exploring the information seeking behavior of Greek graduate students: a case study set in the University of Macedonia. *International Information & Library Review, 43*(2), 79–91.

Mansourian, Y. (2008). Keeping a learning diary to enhance researchers' understanding of and users' skills in web searching. *Library Review, 57*(9), 690–9.

Marchionini, G. (1995). *Information Seeking in Electronic Environments.* Cambridge, UK: Cambridge University Press.

Marchionini, G. & Liebscher, P. (1991). Performance in electronic encyclopedias: implications for adaptive systems. In J. Griffiths (ed.), *Proceedings of the 54th Annual Meeting the American Society for Information Society* (pp. 39–48). Medford, NJ: Learned Information, Inc.

Markauskaite, L. (2007). Exploring the structure of trainee teachers' ICT literacy: the main components of, and relationships between, general cognitive and technical capabilities. *Educational Technology Research and Development, 55*(6), 547–72.

Markey, K. (2007). Twenty-five years of end-user searching, part 1: research findings. *Journal of the American Society for Information Science & Technology, 58*(8), 1071–81.

Markman, E. (1981). Comprehension monitoring. In W. P. Dickson (ed.), *Children's Oral Communication Skills* (pp. 61–83). New York: Academic Press.

Markman, E. M. (1977). Realizing that you don't understand: a preliminary investigation. *Child Development, 48*(3), 986–92.

Marks, D. (2009). Literacy, instruction, and technology: meeting millennials on their own turf. *AACE Journal, 17*(4), 363–77.

Martin, J. L. (2013). *Learning from Recent British Information Literacy Models: A Report to ACRL's Information Literacy Competency Standards for Higher Education Task Force.* Unpublished manuscript. Retrieved from *http://mavdisk.mnsu.edu/martij2/acrl.pdf.*

Mason, L., Boldrin, A., & Ariasi, N. (2010). Searching the web to learn about a controversial topic: are students epistemically active? *Instructional Science, 38*(6), 607–33.

Masui, C. & De Corte, E. (1999). Enhancing learning and problem solving skills: orienting and self-judging, two powerful and trainable learning tools. *Learning and Instruction, 9*(6), 517–42.

Mayer, R. E. (1998). Cognitive, metacognitive, and motivational aspects of problem solving. *Instructional Science, 26*(1–2), 49–63.

McGill, L., Nicol, D., Littlejohn, A., Grierson, H., Juster, N., & Ion, W. J. (2005). Creating an information-rich learning environment to enhance design student learning: challenges and approaches. *British Journal of Educational Technology, 36*(4), 629–42.

Mead, S. E., Sit, R. A., Rogers, W. A., Jamieson, B. A., & Rousseau, G. K. (2000). Influences of general computer experience and age on library database search performance. *Behaviour & Information Technology, 19*(2), 107–23.

Merriam, S. (1998). *Qualitative Research and Case Study Applications in Education.* San Francisco, CA: Jossey-Bass Publishers.

Mestre, L. S. (2010). Matching up learning styles with learning objects: what's effective? *Journal of Library Administration, 50*(7), 808–29.

Mestre, L. S. (2012). Student preference for tutorial design: a usability study. *Reference Services Review, 40*(2), 258–76.

Miao, Y., Engler, J., Giemza, A., Weinbrenner, S., & Hoppe, H. U. (2012). Development of a process-oriented scaffolding agent in an open-ended inquiry learning environment. *Research and Practices in Technology Enhanced Learning, 7*(2), 105–28.

Miholic, V. (1994). An inventory to pique students' metacognitive awareness of reading strategies. *Journal of Reading, 38*(2), 84.

Miles, M. B. & Huberman, A. M. (1994). *Qualitative Data Analysis: An Expanded Sourcebook* (2nd ed.). Thousand Oaks, CA: Sage Publications, Inc.

Miller, G. A. (1956). The magical number seven, plus or minus two: some limits on our capacity for processing information. *Psychological Review, 63*(2), 81–97.

Miller, G. A., Galanter, E., & Pribram, K. H. (1960). *Plans and the Structure of Behavior*. New York: Holt, Rinehart and Winston, Inc.

Miller, W. D., & Irby, B. J. (1999). An inquiry into the exigency of a beginning doctoral cohort in educational leadership. *College Student Journal, 33*(3), 358.

Moore, P. (1995). Information problem solving: a wider view of library skills. *Contemporary Educational Psychology, 20*(1), 1–31.

Moulaison, H. L. (2008). OPAC queries at a medium-sized academic library: a transaction log analysis. *Library Resources & Technical Services, 52*(4), 230–7.

Mukama, E. (2009). The interplay between learning and the use of ICT in Rwandan student teachers' everyday practice. *Journal of Computer Assisted Learning, 25*(6), 539–48.

Murry, J. W., Jr., McKee, E. C., & Hammons, J. O. (1997). Faculty and librarian collaboration: The road to information literacy for graduate students. *Journal on Excellence in College Teaching, 8*(2), 107–21.

Mutch, A. (1997). Information literacy: an exploration. *International Journal of Information Management, 17*(5), 377.

Narciss, S., Proske, A., & Koerndle, H. (2007). Promoting self-regulated learning in web-based learning environments. *Computers in Human Behavior, 23*(3), 1126–44.

Nash-Ditzel, S. (2010). Metacognitive reading strategies can improve self-regulation. *Journal of College Reading and Learning, 40*(2), 45–63.

Navarro-Prieto, R., Scaife, M., & Rogers, Y. (1999). *Cognitive Strategies in Web Searching. Paper Presented at the 5th Conference on Human Factors and the Web, Gaithersburg, MD*. Unpublished manuscript.

Nazim, M. (2008). Information searching behavior in the internet age: a users' study of Aligarh Muslim University. *International Information & Library Review, 40*(1), 73–81.

Nesset, V. (2013). Two representations of the research process: the preparing, searching, and using (PSU) and the beginning, acting and telling (BAT) models. *Library & Information Science Research, 35*(2), 97–106.

Newell, A., Shaw, J. C., & Simon, H. A. (1957). Empirical explorations with the Logic Theory Machine: a case study in heuristics. *Proceedings of the Western Joint Computer Conference, 15*, 218–39.

Newell, A., Shaw, J. C., & Simon, H. A. (1958). Elements of a theory of human problem solving. *Psychological Review, 65*(3), 151–66.

Newell, A. & Simon, A. (1972). *Human Problem Solving*. Englewood Cliffs, NJ: Prentice Hall Inc.

Norman, D. (1983). Some observations on mental models. In D. Gentner & A. Stevens (eds), *Mental Models* (pp. 7–14). Hillsdale, NJ: Lawrence Erlbaum Associates.

Northcutt, N. & McCoy, D. (2004). *Interactive Qualitative Analysis.* Thousand Oaks, CA: Sage Publications.

Nowicki, S. (2003). Student vs. search engine: Undergraduates rank results for relevance. *Portal: Libraries & the Academy, 3*(3), 503–15.

Online Computer Library Center (2002). *How academic librarians can influence students' web-based information choices.* OCLC White Paper on the Information Habits of College Students. Dublin, OH.

O'Hanlon, N. (1988). The role of library research instruction in developing teachers' problem solving skills. *Journal of Teacher Education, 39*(6), 44–9.

Oliver, K. & Hannafin, M. J. (2000). Student management of web-based hypermedia resources during open-ended problem solving. *Journal of Educational Research, 94*(2), 75.

Onwuegbuzie, A. J. (2000). *Validity and Qualitative Research: An Oxymoron?* Paper presented at the Annual Meeting of the Association for the Advancement of Educational Research (AAER), Ponte Vedra, Florida.

Onwuegbuzie, A. J. & Johnson, R. B. (2006). The validity issue in mixed research. *Research in the Schools, 13*(1), 48–63.

Onwuegbuzie, A. J. & Leech, N. L. (2007). Validity and qualitative research: an oxymoron? *Quality & Quantity, 41*(2), 233–49.

Onwuegbuzie, A. J. & Teddlie, C. (2003). Framework for analyzing data in mixed method research. In A. Tashakkori & C. Teddlie (eds), *Handbook of Mixed Methods in Social and Behavioral Research* (pp. 351–84). Thousand Oaks, Ca: Sage Publications.

Ortlieb, E. & Norris, M. (2012). Using the think-aloud strategy to bolster reading comprehension of science concepts. *Current Issues in Education, 15*(1), 1–9.

Osman, M. E. & Hannafin, M. J. (1992). Metacognition research and theory: analysis and implications for instructional design. *Educational Technology Research and Development, 40*(2), 83–99.

Osman, M. E. (2010). Virtual tutoring: an online environment for scaffolding students' metacognitive problem solving expertise. *Journal of Turkish Science Education (TUSED)*, 7(4), 3–12.

Owens, W. T. (1999). Preservice teachers' feedback about the internet and the implications for social studies educators. *Social Studies*, 90(3), 133–40.

Palincsar, A. S. (1986). Metacognitive strategy instruction. *Exceptional Children*, 53(2), 118–24.

Palincsar, A. S. & Brown, D. A. (1987). Enhancing instructional time through attention to metacognition. *Journal of Learning Disabilities*, 20(2), 66–75.

Paris, S. G. & Oka, E. R. (1986). Self-regulated learning among exceptional children. *Exceptional Children*, 53(2), 103–8.

Park, B. (1986). Information needs: implications for the academic library. (Report No. IR 052 140). East Lansing, MI: National Center for Research on Teacher Learning (ERIC Document Reproduction Service No. ED 288525).

Park, T. K. (1994). Toward a theory of user-based relevance: a call for a new paradigm of inquiry. *Journal of the American Society for Information Science*, 45(3), 135–41.

Partnership for 21st Century Skills. (2009). *The MILE Guide: Milestones for Improving Learning and Education*. Washington DC: Partnership for 21st Century Skills.

Partnership for 21st Century Skills. (2003). *Learning for the 21st Century: A Report and MILE Guide for 21st Century Skills*. Washington DC: Partnership for 21st Century Skills.

Pellegrino J. W. & Schadler, M. (1974). *Maximizing Performance in a Problem Solving Task*. Unpublished manuscript, University of Pittsburgh Learning Research and Development Center.

Perkins, D. N. & Salomon, G. (1989). Are cognitive skills context-bound? *Educational Researcher*, 18(1), 16–25.

Pickert, S. M. & Chwalek, A. B. (1984). Integrating bibliographic research skills into a graduate program in education. *Catholic Library World*, 55(9), 392–4.

Pink, S. (2007). *Visual Ethnography*. Thousand Oaks, CA: Sage.

Polkinghorne, S. & Wilton, S. (2010). Research is a verb: exploring a new information literacy--embedded undergraduate research methods course. *Canadian Journal of Information & Library Sciences*, 34(4), 457–73.

Porter, B. (2011). Millennial undergraduate research strategies in web and library information retrieval systems. *Journal of Web Librarianship, 5*(4), 267–85.

Prvan, T., Reid, A., & Petocz, P. (2002). Statistical laboratories using Minitab, SPSS and Excel: a practical comparison. *Teaching Statistics, 24*(2), 68.

Quintana, C., Zhang, M., & Krajcik, J. (2005). A framework for supporting metacognitive aspects of online inquiry through software-based scaffolding. *Educational Psychologist, 40*(4), 235–44.

Raes, A., Schellens, T., De Wever, B., & Vanderhoven, E. (2012). Scaffolding information problem solving in web-based collaborative inquiry learning. *Computers & Education, 59*(1), 82–94.

Ragains, P. (1997). Evaluation of academic librarians' instructional performance: Report of a national survey. *Research Strategies, 15*(3), 159–75.

Rastgoo, A., Naderi, E., Shariatmadari, A., & Seifnaraghi, M. (2011). Investigating the effect of internet information literacy on the development of university students' metacognitive skills. *Australasian Journal of Basic and Applied Sciences, 5*(8), 959–68.

Reeve, R. A. & Brown, A. L. (1984). *Metacognition Reconsidered: Implications for Intervention Research* (Technical report no. 328). Illinois University, Urbana Center for the Study of Reading Cambridge, MA: Bolt, Beranek and Newman, Inc.

Resnick, L. B. & Glaser, R. (1976). Problem solving and intelligence. In L. B. Resnick (ed.), *The Nature of Intelligence* (pp. 205–30). New York: John Wiley & Sons.

Rozencwajg, P. (2003). Metacognitive factors in scientific problem-solving strategies. *European Journal of Psychology of Education, 18*(3), 281–94.

Saito, H. & Miwa, K. (2007). Construction of a learning environment supporting learners' reflection: a case of information seeking on the web. *Computers & Education, 49*(2), 214–29.

Salomon, G. & Perkins, D. N. (1989). Rocky roads to transfer: rethinking mechanism of a neglected phenomenon. *Educational Psychologist, 24*(2), 113.

Santamaria, M. & Petrik, D. (2012). Cornering the information market. *College & Research Libraries News, 73*(5), 265–72.

Saracevic, T. (1975). RELEVANCE: a review of and a framework for the thinking on the notion in information science. *Journal of the American Society for Information Science, 26*(6), 321–43.

Saracevic, T. (2008). Effects of inconsistent relevance judgments on information retrieval test results: a historical perspective. *Library Trends, 56*(4), 763–83.

Šauperl, A., Novijan, S., & Grcr, A. (2007). INTERNATIONAL PERSPECTIVES ... information literacy programs at the University of Ljubljana. *Journal of Academic Librarianship, 33*(2), 294–300.

Schauble, L. & Glaser, R. (1996). *Innovations in Learning: New Environments for Education.* Mahwah, NJ: Lawrence Erlbaum Associates.

Schoenfeld, A. H. (1982). *Beyond the Purely Cognitive: Metacognition and Social Cognition as Driving Forces in Intellectual Performance.* Paper presented at the Annual Meeting of the 66th American Education Research Association, New York, New York.

Shadish, W. R., Cook, T. D., & Campbell, D. T. (2002). *Experimental and Quasiexperimental Designs for Generalized Causal Inference.* Boston: Houghton Mifflin.

She, H., Cheng, M., Li, T., Wang, C., Chiu, H., Lee, P., Chou, W., & Chuang, M. (2012). Web-based undergraduate chemistry problem-solving: the interplay of task performance, domain knowledge and web-searching strategies. *Computers & Education, 59*(2), 750–61.

Shen, C. & Liu, H. (2011). Metacognitive skills development: a web-based approach in higher education. *Turkish Online Journal of Educational Technology – TOJET, 10*(2), 140–50.

Siegel, M. A. (2012). Filling in the distance between us: group metacognition during problem solving in a secondary education course. *Journal of Science Education and Technology, 21*(3), 325–41.

Siegfried, S., Bates, M. J., & Wilde, D. N. (1993). A profile of end-user searching behavior by humanities scholars: The Getty online searching project report no. 2. *Journal of the American Society for Information Science, 44*(5), 273–91.

Simon, C. E. (1995). *Information retrieval techniques: The differences in cognitive strategies and search behaviors among graduate students in an academic library (Doctoral dissertation).* Retrieved from *http://www.eric.ed.gov.proxy-tu.researchport.umd.edu/contentdelivery/servlet/ERICServlet?accno=ED390394.*

Slone, D. J. (2002). The influence of mental models and goals on search patterns during web interaction. *Journal of the American Society for Information Science & Technology, 53*(13), 1152–69.

Somoza-Fernández, M. & Abadal, E. (2009). Analysis of web-based tutorials created by academic libraries. *Journal of Academic Librarianship, 35*(2), 126–31.

Sosin, A. A. & Deleo, P. A. (2005). Uniting information literacy and teacher education. *Academic Exchange Quarterly, 9* (4), 209–13.

Spink, A. & Heinnström, J. (2011) Conclusions and further research. In A. Spink & J. Heinnström (eds), *New directions in information behavior* (pp. 291–7). UK: Emerald.

Stadtler, M. & Bromme, R. (2007). Dealing with multiple documents on the WWW: The role of metacognition in the formation of documents models. *International Journal of Computer-Supported Collaborative Learning, 2*(2–3), 191–210.

Stadtler, M. & Bromme, R. (2008). Effects of the metacognitive computer-tool met.a.ware on the web search of laypersons. *Computers in Human Behavior, 24*(3), 716–37.

Steif, P. S., Lobue, J. M., Kara, L. B., & Fay, A. L. (2010). Improving problem solving performance by inducing talk about salient problem features. *Journal of Engineering Education, 99*(2), 135–42.

Stephan, E., Cheng, D. T., & Young, L. M. (2007). A usability survey at the University of Mississippi libraries for the improvement of the library home page. *Journal of Academic Librarianship, 32*(1), 35–51.

Sternberg, R. A. & Frensch, A. (1990). Intelligence and cognition. In M. W. Eysenck (ed.), *Cognitive Psychology: An International Review* (pp. 57–103). Chichester: John Wiley & Son.

Sternberg, R. J. (1986). Critical thinking: its nature, measurement, and improvement. (Report No. CS 209962). East Lansing, MI: National Center for Research on Teacher Learning. (ERIC Document Reproduction Service No. ED 272882).

Storrs, G. (1994). A conceptualization of multiparty interaction. *Interacting with Computers, 6*(2), 173–89.

Stronge, A. J., Rogers, W. A., & Fisk, A. D. (2006). Web-based information search and retrieval: effects of strategy use and age on search success. *Human Factors, 48*(3), 434–46.

Sutcliffe, A. & Ennis, M. (1998). Towards a cognitive theory of information retrieval. *Interacting with Computers, 10*(3), 321–51.

Sutcliffe, A. G., Ennis, M., & Watkinson, S. J. (2000). Empirical studies of end-user information searching. *Journal of the American Society for Information Science, 51*(13), 1211–31.

Swanson, H. L. (1990). Influence of metacognitive knowledge and aptitude on problem solving. *Journal of Educational Psychology, 82*(2), 306–14.

Switzer, A. & Perdue, S. W. (2011). Dissertation 101: a research and writing intervention for education graduate students. *Education Libraries, 34*(1), 4–14.

Sylwester, R. (1985). Research on memory: major discoveries, major educational challenges. *Educational Leadership, 42*(7), 69–75.

Tabatabai, D. & Luconi, F. (1998). Expert-novice differences in searching the web. *AMCIS 1998 Proceedings Paper 132.* pp. 390–2.

Tabatabai, D. & Shore, B. M. (2005). How experts and novices search the web. *Library & Information Science Research, 27*(2), 222–48.

Taft, R. J. (2011). Utilizing a self-questioning strategy designed within a self-regulated strategy development instructional approach to promote idea generation in students with learning disabilities. *Dissertation Abstracts International Section A: Humanities and Social Sciences, 72* (1-A), 157.

Tajika, H., Nakatsu, N., Nozaki, H., Neumann, E., & Maruno, S. (2007). Effects of self-explanation as a metacognitive strategy for solving mathematical word problems. *Japanese Psychological Research, 49*(3), 222–33.

Tal, N. (2006). Which one to choose?: a comparison between three aggregators. *Knowledge Quest, 34*(3), 24–9.

Tasakkori, A. & Teddlie, C. (1998). *Mixed Methodology: Combining Qualitative and Quantitative Approaches.* Thousand Oaks, CA: Sage Publications, Inc.

Taylor, R. S. (1962). The process of asking questions. *American Documentation, 13*(4), 391–6.

Taylor, A. (2012). A study of the information search behaviour of the millennial generation. *Information Research, 17*(1).

Tenopir, C. (1984). TO ERR IS HUMAN: seven common searching mistakes. *Library Journal, 109*(6), 635.

Tenopir, C., Wang, P., Zhang, Y., Simmons, B., & Pollard, R. (2008). Academic users' interactions with ScienceDirect in search tasks: affective and cognitive behaviors. *Information Processing & Management, 44*(1), 105–21.

Tessmer, M., Wilson, B., & Driscoll, M. (1990). A new model of concept teaching and learning. *Educational Technology, Research and Development, 38*(1), 45–53.

Thelwall, M. (2004). Digital libraries and multi-disciplinary research skills. *LIBRES: Library & Information Science Research Electronic Journal, 14*(2), 4.

Thornes, S. L. (2012). Creating an online tutorial to support information literacy and academic skills development. *Journal of Information Literacy, 6*(1), 81–95.

Tsai, M. (2009). Online information searching strategy inventory (OISSI): a quick version and a complete version. *Computers & Education, 53*(2), 473–83.

Tsai, M. & Tsai, C. (2003). Information searching strategies in web-based science learning: The role of internet self-efficacy. *Innovations in Education & Teaching International, 40*(1), 43.

University of Bristol Library. (2012). *Evaluating your search results.*, Retrieved from *http://www.bris.ac.uk/library/support/findinginfo/evaluation*.

University of Buffalo Libraries. (2012). *Finding and evaluating research materials.* Retrieved from *http://library.buffalo.edu/help/research-tips/evaluate*.

University of Washington. Health Sciences Library. (June 14, 2013). *How to improve database search results.* Retrieved from *http://libguides.hsl.washington.edu/improving*.

Vakkari, P. (2001a). Changes in search tactics and relevance judgements when preparing a research proposal: a summary of the findings of a longitudinal study. *Information Retrieval, 4*(3), 295–310.

Vakkari, P. (2001b). A theory of the task-based information retrieval process: a summary and generalisation (sic) of a longitudinal study. *Journal of Documentation, 57*(1), 44–60.

Van Waes, L. (1998). Evaluating on-line and off-line searching behavior using thinking-aloud protocols to detect navigation barriers. *Proceedings of the Sixteen Annual International Conference on Computer Documentation* (pp. 180–3). New York: ACM Press.

Vezzosi, M. (2009). Doctoral students' information behaviour: an exploratory, study at the University of Parma (Italy). *New Library World, 110*(1), 66–80.

Wagoner, S. A. (1983). Comprehension monitoring: what it is and what we know about it. *Reading Research Quarterly, 18*(3), 328–46.

Walraven, A., Brand-Gruwel, S., & Boshuizen, H. P. A. (2008). Information-problem solving: a review of problems students encounter and instructional solutions. *Computers in Human Behavior, 24*(3), 623–48.

Walraven, A., Brand-Gruwel, S., & Boshuizen, H. P. A. (2009). How students evaluate information and sources when searching the world wide web for information. *Computers & Education, 52*(1), 234–46.

Walraven, A., Brand-Gruwel, S., & Boshuizen, H. P. A. (2010). Fostering transfer of websearchers' evaluation skills: a field test of two transfer theories. *Computers in Human Behavior, 26*(4), 716–28.

Wellman, H. M. (1983). Metamemory revisited. In J. A. Meacham (ed.), *Trends in Memory Development* (pp. 31–52). Basel: S. Karger.

Westbrook, L. (2006). Mental models: a theoretical overview and preliminary study. *Journal of Information Science, 32*(6), 563–79.

Westby, C. (2010). Multiliteracies: The changing world of communication. *Topics in Language Disorders, 30*(1), 64–71.

Wilson, T. D. (1981). On user studies and information needs. *Journal of Documentation, 37*(1), 3–15.

Wilson, T. D. (1997). Information behaviour: an interdisciplinary perspective. *Information Processing & Management, 33* (4), 551–72.

Wilson, T. D. (1999). Models in information behavior research. *Journal of Documentation, 55*(3), 249–70.

Wineburg, S. (1998). Reading Abraham Lincoln: an expert/expert study in the interpretation of historical texts. *Cognitive Science, 22*(3), 319.

Wolf, S. (2007). Information literacy and self-regulation: a convergence of disciplines. *School Library Media Research, 10.*

Wolf, S. E., Brush, T., & Saye, J. (2003). Using an information problem-solving model as a metacognitive scaffold for multimedia-supported information-based problems. *Journal of Research on Technology in Education, 35*(3), 321–41.

Wood, D., Bruner, J. S., & Ross, G. (1976). The role of tutoring in problem solving. *Journal of Child Psychology & Psychiatry & Allied Disciplines, 17*(2), 89–100.

Wopereis, I., Brand-Gruwel, S., & Vermetten, Y. (2008). The effect of embedded instruction on solving information problems. *Computers in Human Behavior, 24*(3), 738–52.

Yang, S. C. (1997). Information seeking as problem-solving using a qualitative approach to uncover the novice learners' information-seeking processes in a Perseus hypertext system. *Library & Information Science Research, 19*(1), 71–92.

Zweizig, D. & Dervin, B. (1977). Public library use, users, uses: advances in knowledge of the characteristics and needs of the adult clientele of American public libraries. In M. Voigt & M. H. Harris (eds), *Advances in Librarianship* (pp. 231–55). New York: Academic Press.

Zhang, Y. (2008a). The influence of mental models on undergraduate students' searching behavior on the web. *Information Processing & Management, 44*(3), 1330–45.

Zhang, Y. (2008b). Undergraduate students' mental models of the web as an information retrieval system. *Journal of the American Society for Information Science & Technology, 59*(13), 2087–98.

Zhang, Y. (2013). The development of users' mental models of Medline Plus in information searching. *Library & Information Science Research (07408188), 35*(2), 159–70.

Zhang, M. & Quintana, C. (2012). Scaffolding strategies for supporting middle school students' online inquiry processes. *Computers & Education, 58*(1), 181–96.

Index

Vakkari, P., 20, 139, 263

Walraven, A., 2–3, 49, 52, 153, 240, 263

Wilson, T. D., 2, 11, 14–15, 20–1, 262–3

Wolf, S., 23, 49, 87, 92, 94, 187, 196–7, 202, 263–4

Wopereis, I., 3, 46, 51, 92, 213, 240, 264

Zhang, Y., 82

CPSIA information can be obtained at www.ICGtesting.com
Printed in the USA
LVOW04s1924120515

438205LV00004B/60/P